Also by Kurt Struckmeyer:

...racy of Love: Following Jesus in a Postmodern World
...dox Faith: A New Reformation for a Postmodern World

P

A Conspi

An Ortho

People of the Way

Passion and Resistance in a Postmodern World

KURT STRUCKMEYER

RESOURCE *Publications* · Eugene, Oregon

PEOPLE OF THE WAY
Passion and Resistance in a Postmodern World

Resource Publications
An Imprint of Wipf and Stock Publishers
199 W. 8th Ave., Suite 3
Eugene, OR 97401

www.wipfandstock.com

PAPERBACK ISBN: 978-1-4982-3455-9
HARDCOVER ISBN: 978-1-4982-3457-3
EBOOK ISBN: 978-1-4982-3456-6

03/30/23

To my grandchildren
Henry, Jasper, Wyatt, and Phoebe.

May you work toward a better world
where children no longer weep from poverty and hunger,
where they no longer live in fear from violence,
and where they are taught kindness, compassion, and love.

Love freely.
Act compassionately.
Live justly.
Seek peace.

Contents

acknowledgment

I'D LIKE TO THANK Jean Struckmeyer, my closest and dearest friend, life partner, and true love for her ongoing support and encouragement. She has been my role model for passionate living and my inspiration for compassionate service. I am ever grateful to have her in my life.

abbreviations

BCE	Before the Common Era
CE	the Common Era
Gen	Genesis
Exod	Exodus
Lev	Leviticus
Isa	Isaiah
Thom	Gospel of Thomas
Matt	Gospel of Matthew
Acts	Acts of the Apostles
Rom	Romans
I Cor	I Corinthians
II Cor	II Corinthians
Gal	Galatians
Eph	Ephesians
Col	Colossians
I Tim	I Timothy
I Pet	I Peter
Rev	Revelation

Introduction:
a passionless church

I want to see a Christianity that is robust, that can actually lead the Western world out of the postmodern morass . . . We've got to be creative. We haven't been this way before. This calls for innovation, for thinking outside the box and all that, but if we read the gospels and say our prayers, we should be able to do it.[1]

—N. T. Wright (b. 1948)

I wish you were either hot or cold; if I had my way, you'd be one way or the other, all the way, but you lukewarm types, you passionless types, you make me want to vomit.[2]

—John of Patmos, speaking for God in the book of Revelation (late first century)

In the town of Bland, Missouri, stands a church unfortunately named Bland Christian Church. But that name could be extended to many congregations throughout the United States today. Danish theologian Søren Kierkegaard (1813–1855) once said, "This age will die not from sin, but from lack of passion." Passion is simply missing in many churches. There is a lack of zeal, an absence of fire in the belly.

Let me be clear from the outset by what I mean when I use the term "passion." The dictionary defines the word as an intense, driving, or

---

1. Malkinson, "N.T. Wright's Vision."

2. A creative paraphrase of Rev 3:15–16. These are the words that John of Patmos, the author of Revelation, reports that he was commanded by Christ to write to the church community in the city of Laodicea, criticizing them for a lack of passion, zeal, and courage in the face of empire.

overmastering feeling or conviction. Certainly, there is an emotional aspect to passion, but I am not talking about the emotive nature of faith as expressed in some Christian worship services. Passion also has a romantic aspect, but I am not discussing sexual desire. In the church, the word passion has long been associated with the final days of Jesus—the story of his suffering and death. But I am not talking about the death of Jesus either. Instead, I am describing the focus of his life—his ardent passion for loving and serving others, and his passionate confrontation with the power politics, unjust economics, and institutional religion of his day. Jesus pursued life-giving relationships and strived for a just society that cares for the least among us. He espoused a lifestyle of radical love, lavish generosity, extravagant forgiveness, inclusive hospitality, compassionate action, selfless service, a passion for justice, creative nonviolence, and simple living. These are the things he was passionate about, the things he preached about, the things he dedicated his life to, and the things he was willing to die for.

Many churches are focused almost solely on their internal welfare and seem to be missing a strong sense of the social mission of Jesus: a desire to work among poor, broken, and trampled people; an eagerness to be change agents in a broken and divided society; a willingness to engage in both compassionate service and radical action for social justice; a prophetic calling to challenge political manipulation by corporate owners, wealthy oligarchs, and autocratic leaders for their own benefit. Apart from applying a comforting bandage and soothing balm here and there, many churches do little or nothing to substantially make the world a better place for those who are suffering from the domination system of our time. Perhaps this is because far too many Christians support and materially benefit from the current situation. And many see no conflict between the gospel of Jesus and the American appetite for white nationalism, unquestioned militarism, and neoliberal capitalism.

THE YOUTH EXODUS

Without finding a strong spiritual dimension or a passionate expression of the radical teachings of Jesus in their church experience, the post-war Baby Boomers (born between 1946 and 1964) began to drift away as they reached young adulthood in the late 1960s and early 1970s, looking for something more—a more vibrant and relevant faith. As they became radicalized and transformed by the war in Viet Nam (1955–1975) and the violent suppression of the civil rights movement, they saw their churches blessing the status quo of militarism and racism either overtly or by their pious silence.

Throughout my college years (1965–1969), my emerging religious convictions were put to the test by the reality of the war in Viet Nam. At the age of twelve, I had been inspired by Jesus' Sermon on the Mount in the gospel of Matthew (chapters 5–7) that called his followers to react nonviolently when provoked, to love one's enemies, and to become agents of peace and justice. Yet my conservative Protestant church never discussed any of these elements of a faithful life. All that really mattered was to believe that Jesus died for my sins and that his sacrificial death would grant me eternal life in heaven. This was, after all, our major objective as members of the Lutheran Church—Missouri Synod (LCMS), a heavenly afterlife. On the Sunday before my confirmation, my pastor interrogated the confirmands in front of the congregation regarding our knowledge of Luther's Small Catechism. Out of the one hundred questions posed to us, none were about seeking peace and justice in the world. In the sanctuary before us, stood an American flag, symbolizing that loyalty to the state was of equal importance to our commitment to God, the church, and the way of Jesus.

When I was in high school, a Lutheran youth counselor from a local seminary recommended reading *The Cost of Discipleship* by Dietrich Bonhoeffer (1906–1945), which, among other things, was structured as a commentary on the Sermon on the Mount. Bonhoeffer contrasted "cheap grace" (passively accepting God's grace without substantive transformation of one's life) and "costly grace" (responding to God's love by following the way of Jesus, no matter the cost). For Bonhoeffer, following Jesus meant adopting a nonviolent stance, which in his understanding meant a passive nonresistance to evil. His understanding of Christian nonviolence was based on the words of Jesus in Matthew's gospel: "Do not resist an evildoer."[3] This was a common misunderstanding of the text based on misleading translations from the original Greek. But Jesus always resisted evil; he simply and emphatically did it nonviolently. The text should read: "Don't react violently against one who is evil,"[4] or "Do not oppose the wicked man by force."[5]

In college, I furthered my meager understanding of nonviolence by reading a few works by Tolstoy and Gandhi. Gandhi's campaign in India involved nonviolent direct action that was very different from a passive resistance to evil; it was an active nonviolence. Apart from that young seminarian, my church offered no resources or encouragement on how to live nonviolently in a violent world. Despite this, I became convinced that it was

---

3. Matt 5:39. See Wink, *Powers That Be*, 98–101. Walter Wink reports the Greek word translated as *resist* (*antistenai*, pronounced *ahn-tee-STEN-ah-ee*) was a technical military term that indicated that one should take a strong stand (*stenai*) against (*anti*) evil.

4. Funk and Hoover, *Five Gospels*, 143.

5. Hart, *New Testament*, 9.

necessary to take a personal stand against participation in war and other acts of collective violence. I decided to register as a conscientious objector to war, not knowing how that would eventually play out. On Valentine's Day 1969, I sent a letter to my local draft board explaining why my understanding of Jesus' call to love our neighbors and our enemies compelled me not to enter military service as an armed combatant. The senior pastor of my congregation told me that although he could not agree with my position to refuse military service because the requirement to obey the state as found in the 13th chapter of Paul's letter to the Romans was too important to his theology.[6] He did however respect my conscientious stance, which has been a Lutheran tradition dating back to Martin Luther's own actions before civil and ecclesial authorities.[7]

As the war in Vietnam raged over the next four years, I became convinced that most American churches, afraid of taking a controversial stand during the war, were being unfaithful to Jesus by tacitly supporting their government's military objectives with little objection. By their silence, I believed that these churches were complicit in the evils of that war. I could not understand how they could so willingly send young parishioners off to kill without any significant challenge regarding the war and its justification. And I reasoned, if the church was willing to support nearly any war in history in contrast to the teachings of Jesus, what else had they missed, ignored, or distorted about Jesus over the centuries? I was not alone in asking that question.

THE NEED FOR A PASSIONATE FAITH

According to Kenda Creasy Dean (b. 1959), Associate Professor of Theology at Princeton Theological Seminary, young adults are looking for a

---

6. Romans 13:1–7. This passage in Paul's letter to the churches of Rome states that everyone must submit themselves to the governing authorities and that those who rebel against authority are rebelling against God. A few scholars believe that this was not part of the original letter by Paul but was a later reactionary insertion that interrupts the flow of Paul's thoughts before and after the insertion. To see what the uninterrupted original text might have been, read Romans 12:9–21 and then jump to Romans 13:8–10.

7. In 1520, Pope Leo X issued a papal bull (public decree) of excommunication against Martin Luther for heretical writing. The following year, Luther was ordered by Holy Roman Emperor Charles V to appear before the Imperial Diet (assembly) at the city of Worms to recant or reaffirm the "errors" in his writings. At the Diet, Luther reportedly responded, "I cannot and will not recant anything, for to act against our conscience is neither safe for us, nor open to us. On this I take my stand. I can do no other. God help me."

passionate church. What they find in many Mainline Protestant churches is a passionless theology.

> *What if Mainline Protestantism's disappointing track record with young people (in and beyond the church) has not been primarily a failure of models, educational strategies, historical cycles, or institutional support, but a failure of theology? Is it possible that the "problem" facing youth ministry reflects all too accurately a malaise infecting Mainline denominations generally: a flabby theological identity due to an absence of passion? That would be ironic. Most young people come to us brimming with passion. Could it be that, instead of fanning this youthful zeal into holy fire, we have more often doused it, dismissed it, or drowned it in committee meetings?*
>
> *The theological challenge youth pose to the church is blunt: Are we who we say we are? Do we practice passion, transformed by a Love who never disappoints, and live by a faith so convincing that we stake our lives on it? Or are we just another sagging social convention, like Dracula, that needs young blood to survive?*[8]
>
> *Passionless Christianity has nothing to die for: it practices assimilation, not oddity. Passionless Christians lead sensible lives, not subversive ones; we are benignly nice instead of dangerously loving.*[9]

Dean reports that because youth are such passionate people, the solution to reaching them, retaining them, and harnessing their passion is for churches to become passionate about the gospel they share. A passionless church will never address passionate youth. But which gospel are churches passionate about?

To produce ardent young Christians, Dean argues, churches must rediscover their sense of mission and model an understanding of being Christian as not something you do for yourself, but something that calls you to share God's love—in word and deed—with others.

The alternative understandings of the gospel are reflected in different interpretations of the mission of the church. The word "mission" derives from the Latin *missiō* (*MEE-see-oh*), which means "sending." At one time, the mission of the church was clear, summed up in the words of the old hymn: "to tell the old, old story of Jesus and his love."[10] Missionaries were sent from Europe and North America to convert the "heathens" of Africa and Asia. The mission of the church was to save souls from an eternal

8. Dean, *Practicing Passion*, 25.

9. Dean, *Practicing Passion*, 52.

10. Hankey, "Old, Old Story."

damnation in hell to an eternal life in heaven. But today, mission is gradually being redefined as the church once more recovers the authentic identity and message of Jesus. The mission of the church is increasingly seen as following Jesus in the proclamation and implementation of the kingdom of God. The earlier understanding of mission in the fifteenth through nineteenth centuries was exclusively about Jesus as a means of personal salvation. The newer understanding is a recovery of the mission of Jesus himself—the reign of God on earth. And it is accomplished by simple things.

> *For I was hungry and you gave me something to eat, I was thirsty and you gave me something to drink, I was a stranger and you invited me in, I needed clothes and you clothed me, I was sick and you looked after me, I was in prison and you came to visit me . . . Truly I tell you, whatever you did for one of the least of these brothers and sisters of mine, you did for me.*[11]

Dean contends that the imitation of Christ is the primary objective of youth ministry. She argues that Christ's passionate life transforms adolescent passion from self-fulfilling activities to self-giving love and service.

But it's hard for congregations to be passionate about a mission to the poor, the lonely, the lost, and the desperate in a violent and unjust society. All too often our churches lack the courage to address the real social issues that face us. They are not speaking and acting clearly, and as a result people are leaving, looking for answers. The churches tell the story of Jesus as if he existed in a fantasy world and did not face similar problems in the first century as we face in the twenty-first. The Jesus of our churches often has no place in the real world—no history, geography, passion, or politics.

For the most part congregational energies are dedicated to the survival and maintenance of the institution. Churches build new sanctuaries, repave parking lots, plan educational programs, print bulletins, rehearse choirs, and devise worship services—the fundamental things necessary to keep the institution humming. Just look at any pastor's datebook to see where the priorities are. But when does the real mission of the church take place? Do the priorities of the local congregation match Jesus' call to "strive first for the kingdom of God and his justice"?[12] Perhaps the greatest hindrance to practicing a kingdom theology of youth ministry is the lack of the palpable presence of living, breathing adult disciples in the church.

William Strauss (1947–2007) and Neil Howe (b. 1951), authors of *The Fourth Turning*, stated in 1995 that one of the defining characteristics of the Millennial generation (1981–1996) is that "their B.S. Detectors are always

11. Matt 25:35–36, 40.
12. Matt 6:33.

on." What this means is that this generation has a well-developed, intuitive olfactory sense for finding stink in lip-service Christianity. It doesn't pass the smell test. This is also the case for the current generations of young people—Generation Z (1997–2012) and Generation Alpha (2013–2025).

According to Kenda Creasy Dean,

> *The point is that practical theological reflection leads to radical congruency between the theology we espouse and the one we live . . . Youth ministry that emphasizes evangelism, without simultaneously giving adolescents opportunities to serve in substantive ministry, eviscerates discipleship. Youth ministry that seeks Christian action without a growing relationship with Jesus reduces it to good works. In short, if adolescents are to become practical theologians in their own right, we have to get them into the pool. And that means you and I have to stand in the middle of the pool ourselves, practicing our faith while holding out our hands, inviting the youth we love to jump into the Christian community alongside us.*[13]

What if we really gave young people something to sink their teeth into, something to get excited about, something that would generate a passionate response and a lifelong commitment? Kenda Creasy Dean wants to connect the passion of youth to the passion of Jesus—a passion for justice and peace, service and compassion, generosity and inclusion, love, and forgiveness. It is the life that Jesus lived and the subversive wisdom that he shared that is at the center of a passionate church.

13. Dean, *Starting Right*, 33.

PART 1

a social justice Jesus

Chapter 1

the two gospels

The spirit of Yahweh is upon me, because he has anointed me to bring good news to the poor.[1]

—Jesus of Nazareth (c. 6 BCE–30 CE), quoting the prophet Isaiah

It ain't what you don't know that gets you into trouble. It's what you know for sure that just ain't so.

—Mark Twain (1835–1910)

In my first book, *A Conspiracy of Love*, I described the fact that two widely different gospel messages separate us into two divergent camps. I will briefly repeat that assertion here.

Two competing streams of faith have shaped the churches in our society. Both have their roots in the earliest days of the Christian church. A theological battle has been waging for the past century between two opposing viewpoints about the Bible and two different gospel messages of the New Testament. Moreover, these biblical viewpoints are just part of a larger theological divide about the essence of the Christian faith and the content of the Christian life.

In *The Heart of Christianity*, scholar Marcus Borg (1942–2015) described two very different ways of seeing what the Christian life is all about—two different visions of Christianity. Borg labeled these as an "earlier paradigm" and an "emerging paradigm."[2] Others might call them

---

1. Luke 4:18 / Isa 61:1.
2. Borg, *Heart of Christianity*, 17–18.

conservative Christianity and liberal Christianity, or traditional Christianity and progressive Christianity, although Borg did not prefer those terms.

The earlier paradigm is still the majority voice in American Christianity today, but according to Borg, it no longer speaks to millions of Christians who are uncomfortable with its definition of the faithful life.

> *This earlier way of being Christian views the Bible as the unique revelation of God, emphasizes its literal meaning, and sees the Christian life as centered in believing now for the sake of salvation later—believing in God, the Bible, and Jesus as the way to heaven. Typically, it has also seen Christianity as the only true religion.*[3]

The dominance of the earlier paradigm causes many progressive Christians to wonder if they can still call themselves "Christian" if they do not buy into biblical literalism, religious exclusivity, and a heavenly afterlife as the goal of the Christian life. According to Borg, an emerging alternative paradigm has been developing steadily for the last century and has become a kind of grassroots movement within the Mainline denominations.

> *The emerging paradigm sees the Christian life as a life of relationship and transformation. Being Christian is not about meeting requirements for a future reward in an afterlife, and not very much about believing. Rather, the Christian life is about a relationship with God that transforms life in the present.*[4]

Borg, in his characteristically compassionate pastoral manner, was careful to say that "the issue isn't that one of these paradigms is right and the other wrong. Rather, the issue is functionality, whether a paradigm 'works' or 'gets in the way.'"

> *The earlier paradigm has nourished and continues to nourish lives of deep devotion, faith, and love. The Spirit of God can and does work through it. It has for centuries and still does. When it leads to a strong sense of the reality and grace of God, to following Jesus, and to lives filled with compassion and a passion for justice, as it sometimes does, all one can say is, "Praise the Lord."*
>
> *But for millions of others, the earlier paradigm no longer works. Unpersuasive to them, it has become a stumbling block. What is the Christian message, the Christian gospel, for people who can't be literalists or exclusivists? What do we have to say to them? In an important sense, this is an issue of evangelism. For*

---

3. Borg, *Heart of Christianity*, xii.

4. Borg, *Heart of Christianity*, 14.

these millions, the emerging paradigm provides a way of taking Christianity and the Christian life seriously.[5]

TWO DIFFERENT GOSPELS

I believe that these alternate forms of Christianity are based on two very different gospel messages found in the pages of the New Testament. The term *gospel* derives from an Old English word meaning *good news* or *glad tidings*. In Greek, it is *euaggelion* (*yoo-ang-GHEL-ee-on*). From this Greek word, we derive the English terms *evangelical* and *evangelism*.

As one reads the four gospels and the letters of Paul, it becomes evident that there are two distinctly different messages of good news proclaimed in those ancient writings—two contrasting narratives at the heart of Christianity. The first message of good news that we encounter in the New Testament is presented in the gospels of Matthew, Mark, and Luke: the good news announced by Jesus. This message is focused on the life of Jesus and his teachings: the kingdom of God and the good news to the poor. The second gospel is the good news announced by Paul in his letters or epistles, and in the gospel of John. This message of good news is focused on the death of Jesus, his resurrection from the dead, and the consequences for our salvation. It is summarized in the historic creeds of the Christian faith. To clarify the difference between the two, we might say that the first is the "gospel *of* Jesus," while the second is a "gospel *about* Jesus."

The gospel *of* Jesus is primarily a social gospel. It is the proclamation of the present and future kingdom of God—a just and peaceful human society. The most authentic message proclaimed by Jesus was never about himself or his role in the salvation of the world. Those ideas were later developed by Hellenistic Gentile and Jewish worshipers.[6] Instead, the gospel *of* Jesus was about what he believed God desired in the world, about the radical transformation that God was seeking in human lives and social relationships. It was and is a gospel about redeeming our life together in the here and now. It seeks the common good by elevating the status of those at the bottom of the economic ladder. The gospel *of* Jesus is truly "good news to the poor."

The gospel *about* Jesus changes all that. Paul is very clear about the gospel he is proclaiming. In a letter to the house churches of Rome, he declares that he has been:

5. Borg, *Heart of Christianity*, 18.

6. Hellenism referred to the Greek language, culture, and values.

> *Set apart for the gospel of God . . . the gospel concerning his Son,
> who was . . . declared to be Son of God . . . by resurrection from the
> dead, Jesus Christ our Lord."*[7]

In another letter to the house church at Corinth, he says:

> *Now I should remind you, brothers and sisters, of the good news
> that I proclaimed to you . . . that Christ died for our sins in ac-
> cordance with the scriptures, and that he was buried, and that
> he was raised on the third day in accordance with the scriptures.*[8]

The good news proclaimed by Paul puts the emphasis on Jesus himself
and the salvation from sin that Paul believed resulted from the death and
resurrection of the Christ. Someone once said that as Jesus taught his disciples, he pointed their attention toward the centrality of the kingdom of God,
but all the disciples could see was his pointed finger. It was the messenger
and not the message that ultimately dominated and shaped the history of
the church. The gospel *about* Jesus is a message of good news that the death
and resurrection of Jesus has changed everything for humanity in relation to
a wrathful God. It is a gospel aimed at individual lives and their eternal fate.

John's gospel enhances Paul's gospel *about* Jesus. In John's narrative, Jesus repeatedly speaks about himself and his close relationship to God, who
he regarded as a metaphorical father. A series of "I am" statements in John's
gospel are intentionally designed to recall the words of God to Moses in the
book of Exodus. When Moses asks God's identity, *Elohim (el-o-HEEM)*—a
Hebrew word meaning *god* or *gods*—responds in this way:

> *Elohim said to Moses, "I AM WHO I AM." He said further, "Thus
> you shall say to the Israelites, 'I AM has sent me to you.'"*[9]

In John's gospel, Jesus declares:

> *I am the bread of life . . . I am the light of the world . . . I am the
> gate for the sheep . . . I am the good shepherd . . . I am the resur-
> rection and the life . . . I am the way, and the truth, and the life . . .
> I am the true vine.*[10]

John's readers and listeners did not miss the point.

---

7. Rom 1:1–4.

8. 1 Cor 15:1–4. (References to "according to the scriptures" are unclear).

9. Exod 3:13.

10. John 6:35, 8:12, 10:9, 10:11, 11:25, 14:6, 15:1.

MISSING THE SUBSTANCE

What is missing from the gospel *about* Jesus is the kingdom of God. Paul and John rarely refer to it. Paul, in fact, says little about the wisdom tradition of Jesus except his focus on a loving community. The alternative wisdom teachings of Jesus—his stories, his aphorisms, his parables, his moral clarity—are all missing. The life and teachings of Jesus are not central to Paul's message. John's gospel includes none of Jesus' parables but instead offers us lengthy discourses like those of ancient Greek philosophers. It doesn't even sound like Jesus. Together, Paul and John present us with a very different figure than the Jesus of Matthew, Mark, and Luke. Paul clearly states in his letters that the human Jesus is of no real concern to him. He in fact never met the living Jesus, although their lives overlapped. All that matters is the fictional Christ figure that Paul created, or at least elaborated from the earliest cult members.

> *Even though we once knew Christ from a human viewpoint and
> as a man, that isn't how we know him now.*[11]

Marcus Borg differentiates between the Jesus of history—a real human being who lived and taught among us—and the cosmic Christ of the Christian faith, a product of Paul and the Hellenistic Christian community who were focused on an impending apocalyptic event: the future appearance of the mystical Son of Man, the resurrection of the dead, and a final judgment of humanity. Borg calls these contrasting images the pre-Easter Jesus and the post-Easter Jesus. In other words, the pre-Easter Jesus was a human teacher of love and compassion, while the post-Easter Jesus was an apocalyptic figure of judgment, reward, and punishment. They are simply not the same.

The distinction between these competing New Testament gospels and their images of Jesus is extremely important because which message one hears and responds to will shape one's Christian faith and life. The gospel *of* Jesus focuses on a personal and social transformation in this life while the gospel *about* Jesus focuses almost exclusively on individual salvation from God's wrath and an eternal life in heaven. The gospel *of* Jesus is primarily a social and public gospel; the gospel *about* Jesus is an individualistic and private gospel.

The great divide between Christians is whether the *life* of Jesus or the *death* of Jesus is more important. The creeds of the church favor the latter. None of Jesus' teachings about how to live in the present—the need for love,

11. II Cor 5:16.

compassion, forgiveness, generosity, and justice—is considered important in the key confessions of the church.

JESUS OR PAUL

One's orientation to the gospel *of* or *about* Jesus will determine one's central mission as a believer or a follower. The atonement gospel of Paul calls his adherents to a mission of evangelization and conversion so that others may experience a heavenly afterlife with God and be saved from an eternal life in Hell. The social gospel of Jesus calls his followers to transform both individual lives and social structures to deal with the pervasive issues of human suffering: poverty, hunger, shelter, education, and employment. One gospel is afterlife oriented; the other is centered in the present. It is all a question of whether one puts an emphasis on the teachings of Jesus or the teachings of Paul.

These two streams of Christianity have existed side by side since the beginning, often integrated by Jesus' followers in the early church. But today, these two competing gospels are dividing Christians around the world into irreconcilable camps. In the twentieth century, historian Martin Marty (b. 1928) saw these expressed in the United States as what he termed as *Public Protestantism* and *Private Protestantism*. The Public Protestants responded to the Social Gospel in the Progressive Era from the 1870s to the 1920s and sought to remake American society as an expression of God's kingdom. They focused on eradicating poverty, ignorance, disease, and crime. Private Protestants sought to keep the church solidly within the individualistic sphere, focused instead on the condition of the human soul. One could easily extend Marty's terminology beyond the Protestant denominations to include Roman Catholics and others with the broader terms *Social Christianity* and *Private Christianity* in the current debate over the understanding of the gospel message.

Traditionally, Christian theology and practice has concentrated on issues of sin and salvation. Personal redemption from God's righteous wrath has become more important than the transformation of human behavior or the struggle for justice in human society. In orthodox theology, we are passive recipients of God's grace, not hands-on actors in the transformation of the world.

But, according to social gospel theologian and pastor Walter Rauschenbusch (1861–1916), until Paul developed his doctrine of sin and salvation, the temptation and fall of humanity in the Garden of Eden was not of theological importance in the Hebrew Bible. The idea of original sin and our need for redemption is simply not there. Although the church has built its entire doctrine of human redemption on the story of the fall, Jesus and the earlier Hebrew prophets paid little attention to it. Once again, we see the difference between the gospel *of* Jesus and the gospel *about* Jesus. The latter is immersed almost entirely in personal salvation from the inherited guilt of original sin—something Jesus said nothing about.

THE DOMINATION SYSTEM

But there is a larger form of sin that Jesus sought to correct. Throughout history, nearly every society has favored an elite group of individuals and families at the expense of most less-fortunate inhabitants. For thousands of years, economic elites have rigged society in their favor by crafting systems that would benefit their prosperity and ensure their control over the nation's political and economic affairs. Historically, they have used unjust economic systems to extract wealth from the sweat of slaves, peasants, serfs, laborers, and the working class while contributing little to the common welfare. Social control has been maintained with violence and military might, often supported by religious institutions. These societies have invariably been patriarchies where the authority and desires of men have dominated the lives of women and children. The system has frequently favored one race, tribe, or ethnic group over others.

Biblical scholar Walter Wink (1935–2012) has referred to these societies as manifestations of an enduring "domination system" that has been part of the human story since the rise of civilization in the ancient Near East. Wink describes the domination system in this way:

> *It is characterized by unjust economic relations, oppressive political relations, biased race relations, patriarchal gender relations, hierarchical power relations, and the use of violence to maintain them all. No matter what shape the dominating system of the moment might take (from the ancient Near Eastern states to the Pax Romana to feudal Europe to communist state capitalism to modern market capitalism), the basic structure has persisted now for at least five thousand years, since the rise of the great conquest states of Mesopotamia around 3000 BCE.*[12]

We easily observe the domination system in the structure of kingdoms, empires, and dictatorships. It has been embodied in traditional customs and religious teachings throughout history. But when democratic systems in a largely secular culture are controlled by wealthy and powerful

12. Wink, *Powers That Be*, 39–40.

forces, the same results occur. Massive tax cuts for the wealthiest, bloated military budgets, welfare for giant corporations, authoritarian leaders who cling to power, vast prison systems, and cuts to social services for the poorest Americans are all signs of a domination system.

Walter Wink notes that the teachings of Jesus were a prescriptive remedy to the domination system of his time. The kingdom of God that he described is an antidote to the disease of the domination system. The vision of Jesus stands in direct opposition to the political and economic aims of these pervasively unjust social structures. It is a vision of the domination system turned upside-down. Therefore, every act of resistance to the domination system, every protest of its unjust laws and structures, every effort to transform it for the common good is a sign of the inbreaking kingdom of God that Jesus proclaimed.

In the reign of God, all typical domination values are reversed. The first shall be last and the last shall be first. The greatest people in the kingdom shall be servants. The powerful shall be brought low and the lowly lifted up. The hungry shall be filled with good things and the rich sent away empty. The kingdom of God particularly belongs to the poor, the hungry, and the mourning because they will gladly welcome its coming. The rich will find it almost impossible to enter because they are too entrenched in the current domination system and its benefits and will resist the change the kingdom of God promises.

We cannot eliminate the dark side of our human condition, but we can summon the better angels of our nature to make us a more humane, kind, and decent people. Even if persistent social selfishness cannot be eliminated, it can be mitigated and minimized by people of good will. The hope of the reign of God is that a transformation of the politics of selfishness is possible through the efforts of transformed individuals who are committed to nonviolent social change motivated by love and compassion.

JOURNEY OF TRANSFORMATION

Following Jesus involves a movement away from self-obsession and toward the needs of other people. We begin the journey of transformative discipleship by denying ourselves and emptying our hearts of self-centered devotion.

> *Then he said to them all, "If any want to become my followers, let them deny themselves and take up their cross daily and follow me."*[13]

13. Luke 9:23.

Although most New Testament translations use the phrase "let them deny themselves," a few offer variations of "let them forget themselves" or "let them give up the things they want." The New Living Translation (NLT) says, "You must turn from your selfish ways." Selfishness is the fundamental nature of individual sin and is the root cause of the social sin of the domination system that causes so many people around the world to be oppressed, disenfranchised, and forgotten. But Jesus calls us out from the lordship of selfishness to a new mode of life. He calls us to risk everything for that new way of thinking and living.

Social activist and journalist Dorothy Day (1897–1980) said that our hearts must change to follow Jesus.

> *The greatest challenge of the day is: how to bring about a revolution of the heart, a revolution which has to start with each one of us? When we begin to take the lowest place, to wash the feet of others, to love our brothers with that burning love, that passion, which led to the cross, then we can truly say, "Now I have begun."*[14]

The gospel *of* Jesus invites us to go beyond ourselves and live for others—feeding those in need, sheltering them, clothing them. Followers of Jesus do not undertake good works to get to heaven; they do so because charity, service, and a commitment to justice represent the faithful lifestyle that Jesus invites us to enter.

To fully understand the social gospel *of* Jesus and to follow his distinctly countercultural Way, it is important to recover the message and mission of the kingdom of God that has been lost, hidden, or misrepresented in far too many Christian churches. The kingdom of God is about engaging in a conspiracy of love to change the world.

14. Day, *Loaves and Fishes*, 215.

Chapter 2

context for a life

Justice, and only justice, you shall pursue.
—Deuteronomy 16:20 (the Law)

What does the Lord require of you but to do justice?
—Micah 6:8 (the Prophets)

Strive first for the reign of God and God's justice.
—Matthew 6:33 (the Gospels)

The biblical call to social justice flows through the entire Bible. In the Hebrew Bible, we find it in the law (Torah) and in wisdom literature, including the Psalms and Proverbs. We find it repeatedly in the words of the prophets—Isaiah, Amos, Micah, Zechariah, Ezekiel. And the call to justice flows through the New Testament—in the life of Jesus recorded in the gospels and life of the early church as recorded in Acts.

At its heart, the Bible tells the story of a God who liberated an oppressed people from a powerful empire and created a remarkable covenant with them: to worship no other God and to demonstrate their devotion by creating a just society that would stand in contrast to the oppressive empires of the world. The essential message of the covenant is to love God and to love your neighbor.

Many people believe that Jesus of Nazareth taught only spiritual truths and did not care about the politics and economics of his day, even though they had a great impact on the poor peasants—fishermen, farmers, prostitutes, and tax collectors—who followed him. An unbiased reading of the gospels tells a different story. Jesus lived during a time of political turmoil—a tense situation in which the poor suffered at the hands of the domination system of their time.

If Jesus accepted any messianic role, it was that of a social prophet—one who is called by God to voice God's demand for justice to those who hold economic, political, and religious power. It is a decidedly political task. That is because the pursuit of justice is always political.

Jesus worked to fulfill the hopes and dreams of his people but not in the way many imagined or expected. Make no mistake, even though Jesus was filled with the spirit of God—the spirit of love and compassion and justice—he was not offering a solely spiritual solution. He was concerned about oppressive political regimes and an economy of commercialized agriculture that was impoverishing the peasants of Palestine at an alarming rate, and he offered a contrasting vision of society—the kingdom of God. He developed a political platform for a new social movement, one that would lead to a more just and equitable society.

POLITICS IN THE FIRST CENTURY

When we discuss the social and political stance of Jesus, we must first understand the political structures of first-century Roman Palestine, which was an occupied province of the Roman Empire. Jesus experienced three despotic structures of government organized for a privileged few at the expense of the vast majority. Galilee was a monarchy ruled by Herod Antipas. After the removal of his brother Herod Archelaus by Rome in 6 CE, nearby Judea was ruled directly by a Roman Procurator who reported to the governor of Syria. However, the day-to-day operations were entrusted to a wealthy oligarchy (meaning "the ruling few") of the Sadducees, sometimes referred to in the gospels as "the leaders of the people," or "the chief priests and the elders." In conquered territories, it was always Rome's practice to find indigenous collaborators to rule on their behalf. And they always chose people from the wealthy class who saw it in their personal interest to support power when it advantaged them. On top of these structures was an emperor in Rome who was essentially a self-appointed dictator. So, Jesus was confronted by a monarchy in Galilee, an oligarchy in Jerusalem, and a dictatorship in Rome.

People living under the oppression of a domination system generally respond to the situation in one of four ways. They may become part of the establishment; but that course is only available to a few with the most wealth and power. They may simply try to cope or compromise to some degree with the ruling authorities to survive—go along to get along. They may emigrate or withdraw from society in isolated communities. Or they may take up arms and revolt. The people of first-century Palestine certainly fit this pattern of multiple responses. There were several different influential groups or parties active in the culture: Sadducees (establishment), Pharisees (compromise), Essenes (withdrawal), Zealots (revolution). Except for the Sadducees, the other three groups all hoped for a political savior to drive out Rome and set up a new rule.

These parties were notable factions with various political impacts, but they represented only a small minority of the population. They were largely composed of literate elites who had the luxury of engaging in positions of political and religious cooperation or opposition. Most of the people were subjugated and defeated peasants who were buffeted by political winds and degraded by poverty. They just tried to survive until events pushed them to the point of subversive action and rebellion. According to the Talmud, these illiterate and uneducated peasants were commonly known as *am ha'aretz* (*ahm hah-AHR-etz*), meaning "the people of the land." This was a derogatory term suggesting that they were ignorant, illiterate, and uneducated rubes. In John's gospel, they are referred to as the "rabble who know nothing about the law [Torah]."[1] The peasants found it hard to make any significant response to oppression when they were trying to eke out an existence from the land. But as some saw their lives spiral out of control and they lost lands, homes, and employment, violent rebellion must have been a tempting option.

ECONOMICS OF EXPLOITATION

Significant changes in the global economy of the first century had created a crisis for the peasant class in Israel. Under Rome, they had transitioned from a traditional agrarian economy to a commercialized agrarian economy that required the creation of large estates. At one time the elites were satisfied to take the agricultural surplus of the peasant producer's efforts; now they began to take the land. Peasants moved in a downward spiral from small freeholders to tenant farmers, to day laborers, and finally to either beggars or bandits. Throughout his life, Jesus identified with the poor and their plight because he was one of them.

Debt was the tool used by the wealthy elites to acquire large plots of land that were then converted from subsistence farms to large estates and

1. John 7:49.

vineyards growing crops for export. When you understand this economic scenario, you really begin to understand many of the parables told by Jesus—populated with characters like workers in the vineyards, day laborers, and dishonest stewards.

When peasants were unable to keep their farms going—either through drought, illness, or mismanagement—they were forced to borrow money, using their land as collateral, from wealthy elites toward the next harvest to survive. Even if the crops failed, they still had to pay taxes and tithes. That usually required cash, not crops. Eventually, if they could not pay their debts, their land was foreclosed and taken from them. Debt was a big deal for the peasant class and forefront in their minds. It is revealed in the prayer Jesus taught his disciples, "Forgive us our debts as we forgive those indebted to us."[2]

According to the Hebrew Bible, justice is what God desires, what God demands. And social injustice stirs God's anger at nations and their leaders. But what kinds of things constitute social injustice? They include activities that prevent people from having access to the basic conditions for life and societal structures that favor the rich and disadvantage the poor.

A JEWISH PEASANT LIFE

Jesus was probably born in Nazareth (*Natzeret*), not in Bethlehem (*Beit-Lechem*) as Matthew and Luke contend. Located in the northern province of Galilee, Nazareth was a small farming village nestled in a hollow in the hills at the site of an ancient spring. It was surrounded by olive orchards and cypress trees. Archeological evidence suggests that the village was less than 200 years old in the first century. It stood at an elevation of about 1,200 feet and commanded a panoramic view of its corner of the world. Its population was somewhere between 200 to 400 people, or perhaps twenty to forty families.[3]

The region of Galilee was a small area about fifty miles long and thirty-five miles across. It was within this limited area that Jesus later lived and worked. The town of Nazareth was located about twenty miles inland from

2. Matt 6:9–13 / Luke 11:2–4.

3. Today, Nazareth is known as "the Arab capital of Israel" with a population of nearly 80,000. The inhabitants are now predominantly Arab citizens of whom 70 percent are Muslim and 30 percent Christian. It is home to the Basilica of the Annunciation which Catholic tradition contends is built over the site of the house of the Virgin Mary, and where the angel Gabriel appeared to her and announced that she would conceive and bear Jesus.

the Mediterranean Sea, fifteen miles from the Lake of Galilee to the east, and roughly one hundred miles north of Jerusalem.

Jesus spent most of his life in Nazareth, around 30 years. A backwater village in an insignificant outpost of the vast Roman Empire, Nazareth was not much of a place to grow up in. It was never mentioned in the Hebrew Bible, in the Talmud, or in the writings of the Jewish historian Josephus. *"Can anything good come out of Nazareth?"*[4] people would later ask.

Nazareth was in a beautiful and fertile area. Its favorable location would have attracted absentee landlords, who owned nearby fields, flocks, vineyards, orchards, and gardens. These wealthy landowners may have built residences in the neighboring cities of Sepphoris, Tiberius, Ptolemais, or even distant Jerusalem.

Even though Jesus spoke in largely rural terms about the reign of God, reflecting the background of his listeners, he grew up an hour's walk (two and a half miles) from Sepphoris, one of the most cosmopolitan areas of the Mideast. Standing along one of the busiest trade routes in ancient Palestine, Jesus could observe a typical Hellenistic city with its baths, temples, theaters, statues, and festivals. The city boasted a population of 30,000 and was a center for culture and art in Galilee. Growing up in Galilee, he could observe a culture in which ancient Jewish traditions and contemporary Greco-Roman urban values collided.

FAMILY LIFE

Jesus was probably the first child of a carpenter and construction worker named Yosep (Joseph) and his wife Myriam (Mary). The Gospel of Luke tells us that Nazareth was the home village of Myriam.[5] When Yosep had Jesus circumcised, eight days after birth, he named his child after Moses' successor, Joshua. In Hebrew, the name is Yehoshua ("Yahweh saves" or "Yahweh is salvation"), and in those days the name was usually shortened to Yeshu'a or even to Yeshu, which is how Jesus was popularly known.[6] Yeshu was a common name in those days. To the Jews, the name meant freedom and liberation.

Most of Yeshu's neighbors would have been farmers who lived in the village and worked the fields nearby, or workers in the relatively small number of trades necessary to support agricultural life. Yosep is identified in Matthew's gospel as a carpenter. The Greek word is *tekton* (*TEK-tone*) which

4. John 1:46.

5. Luke 1:26.

6. Luke 1:31.

can be translated in the broad sense as any craftsman or workman, but particularly a carpenter or builder. Because a father normally taught his trade to his sons, Yeshu probably followed his father's building and woodworking trade. Yeshu is identified as "the carpenter"[7] and "the carpenter's son."[8] Yosep, as a craftsman and builder, was probably an itinerant workman, going wherever there was construction work to be done. Nazareth could probably not provide enough business for a builder to support his family, and Joseph may have worked in other towns and villages. Joseph and Jesus could possibly have worked on the construction projects in Sepphoris, four miles to the north, where the city was being reconstructed after having been destroyed by the Roman army. In 3 BCE, Herod Antipas began rebuilding the city as his capital.

Yeshu was probably joined in Yosep's construction trade by his brothers Ya'akov (Jacob/James), Yosef (Joses), Yehudah (Judas), and Shemon (Simon). He had at least two sisters whose names are not recorded in the gospels. It was a large family—at least seven children—and not particularly well off. They would have likely had a diet based on bread and olive oil supplemented by fruits and vegetables from nearby fields and orchards.

As members of the *artisan* class, Yosep and his family were on the lower end of the economic and social scale. Another way of saying that, is they likely lived in poverty. Although a construction worker would be considered middle class today, there was no middle class in antiquity. In this period, these itinerant workers were generally peasants who had lost their land through indebtedness. Thus, on both the social and economic scales, they ranked below the *peasants* who still worked their own land.

However, Jesus and his family were not at the bottom of the economic ladder in his society. There were others worse off. The lowest level in the class structure were the "expendables." These people existed because—despite the high mortality rates, disease, famine, and war—the lower classes produced more people than the upper classes found it profitable to employ in a commercialized agrarian economy. If they found work at all, it was as day laborers. In any event, their lives were brutal and short. The effects of poverty, disease, and violence were probably like that of the poor urban and rural areas in Third World countries today. The average life expectancy for a Jewish male in Palestine was 29 years, because many children died before the age of five.

Somewhere between 80 and 95 percent of the population were illiterate. The gospels indicate that Jesus could read, but it is very unlikely. Like

7. Mark 6:3.

8. Matt 13:55.

other Jews of his day, Yeshu spoke Aramaic, presumably with a distinctive Galilean accent. He probably also spoke some Greek, which was the language of the urban areas of Galilee. Any Jewish artisan or merchant wanting to do business with the Hellenistic upper class needed to converse in the common dialect of Greek known as *Koine* (*koy-NAY*).

RELIGION

Yeshu was a Jew. While growing up, he would have attended the synagogue every Shabbat (Sabbath) that ran from sundown Friday to sundown Saturday. In Nazareth, the synagogue (meaning "gathering" or "assembly") may have met in a building dedicated to that purpose, but more likely they probably gathered in an open village meeting place where at other times disputes were settled by village elders.

There he would participate in services of scripture recitations and prayer. He would have heard the stories and words of the prophets—of Elijah, Samuel, Isaiah, and Amos. Perhaps he sang the poetic verses of the Psalms. He may have known portions or all of them by memory, a feat not uncommon among learned illiterates. In an oral culture, most people knew the basic stories and foundational narratives of their tradition. An intellectual prodigy, Jesus developed a very strong command of his religious heritage. He would have recited the *Shema* every morning and evening, which affirmed:

> *Hear O Israel: The Lord our God is one Lord; and you shall love the Lord your God with all your heart, and with all your soul, and with all your might.*[9]

Yeshu would have participated in the five major Jewish festivals and presumably went on pilgrimages to Jerusalem. Three of the major festivals are agricultural and are tied to the seasons of the land in Palestine. *Pesach* (Passover), the spring festival, marks the beginning of the barley season. *Shabouth* (Weeks or Pentecost) marks its conclusion 50 days later. *Sukkoth* (Tabernacles) celebrates the autumn harvest and is a time of thanksgiving. It is preceded by a ten-day period of communal purification. From an early date these agricultural festivals came to be associated with formative events in Israel's historic memory. Pesach commemorated the Passover by the angel of death in Egypt with the eating of unleavened bread. The other two major festivals were in the fall. *Rosh Hashanah*, the Jewish New Year,

9. Deut 6:4–5.

commemorates creation. Ten days later the people fasted on *Yom Kippur*, the Day of Atonement.

It was a superstitious world. Magic and witchcraft, demons and angels, possession and exorcism, miracles and prophecies, divination and astrology were taken for granted. Wonder workers and healers toured the towns, performing cures and miracles.

This is about all we can know or suppose about Jesus, prior to his adult ministry. He appeared on the world stage when he was a young man, about 30 years old. That was when he met the wilderness preacher, who set him on the road to his destiny.

JOHN, THE PROPHET OF JUSTICE OR DOOM

John the baptizer appeared in the wilderness, proclaiming a baptism of repentance for the forgiveness of sins. And people from the whole Judean countryside and all the people of Jerusalem were going out to him, and were baptized by him in the river Jordan, confessing their sins.[10]

In those days Jesus came from Nazareth of Galilee and was baptized by John in the Jordan.[11]

Jesus was profoundly moved by the message of Yochanan (John) the baptizer. John's prophetic message was a simple one. God was angry with the chosen people and planned to punish them unless a change took place. God's anger was not due to individual sins, or even over a nation that had turned away from the worship of God. Instead, John declared that the issue was a lack of social justice.

Peasants were losing their land. Poor people were going hungry. They were suffering from illness and deprivation, and many were without adequate clothing. People were not helping one another in the face of desperate circumstances. Individuals were left on their own to suffer from an oppressive and unjust system. They were desperate and on the verge of rebellion against the wealthy elites and the Roman Empire.

John warned that God would intervene in history to condemn and destroy Israel, bringing an end the present situation. God would do this through a foreign agent—the empire of Rome and Roman legions—just as God had done centuries earlier to Israel and Judah with the armies of Assyria and Babylon. In John's vision, God's judgment would bring massive

10. Mark 1:4–5.
11. Mark 1:9.

destruction.[12] John pictured these events as a great forest fire before which the snakes of the forest flee,[13] in which trees and chaff are burnt,[14] and in which people will be engulfed in a baptism of fire.[15] He also made use of the metaphors of the ax and the winnowing fan used to separate wheat from chaff. There is no reason to think that John was referring to a burning hell in the afterlife. The forest fire he described is an image of hell on earth. He foresaw not the end of the world, but the Roman destruction of Jewish life, culture, and political hopes in Palestine.

John employed the metaphors of a prophet. The prophets dealt with the concrete actions of God in history. A prophecy is not a prediction; it is a warning or a promise. The prophet warns Israel about God's judgment and promises God's salvation. Both the warning and the promise are conditional. They depend upon the free response of the people of Israel. If Israel does not change, the consequences will be disastrous. If Israel does change, there will be an abundance of blessings.

It did not take special insight to see that the Jewish people were on the verge of a suicidal uprising against the Roman Empire. Recurring episodes of violence were leading toward a dramatic confrontation with the most powerful military force on earth, which would culminate by the destruction of their culture within four decades. The shadow of catastrophe hung over the land and the signs could be clearly seen for those who paused long enough to read them.

Change or be destroyed, John cried. When confronted with John's dramatic words of impending doom and a call to conversion, the people asked, "What then shall we do?" John's response was that religious rituals could not save them. Only acts of charity and justice could avert God's anger and wrath.

> *And the crowds asked him [John], "What then should we do?" In reply he said to them, "Whoever has two shirts must share with someone who has none. Whoever has food should do the same."*[16]

Solidarity and sharing among the people of the villages was a first step toward the kingdom of God. But the call for justice was addressed to others

---

12. John's vision was first reported in the gospels of Matthew and Luke which were written after 85 CE. They wrote following the Great Jewish Rebellion (66–73 CE). So, the gospel writers are looking backward to around 30 CE at a warning of events that already happened.

13. Matt 3:8.

14. Matt 3:10, 12.

15. Matt 3:11.

16. Luke 3:10–11.

who were far away, living in luxurious homes and palaces. In Jerusalem, it was the Sadducees, and the aristocratic families they represented, who needed to change. Closer to hand, it was Herod Antipas, the ruler of Galilee and Perea, who required a new heart. John believed that these uncaring rulers must embrace justice for the poor to forestall a simmering peasant rebellion and a massive Roman military suppression.

JESUS, THE PROPHET OF JUSTICE AND HOPE

John was eventually arrested and later executed by Herod Antipas.

> *But Herod the ruler, who had been rebuked by him because of Herodias, his brother's wife, and because of all the evil things that Herod had done, added to them all by shutting up John in prison.*[17]

After John's arrest and execution, Jesus picked up the mantle of leadership from his mentor. But as he carried on John's work, Jesus began to form a new vision. John was right, of course. If the situation did not change drastically, many people would lose their lives in a futile struggle against the power of Rome. The suffering of poor and oppressed peasants would only increase. The institutions and culture of the Jewish people would be wiped out and replaced with Greek culture and Roman institutions. And the worship of Yahweh would be replaced by the pantheon of Roman Gods.

Jesus did not feel called to save Israel by bringing everyone to a baptism of repentance in the Jordan. He decided that something else was necessary, something that had to do with the poor, the sick, and the outcast—the lost sheep of the house of Israel.

Jesus and John saw God differently. John saw God as an angry judge. Jesus saw God as a compassionate and nurturing father. As a result, Jesus modified John's message. Jesus began to find a new way to address the coming catastrophe. He developed an alternative vision, a way out, a way to avert violent confrontation.

John preached actions of justice, but with his emphasis on the coming catastrophe, these were actions that would have been motivated by fear. Jesus no longer preached John's message of doom. Instead, he preached a vision of the way things could be, the way they would be when God established God's rule on earth. Like John's message, it had to do with acts of compassion and justice. But the way of Jesus was based on hope, not fear. The reign of God operates by invitation, not coercion.

17. Luke 3:19–20.

If people would begin living out the just and peaceful values of God's in-breaking reign. the inevitable destruction could be avoided. Jesus believed that the time to establish God's rule on earth was now, not at some future date. Jesus now clearly saw the way God would act in history, and it was through him.

Jesus gathered the timeless hopes of humanity for a world of peace, justice, and equity. In words and actions, he demonstrated that the time had come for a new way of living. The mission Jesus now embarked on was to make his vision of God's new reign clearly visible to the people of his day, and to invite them to enter in through communities of solidarity and sharing. John relied upon a baptism of conversion; Jesus set out to liberate people from lives of suffering and anguish—present and future. In Jesus' mind, John had already breached the walls of the old order and made the way for Jesus to follow.

> *Up until the time of John the Baptist, we had the law of Moses and the words of the prophets. Since John arrived, the good news about the kingdom of God has been announced. Now people everywhere are pushing to get in.*[18]

18. Matt 11:12 / Luke 16:16.

Chapter 3

a conspiracy of love

Now after John was arrested, Jesus came to Galilee, proclaiming the good news of God, and saying, "The time is fulfilled, and the kingdom of God has come near."

—THE GOSPEL OF MARK 1:14–15

Soon afterwards he traveled through towns and villages, proclaiming and bringing the message of the kingdom of God.

—THE GOSPEL OF LUKE 8:1

From that time Jesus began to proclaim, "Change your life. For the kingdom of God has come near."

—THE GOSPEL OF MATTHEW 4:17

THE DOMINANT THEME IN the gospels, and the center of Jesus' proclamation, was a social and political vision that he described as *the kingdom of God*. This one phrase sums up his whole ministry and his whole life's work. Every thought and saying of Jesus were directed and subordinated to one single thing: the realization of the reign of the God of love within human society. It was never *his* kingdom; it was always *God's* kingdom. Moreover, it was an earthly, not a heavenly, kingdom.

The Greek word that we have translated into English as kingdom is *basileia* (*bas-ih-LEE-ah*), meaning kingship, kingly rule, reign, or sovereignty, but never a place or territory. The expression *kingdom of God—basileia tou theou* (*bas-ih-LEE-ah too THEH-oo*)—points to the ruling activity of God over human relationships. It is the quality of this ruling activity that is important, because it is often diametrically opposed to traditional political establishments. Herod the Great had the title of *basileus* (*bas-ih-LYOOS*) or king. So *basileia* has to do with who governs the common life and what kind of community or society they establish.

When Jesus used the term *kingdom of God,* it expressed a vision of the kind of society God desired for God's people. What would life be like if God and not Herod or Caesar ruled this land? Jesus declared that this new form of society was coming into being. However, it would not come from violent revolution. Instead, it would be the result of subversive noncompliance with the domination system by a people committed to nonviolent resistance and action. He urgently cried out to his contemporaries, "The kingdom of God is at hand!"

When Jesus announced the coming of the kingdom of God, he was announcing a social revolution. Jesus saw himself as the messenger chosen by God to deliver the good news of God's powerful new activity in the world. God's kingdom of justice was coming to replace the authority of ingrained systems of domination. The kingdom of God, as proclaimed by Jesus, was clearly political. Its very name implies the politics of God.

According to Jesus, God is creating a new order in our midst. He declared that God's kingdom is something of great value, yet it is often hidden from view by the overwhelming presence of injustice and violence and must be uncovered or recovered. It is something that has been lost and must be found again. It is something we have long believed is impossible but must now struggle and hope for again. The kingdom is something that cannot be seen in and of itself, yet its effects are plainly visible. To enter the kingdom, in fact to even *see* the kingdom, one must experience a dramatic change—a reorientation, a rebirth, a significant transformation.

Let us be clear, the kingdom that Jesus proclaimed is not a theocracy—a government controlled by a religious institution or officials who are regarded as divinely guided. It is not a rule from on high in which correct behavior is mandated. In many theocracies, like Iran, government leaders are members of the clergy, and the state's legal system is based on religious law. The kingdom of God is not like the government of Gilead as described in Margaret Atwood's (b. 1939) futuristic dystopian novel, *The Handmaid's Tale.* The kingdom of God is very different. It is not a society run by the church, nor is it based on harsh tenets found in the Hebrew Bible or elsewhere. The governing principle is simply love. It is a society of the poor, of people living on the margins, along with many others, whose actions and relationships are shaped by love, peace, and justice.

Jesus painted a vision of God changing the world not through a heavenly decree, but from within through the creation of a new community bonded together in egalitarian social relationships. He described what would happen when love finally broke through the hearts and minds of people to transform their actions and relationships into a society based on compassion, generosity, and equality.

The reign of God must be understood as both personal transformation and social transformation. Everything that Jesus says about the ruling style of God is true in both dimensions. Any attempt to see it as one or the other is an incomplete understanding of the kingdom. Personal transformation must lead to social transformation. And social transformation can only come about through the efforts of transformed people. It is not just about good people offering personal service and charity to those in need, it is about a wholesale transformation of the social order that will eliminate human suffering and need among us.

What made Jesus so unique was his conviction that the reigning style of God had already started happening. It was not to be found in a new king who would ascend the throne of Israel with a trumpet blast, nor would it come about through a bloody military liberation that would overthrow oppressive rulers. The fundamental message of Jesus' proclamation was the day of God's reign has already dawned—it is here in our midst. The liberation from oppression that the prophets proclaimed, and the poor had long desired to see, is now present. Jesus' healing of those who suffered from blindness and leprosy, sharing meals with the unacceptable and outcasts, and announcement of good news to the desperately poor were all signs that God's ruling style had arrived. And it began with establishing small contrast communities amid the domination system.

The kingdom of God was the metaphor Jesus used to describe his vision of the way things were meant to be in human society—how things could be dramatically different within us and among us—and to understand Jesus you must understand the nature and power of a vision. Visions always deal with the future. Indeed, a vision is where tomorrow begins, for it expresses what those who share the vision are working hard to create. The power of a vision is that while it describes the future state to be achieved, it begins to immediately shape the present. A community or organization does not wait for the results of a vision to magically appear, they work together to make it a reality. Jesus chose to take the long-awaited dream of a just and compassionate society, and by articulating and acting on it, make it a vision that would lead to the transformation of the world. When people embrace a vision of the future, they begin to live it out in the present.

A NEW METAPHOR

As a metaphor, the *kingdom of God* does not work very well for us today, nor will it conceivably work any better in the future. Kingdoms and empires are diminishing around the world. Democracies are rising. But no matter what form governments take, domination systems abound. So, it would be helpful to find a new metaphor that people can better understand and connect with in the twenty-first century. We need a fresh language that will better describe the vision of Jesus and our role as his followers in a postmodern world. Brian McLaren (b. 1956) put it this way:

> *When Jesus spoke of the kingdom of God, his language was charged with urgent political, religious, and cultural electricity. But today, if we speak of the kingdom of God, the original electricity is largely gone, and in its place, we often find a kind of tired familiarity that inspires not hope and excitement, but anxiety or boredom . . .*
> *For many people today, kingdom language evokes patriarchy, chauvinism, imperialism, domination, and a regime without freedom—the very opposite of the liberating, barrier-breaking, domination-shattering, reconciling movement the kingdom of God was intended to be! . . . If Jesus were here today, I'm quite certain he wouldn't use the language of kingdom at all, which leaves us wondering how he would articulate his message.*[1]

For some time, I have been using the "conspiracy of love" as a new metaphor for what Jesus was describing, especially considering his parables of the mustard seed and the leaven which have conspiratorial elements. I see the conspiracy of love as the subversive activity of a people focused on Jesus' vision of a better world—a world governed by love. The word *conspiracy* derives from the same root as *spirit*. The Latin root *spirare* (*SPEE-rah-reh*) means *to breathe*. For example, the word *respiration* is *to breathe again*, and *inspiration* means *to breathe in*—to be filled with the spirit. To *conspire* normally connotes agreement or unity in an activity, but it literally means *to breathe together*. Those engaged in a conspiracy are so united around an idea or action that they are seen to breathe as one. I believe that Jesus called his followers to engage in a conspiracy of profound personal and social transformation that would undermine the domination system in every time and place.

I also want to justify my substitution of the word "love" for "God." In my opinion, one does not have to believe in God—at least not in the traditional sense of a supernatural all-powerful being—to engage in the

---

1. McLaren, *Everything Must Change*, 138–139.

conspiracy of love. Let me take a moment to describe what a non-super-natural, non-theistic God looks like. A remarkable document in the New Testament—the first letter of John—introduced a completely different way of thinking about God than our traditional conception.

> *God is love, and he who abides in love abides in God, and God abides in him.*[2]

As far as I know, the New Testament has only three definitions for God: God is spirit,[3] God is light,[4] and God is love.[5] The first definition comes from the gospel of John and the second two derive from the First Letter of John. So, these metaphors may derive from the same community. But of all these definitions, love represents the highest, deepest, and most powerful force in human life. It is the energy that fosters human growth and change. Love is the impulse behind empathy and concern, and the fuel that drives compassion and justice.

In Greek, "God is love" is *theos ein agapē* (*THEY-ohs ayn ah-GAH-pay*). Agapē (*ah-GAH-pay*) is one of four different Greek words that we translate into English as love. Philia (*fil-EE-ah*) refers to loyal friendship or a brotherly love; eros (*ERR-ohs*) is used to describe passionate, erotic, or romantic love; and storgē (*STOR-gay*) is used in relation to the natural affection of family love, like the love of a parent for a child. But agapē (or more commonly—*agape*) implies a selfless love, a self-giving love, often an unconditional love. It is a love directed toward others, putting the needs of others ahead of oneself. This is the kind of love people saw in Jesus.

When the New Testament declares that "God is love," it means that these two language symbols—*God* and *love*—are identical. If God is love, then the converse is also true: Love is God. Therefore, the word "God" is a name we give to the spirit of selfless love found at the depths of our human-ity and experienced in the relationship of human love toward one another. Thus, "God" can be seen as a language symbol that personifies self-giving compassionate love as a divine entity. For millennia, humans have projected this image of God onto a supernatural being. However, according to the First Letter of John, God is not a loving being. God is love itself.

Love, bound up in human flesh, is the manifestation of God in the world. This is another way of looking at divine incarnation. For the early

2. 1 John 4:16.

3. John 4: 24: "God is spirit, and those who worship him must worship in spirit and truth."

4. 1 John 1:5: "God is light and in him there is no darkness at all."

5. 1 John 4:7–8: "Beloved, let us love one another, because love is from God; every-one who loves is born of God and knows God. Whoever does not love does not know God, for God is love."

church, Jesus embodied the image of a God of love, revealed in his words and deeds. Therefore, some saw him as the incarnation of God on earth. However, the radical message of the New Testament is that God is no longer an external being who dwells in heaven; God has come to dwell among us, not just in the person of Jesus, but within every human being. Indeed, God has always—and only—been a part of humanity, located deep within human consciousness and projected as a divine actor in the human story. God, in the form of compassionate love, is a latent presence within each of us, but this God remains hidden until humans outwardly express love toward others. Loving one another is the full expression of God on earth.[6]

I do not believe that one must be a Christian to be engaged in the work of the conspiracy of love. After all, the peasants Jesus spoke to in Galilee, Judea, and Samaria were not Christians, and they were the first ones called to the task. The Jewish concept of *tikkun olam*, a Hebrew phrase that means repairing or healing the world, likewise suggests that as humans we have a shared responsibility to transform the world through social action in the pursuit of justice and peace. Many other faiths have similar calls to work for a better world. The vision of Jesus requires the involvement of people everywhere—people of every faith and people of no faith at all.

German pastor, theologian, and martyr Dietrich Bonhoeffer (1906–1945) wrote from prison in May 1944:

> *The day will come . . . when people will once more be called to speak the word of God in such a way that the world is changed and renewed. It will be in a new language, perhaps quite nonreligious language, but liberating and redeeming like Jesus's language, so that people will be alarmed, and yet overcome by its power—the language of a new righteousness and truth, a language proclaiming that God makes peace with humankind and that God's kingdom is drawing near.[7]*

So, *the conspiracy of love* is my suggested metaphor for the kingdom of God. I believe it is a phrase that is well suited for the postmodern world and may have an appeal to younger generations. Whenever the "kingdom of God" is mentioned going forward, try substituting the phrase the "conspiracy of love" in your mind and see if it brings new excitement and understanding to the text. However, for sake of consistency and historical accuracy, let us continue with the original metaphor from the lips of Jesus—the kingdom of God.

6. 1 John 4:12: "No one has ever seen God. But if we love each other, God lives in us, and His love is brought to full expression in us." (NLT).

7. Bonhoeffer, *Letters and Papers*, 300.

THE INAUGURAL ADDRESS

If we take our spiritual blinders off for a moment, we can begin to see Jesus in a new light. Imagine him in the context of a struggle for social and economic equality like the struggles of Mohandas Gandhi and Martin Luther King Jr as they addressed their respective domination systems. According to Luke's gospel, Jesus began with an inaugural address in Nazareth—his "I have a dream" speech. Jesus called for the implementation of the Jubilee year by quoting the prophet Isaiah.

> *He went to Nazareth, where he had been brought up, and on the Sabbath day he went into the synagogue, as was his custom. He stood up to read, and the scroll of the prophet Isaiah was handed to him. Unrolling it, he found the place where it is written:*

> *"The Spirit of Yahweh is upon me, because he has anointed me to bring good news to the poor. He has sent me to proclaim release to the captives and recovery of sight to the blind, to let the oppressed go free, to announce that this is the year of Yahweh's amnesty."*

> *Then he rolled up the scroll, gave it back to the attendant and sat down. The eyes of everyone in the synagogue were fastened on him. He began by saying to them, "You've just heard scripture make history. It has now come true in this place."*[8]

Jesus was announcing that he had come to establish the ancient Hebrew concept of Jubilee in which the economic debts of the poor were forgiven, debt-slaves were released, and land that had been taken in foreclosure for peasant indebtedness would be returned by rich landowners to the dispossessed. This was good news to the working poor and the completely destitute who were forced to become beggars.

The Jubilee year was the culmination of seven sabbath years. The number seven had magical power for the Hebrews. They believed that God created the world in six days and then rested on the seventh. They were unique among ancient peoples in mandating that people and animals should rest one day a week. The word Sabbath comes from the Hebrew word *shabath*, meaning, "to rest." The Hebrew people believed that the land itself should be allowed to rest from agricultural production every seventh year. They called it the sabbath or sabbatical year.

The book of Deuteronomy mandated in its Sabbatical Year Code that all financial debts must be forgiven[9] and all indentured Hebrew debt-slaves

8. Luke 4:16–21. (Creative combination of NRSV, *Five Gospels*, and *Message*.)

9. Deut 15:1–3.

must be released every seven years,[10] in a form of economic grace. Then, after seven Sabbatical Years, the fiftieth year was to be declared a Jubilee Year. The Jubilee Year Code in Leviticus required that the land—the economic capital of an agricultural economy—must be redistributed to the peasants who had lost their land to the wealthy through indebtedness.[11] People could become indebted through their own fault (laziness, drunkenness, or ineptitude), but they could also become indebted by things beyond their control (like illness, drought, or systemic exploitation).

Once every fifty years, the Law demanded leveling the economic playing field. The Hebrews believed that Yahweh had rescued them from oppression in Egypt. And Yahweh refused to let them oppress one another. Therefore, they could not allow social inequality to become prolonged or endemic. The Jubilee year was a call to the wealthy to give up land they had accumulated and to return it to the landless. It is the rich who must give back what had been taken from the peasants. They must free people from debt, and debtors from prison. They were invited to be like the Yahweh they worshipped—compassionate, gracious, and just.

However, Jesus was not naive. He knew that the call for Jubilee restoration would be rejected by the rich and powerful. It had little chance of succeeding if it required the willing participation of those at the top of society. So, he addressed the domination system in a different way—a revolutionary way of living by those at the bottom of society that would try to mitigate suffering through radical generosity and sharing of resources. Jesus rejected the politics of violent revolution. Instead, he developed a nonviolent approach. He would not try to overthrow the kings, oligarchs, and the wealthy landowners. Instead, he and his followers would create alternative communities—modeling a new social order amid the old. Small changes, he knew, can lead to big results.

And, Jesus taught, the kingdom of God was beginning immediately, starting with powerless groups at the bottom of society. The poor and the outcasts would model life in the kingdom of God for the wealthy and powerful. To the poor peasants and fishermen in the villages and towns of Galilee it came as good news. The decisive moment in time appointed by God had arrived. The oppressive social order was being replaced with God's new order.

> *Then Jesus, filled with the power of the Spirit, returned to Galilee, and a report about him spread through all the surrounding*

---

10. Deut 15:12–15.

11. Lev 25:8–12.

country. He began to teach in their synagogues and was praised by everyone.[12]

Jesus came to Galilee, proclaiming the good news of God, and saying, "The time is fulfilled, and God's kingdom is at hand; reshape your lives, and believe in the good news."[13]

However, the people of his day were looking for a different kind of kingdom and a military messiah to lead it. Jesus would disappoint their expectations. They believed that when God finally acted, it would be with great signs and wonders. Jesus implied that God was already acting through the actions of poor and oppressed peoples. God's actions were already present but could not be seen by people living under the influence of an old paradigm.

Once Jesus was asked by the Pharisees when the kingdom of God was coming, and he answered, "You won't be able to observe the coming of the kingdom of God. People will not be able to say, 'Look, here it is!' or 'There it is!' On the contrary, the kingdom of God is right there in your presence."[14]

"It will not come by watching for it. It will not be said, 'Look, here!' or 'Look, there!' Rather the [kingdom] is spread out upon the earth, and people don't see it."[15]

FORMATION OF A MOVEMENT

Jesus quickly formed a political and cultural movement to create this alternative social reality. The coming of God's new social order required a committed people with a new vision and new values, living in inclusive community. The founding of a new social reality is not a threat to the status quo when it is only a vision in the head of one person. Jesus knew that it would be relatively easy to silence a single voice. But a movement empowered by a shared vision is much more difficult to stop. When a movement galvanizes the hopes and aspirations of a larger community, authorities begin to worry. Movements can quickly get out of control.

So, at the synagogue in Nazareth, Jesus essentially announced he was launching a political movement to bring relief to the suffering and dispossessed peasants and to re-establish God's reign of justice in Roman Palestine.

12. Luke 4:14–15.

13. Mark 1:15.

14. Luke 17:20–21.

15. Thom 113. (Funk and Hoover, *Five Gospels*, 531).

He called others to follow him in proclaiming the kingdom and healing the sick throughout the villages and towns of Galilee. He believed it was his mission to spread the message widely to include others in his vision.

> *But he said to them, "I must proclaim the message of God's kingdom to the other cities also; for I was sent for this purpose."*[16]
> *Let us go on to neighboring towns, so that I may proclaim the message there also; for that is what I came to do.*[17]

He began by commissioning twelve disciples to replicate what he was doing. Jesus first encountered at least two of his followers, Andrew and Simon, at the Jordan River where they too were attracted by the preaching of John the baptizer.[18] Later, Jesus left the Jordan and went north to its source, the Sea of Galilee, to the fishing village of Capernaum to find Simon and Andrew, and to call them and others to follow him.

> *As he walked by the Sea of Galilee, he spotted Simon and Andrew his brother, casting a net into the lake—for they were fishermen. And he said to them, "Follow me, and I will have you fishing for people." Right there and then, they abandoned their nets and followed him.*
> *When he went a little farther, he saw two other brothers, James, son of Zebedee and his brother John, in the boat with their father Zebedee, mending their nets, and he called them. Right there and then, he called to them, and they left the boat and their father and followed him.*[19]

Jesus then expanded his movement to include at least eighty-two disciples, chose twelve to be in a leadership role, and gave them marching orders.

> *And when day came, he called his disciples and chose twelve of them: Simon, whom he called Peter ["Petros" meaning Rock], and his brother Andrew, and James, John, Philip, Bartholomew, Matthew, Thomas, James, Simon (who was called the Zealot), Thaddeus, and Judas Iscariot.*[20]
> *Then Jesus called the twelve together and gave them power and authority over all demons and to cure diseases, and he sent them out to proclaim the kingdom of God and to heal . . . They*

16. Luke 4:43.

17. Mark 1:38.

18. John 1:35–41.

19. Matt 4:18–22.

20. Mark 3:16–19.

departed and went through the villages, bringing the good news and curing diseases everywhere.[21]

As you go, proclaim the good news, "The kingdom of God has come near." Cure the sick, raise the dead, cleanse the lepers, expel demons.[22]

He sent another seventy disciples out ahead of him, in thirty-five pairs, to the villages and towns of Galilee that he planned to visit in the coming days. Sharing food, healing the sick, and announcing the kingdom of God: these were the three assignments to his many disciples.

After this the Lord appointed seventy others and sent them on ahead of him in pairs to every town and place where he himself intended to go. He said to them . . . "Whenever you enter a town and its people welcome you, eat what is set before you; cure the sick who are there, and say to them, 'The kingdom of God has come near to you.'"[23]

TEACHINGS ON THE ROAD

Walking between the towns and villages meant that Jesus and his followers would have spent much of their time hiking through fields and valleys, up mountains and cliffs and relying on others for their sustenance. Along the way he taught using stories and metaphors.

Jesus taught his followers to pray for the kingdom of God to come on the earth as it was in heaven. He taught them to reject selfish concerns and to pray for sufficiency—just enough for tomorrow, "our daily bread." He taught them that the path out of debt is through economic forgiveness. Finally, he taught them not to succumb to tests of their faith.

Say this when you pray: Father, may your name be honored, may your reign begin. Grant us the food we need for each day. Pardon our debts, for we ourselves pardon everyone indebted to us. And do not put us to the test.[24]

He taught that the kingdom of God belongs to the poor and dispossessed who will welcome its arrival. But he said that the rich have already received their consolation and will not welcome the coming kingdom.

21. Luke 9:1–6.

22. Matt 10:7–8.

23. Luke 10:1–9.

24. Q 34. (Powelson, *Lost Gospel Q*, 68, combined with Mack, *Lost Gospel*, 76).

> *Blessed are you who are poor, for yours is the kingdom of God.*
> *Blessed are you who are hungry now, for you will be filled. Blessed*
> *are you who weep now, for you will laugh . . . But woe to you who*
> *are rich, for you have received your consolation. Woe to you who*
> *are full now, for you will be hungry. Woe to you who are laughing*
> *now, for you will mourn and weep.*[25]

That version of the beatitudes from Luke is probably the earliest and most authentic. He addresses the poor, the hungry, the weeping without any qualifications. When combined with the words in his inaugural address we have the poor, the oppressed, the hungry, the weeping, the blind, and the prisoners—all victims of an oppressive segment of society. Add to these the sick, the infirm, and the demon-possessed—all recipients of Jesus' compassionate healing ministry. These were the focus of his concern: forgotten people on the bottom of the social hierarchy, either excluded from or imprisoned by society at large.

A later version from Matthew's gospel may not have been actually spoken by Jesus, but it still may have some validity. In it he reportedly described the kind of people who make up the kingdom of God.

> *Blessed are the spiritually humble, for they are people of Gods new*
> *order. Blessed are those who are deeply concerned, for they will*
> *see their ideas become reality. Blessed are the gentle but strong, for*
> *they will be God's partners across the land. Blessed are those who*
> *hunger and thirst for justice, for they will have plenty to chew on.*
> *Blessed are the compassionate, for they will receive compassion.*
> *Blessed are the pure in heart, for they will see God. Blessed are*
> *those who work for peace, for they will be called children of God.*
> *Blessed are those who have endured much for the sake of justice,*
> *for they are people of God's new reign.*[26]

Jesus taught his followers many things, but there are nine teachings that are key to understanding what he stood for: radical love, lavish generosity, extravagant forgiveness, inclusive hospitality, compassionate action, selfless service, a passion for justice, creative nonviolence, and simple living. For the sake of brevity, I'll only include two or three specific examples of each of his teachings, but there are many more.

Jesus taught the disciples about the importance of radical love as they walked along the roads of Galilee. To follow Jesus is to incarnate love; not love as a feeling, but selfless, self-giving love in action—agape love. Beyond loving your neighbor as proscribed in the Hebrew Bible, Jesus taught us to

25. Luke 6:17–25.

26. Matt 5:3–10. (NRSV combined with Jordan, *Cotton Patch Version*, 22).

love one's enemies, haters, abusers, and persecutors. He instructed his followers to treat everyone the way they wanted to be treated.

> *You have heard that it was said, "You shall love your neighbor and hate your enemy." But I say to you, love your enemies and pray for those who persecute you, so that you may be children of your Father in heaven.*[27]
>
> *Love your enemies. Do good to those that hate you. Bless those who curse you. Pray for your abusers.*[28]
>
> *Do to others as you would have them do to you.*[29]

And Jesus taught them the importance of generosity. To follow Jesus is to share what we have with others. It calls us to a lavish generosity—graciously sharing our lives and resources. It means giving freely without thought of return.

> *Give to everyone who begs from you.*[30]
> *Do not refuse anyone who wants to borrow from you.*[31]
> *Lend, expecting nothing in return.*[32]

Non-reciprocity is a key value of the kingdom. We are not to pay back hatred or violence. But Jesus also advises against operating primarily out of reciprocity when it comes to doing good things as well. Just as we should not repay evil for evil, we should also not expect repayment of good for good. Doing good and being generous to all is our call.

Jesus knew that it would be difficult for the rich to share their wealth with others. He taught about the danger of wealth more than anything other than the kingdom of God.

> *How hard it is for those who have wealth to enter the kingdom of God!*[33]
>
> *It is easier for a camel to go through the eye of a needle than for someone who is rich to enter the kingdom of God.*[34]
>
> *You cannot serve God and money.*[35]

27. Matt 5:44–45.

28. Matt 5:44, 46 / Luke 6:27–28.

29. Luke 6:31.

30. Luke 6:30.

31. Matt 5:42.

32. Luke 6:35.

33. Mark 10:23 / Luke 18:24.

34. Mark 10:25 / Matt 19:24 / Luke 18:25.

35. Matt 6:24 / Luke 16:13.

To follow Jesus is to forgive each other. It is a life of extravagant forgiveness—reconciling with those we have hurt and those who have hurt us, forgiving again and again and again.

> *Then Peter came to Jesus and asked, "Lord, how many times shall I forgive my brother or sister who sins against me? Up to seven times?" Jesus answered, "I tell you, not seven times, but seventy-seven times."*[36]
>
> *For if you forgive other people when they sin against you, your heavenly Father will also forgive you.*[37]
>
> *Forgive, and you will be forgiven.*[38]

To follow Jesus is to welcome and accept others. It is the practice of inclusive hospitality—breaking down the barriers that divide us and accepting others without judgment. It means mixing with the unloved and undesirable. To follow Jesus is to welcome and accept everyone into our common life, inviting all to join us in community—the stranger, the alien, the immigrant, the refugee, and people of all races, faiths, and sexual orientations. It means affirming their rights in our society.

> *I have come not to invite the acceptable, but the unacceptable.*[39]
>
> *When you give a banquet, invite the poor, the crippled, the lame, and the blind. And you will be blessed for they cannot repay you.*[40]

To follow Jesus means engaging in compassionate action that binds us to the welfare of all. Marcus Borg said, "For Jesus, compassion was the central quality of God and the central moral quality of a life centered in God."

> *Be compassionate as your Father is compassionate.*[41]
>
> *Blessed are the compassionate, for they will be shown compassion.*[42]
>
> *For I was hungry and you gave me food, I was thirsty and you gave me drink, I was a stranger and you welcomed me, I was naked and you clothed me, I was sick and you visited me, I was in prison and you came to me.*[43]

36. Matt 18:21–22.

37. Matt 6:14.

38. Luke 6:47.

39. Mark 2:17 / Matt 9:12–13 / Luke 5:31–32.

40. Luke 14:13.

41. Matt 5:48 / Luke 6:36.

42. Matt 5:7.

43. Matt 25:34–36.

To follow Jesus means a life of selfless service. It means giving up our need for importance to serve the least among us as an equal, not as a superior.

> *The greatest among you will be your servant.*[44]
> *Whoever wants to be first must be the last of all and servant of all.*[45]
> *Those who grasp and clutch at self will lose it. Those who let go of self and follow me will find it.*[46]

To follow Jesus is to have a passion for justice. It means becoming an agent of change for a world in which everyone gets a fair share of resources and opportunities. It means speaking out on behalf of those who have no voice.

> *Blessed are those who hunger and thirst for justice!*[47]
> *Strive first for the kingdom of God and its justice.*[48]

To follow Jesus means using creative nonviolence in situations of conflict. It means seeking change without resorting to violence and absorbing hostility with nonviolent defiant action.

> *If anyone strikes you on the cheek, offer the other also; and from anyone who takes away your coat do not withhold even your shirt. Give to everyone who begs from you; and if anyone takes away your goods, do not ask for them again.*[49]
> *Blessed are those who work for peace, for they shall be called God's children.*[50]

To follow Jesus means living simply on the earth, living lightly like an itinerant or sojourner. It means not being bound by possessions and a lifestyle of wasteful consumption.

> *Therefore, do not worry, saying, "What will we eat?" or "What will we drink?" or "What will we wear?" For it is the nations of the present system who strive for all these things. But strive first for the*

---

44. Matt 23:11.
45. Mark 9:35.
46. Mark 8:35 / Matt 10:39, 16:25 / Luke 17:33.
47. Matt 5:6.
48. Matt 6:33.
49. Luke 6:29–30.
50. Matt 5:9.

> *kingdom of God and his justice, and all these things will be given to you as well.*[51]
>
> *Do not be blinded by the pursuit of food, clothing, and posses-sions. Stop worrying about these things. Only those who lack spirit and soul pursue them.*[52]

Jesus taught that it is not what one believes that counts, but what one does.

> *Not everyone who says to me "Lord, Lord," will enter the king-dom of God, but only the one who does the will of my Father in heaven.*[53]
>
> *Why do you call me "Lord, Lord," and then not do what I say? I will show you what the person who comes to me, hears what I have to say, and acts accordingly is like. That person is like some-one building a house, who digs deeply and lays the foundation on bedrock. The rain pours down, the floods rise in a torrent, and the winds blow and beat upon the house, but it does not fall. It is built on rock. But the one who listens and does nothing is like the person who builds a house on sand with no foundation. When the river bursts against it, it collapses immediately and is destroyed.*[54]

PROCLAMATION, HEALING, AND MEAL FELLOWSHIP

Proclamation of the kingdom and healing of the sick went together. The healing of the sick and exorcisms brought about renewal at a personal and social level.

> *Jesus went throughout Galilee, teaching in the synagogues and proclaiming the message of the kingdom and curing every disease and every sickness among the people.*[55]
>
> *When the crowds found out about it [that he was in the town of Bethsaida], they followed him; and he welcomed them, and spoke to them about the kingdom of God, and healed those who needed to be cured.*[56]

---

51. Matt 6:31–33 / Luke 12:29–31.

52. Q 53. (Powelson, *The Lost Gospel Q*, 87).

53. Matt 7:21.

54. Matt 7:24–27 / Luke 6:46–49.

55. Matt 4:23, 9:35.

56. Luke 9:11.

In the first century, many diseases were believed to be caused by evil spirits—demons—who were in the service of Satan. Jesus is portrayed as astonishingly effective in casting out demons and evil spirits. Because the kingdom of God was replacing and ultimately defeating the kingdom of Satan (the domination system), exorcism of demons was a visible sign of the strength of God's kingdom over Satan.

> *If it is by the finger of God that I cast out the demons, then the kingdom of God has arrived.*[57]

In his book *Binding the Strong Man*, theologian and activist Ched Myers interprets the healing miracles of Jesus as symbolic actions taken to restore an individual to his or her rightful place in society where illness was perceived as a result of impurity or sin. His healings were symbolic actions that overcame the dominant symbolic system that oppressed and excluded sick people.

> *Throughout this commentary I will interpret the "miracles" of Jesus—exorcism and healing—as "symbolic action." This will undoubtedly trouble some readers, who will take me to be implying that these events did not really take place, that Jesus did not really heal or cast out demons. That is not what I mean by symbolic action . . . I am not suggesting that Jesus did not in fact minister to or care about individual victims . . . I mean action whose fundamental significance, indeed power, lies relative to the symbolic order in which they occurred . . . In the symbolic order of Judaism, illness was associated with impurity or sin, a state that meant exclusion from full status in the body politic . . . Jesus' healing ministry is thus portrayed as an essential part of his struggle to bring concrete liberation to the oppressed and marginal of Palestinian society.*[58]

In addition to teaching about the kingdom of God and healing the sick and demon-possessed, a third element, meal fellowship, was the other component of Jesus' ministry. For Jesus, the beginning of community was the sharing of food. Sharing a meal with someone implied acceptance of them. His table fellowship was for the outsider, the marginalized, and the despised. Since Jesus had no home, no wealth, no banquet table, no food to offer, he modeled inclusive table fellowship by publicly accepting invitations to dinner from others—often from those considered "sinful" people. He is thus introducing an alternative social practice based upon inclusivity. He was accused of being a glutton and a drunkard because of his enjoyment of festive meals with all elements of society.

57. Matt 12:28 / Luke 11:20.
58. Myers, *Binding the Strong Man*, 144–146.

> *The Pharisees and the scribes were grumbling and saying, "This*
> *fellow welcomes outcasts and eats with them."[59]*
> *Now the son of man comes, eating and drinking, and you say,*
> *"Just look at him, a glutton and drunkard, a friend of tax collec-*
> *tors and outcasts!"[60]*

The inclusive banquet became another metaphor for the kingdom of God.

> *I predict that people will come from east and west, from north and*
> *south, and will eat at God's kingdom banquet.[61]*
> *A man once gave a great banquet and invited many guests. As*
> *the dinner hour approached, he sent a servant to tell them, "Come,*
> *everything is ready now." One by one, they started making excuses.*
> *The first guest told the servant, "I'm sorry but I just bought a piece*
> *of land and have to go see it." Another guest said, "You'll have*
> *to excuse me, I'm on my way to take a look at five pairs of oxen*
> *that I've purchased." A third guest explained, "I just got married*
> *and can't come." The servant returned to tell the host about these*
> *excuses. In a fit of anger, the man shouted, "Go out right now into*
> *the streets and alleys and invite the poor, the crippled, the blind*
> *and the lame." Soon the servant reported back, "I've carried out*
> *your orders, but there is still room." "Then go farther out to the*
> *roads and the country lanes," the man responded, "and lead people*
> *back until my house is filled. But not one of those original guests*
> *will share this feast."[62]*

The original guests were preoccupied with concern about possessions and family obligations. The dispossessed and homeless had no distractions to keep them from the feast of the kingdom.

The community that gathered around Jesus left everything to follow him. In joining the Jesus movement, the disciples had entered what is known as a *fictive family*, not related by blood but through bonds of love for one another as sisters and brothers. The gospels tell us that Jesus' mother and brothers sought to restrain him because they thought that he had lost his mind.[63] Once when told that they had come to see him, he replied:

---

59. Luke 15:2.

60. Matt 11:19 / Luke 7:34.

61. Matt 8:12 / Luke 13:29.

62. Matt 22:1–10 / Luke 14:16–24.

63. Mark 3:21: "When his family heard it, they went out to restrain him, for people were saying, 'He has gone out of his mind.'"

"Who is my mother, and who are my brothers?" And pointing to his disciples he said, "Here are my mother and my brothers! For whoever does the will of my Father in heaven is my brother and sister and mother."[64]

My mother and my brothers are those who hear the word of God and do it.[65]

Jesus prioritized the kingdom of God over the pulls of family responsibility, commending his disciples for cutting their ties to their community—leaving home, livelihood, and family behind. He knew this would be a difficult decision and a challenging test. These were strong words meant to open people's eyes to the reality of what Jesus was about, what he was proposing, and where he was going.

Jesus called on his followers to trust that the way of life he taught and modeled had the capability of transforming their lives and changing the world. He invited them to transform their old ways of thinking, and to shed their culture's conventional wisdom to follow him. He asked them to risk their lives for this new way of living when he said, "If any want to become my followers, let them deny themselves and take up their cross daily and follow me." Taking up one's cross in the context of first-century Roman Palestine meant a willingness to sacrifice one's life in an engagement with political and economic power and a challenge to the unjust systems of the world.

Trusting others is often a daring and risky venture. It requires the commitment of a faithful relationship and the sustaining courage of hope. But this was the risk taken by Jesus' followers. He called them to live in a way that does not make sense if trust in others is absent. He asked them to live recklessly, but not without the safety net of a community. He invited them to share their resources generously with others, even with strangers, trusting that this generosity would be shown to them in their time of need.

THE MARCH TO JERUSALEM

According to the synoptic gospels (Matthew, Mark, and Luke), toward the end of his year of building a movement in Galilee, Jesus set his sights on Jerusalem in Judea. He decided to go there to confront the Sadducees—the rich and powerful rulers of the people—at their symbolic seat of power. He would interrupt the operations of the Jerusalem Temple with a demonstration aimed at the Sadducees as thieves and swindlers of the poor multitudes.

64. Mark 3:35 / Matt 12:48–50.

65. Luke 8:21.

Jesus clearly understood that arrest and death are always potential and likely consequences of the pursuit of justice in an unjust society. He cautioned his followers that to follow him, they must be willing to risk public execution on a cross—the penalty for civil disobedience and insurrection by common people. It was a time of decision. Jesus was heading towards a confrontation with power that risked his life and the lives of his followers.

Jesus' entry into the city on the Sunday before Passover was a noisy demonstration that attracted wide attention. Jesus was hailed as a messiah with leafy branches cut from date palm trees and strewn in his path.

> *Then those who went ahead and those who followed were shouting, "Hosanna!"*[66]

Hosanna was originally a Hebrew cry for help—*yasha-na, (yaw-SHAH-naw)* meaning "Save us now!" As an exclamation of adoration, it became more of an expression of thanks: "Our salvation has arrived!" The Hebrew word *yasha (yaw-SHAH)* and the Greek term *sózó (SODE-zo)* appear in most English translations of the Bible as "save," yet they also mean "liberate." So, the people may be shouting "Liberate us now!" or "Our liberation has arrived!" They also cried,

> *Blessed is the one who comes in the name of Yahweh! Blessed is the coming kingdom of our ancestor David!*[67]
> *When Jesus entered Jerusalem, the whole city was stirred and asked, "Who is this?" The crowds answered, "This is Jesus, the prophet from Nazareth in Galilee."*[68]

The following day, on Monday morning, Jesus headed straight for the Temple and created a public disturbance in the Court of the Gentiles in full view of the Sadducees and the Roman garrison in the Antonia Fortress that overlooked the Temple.

> *And he entered the Temple and began to drive out those who were selling and those who were buying in the Temple, and he overturned the tables of the money changers and the seats of those who sold doves; and he would not allow anyone to carry anything through the Temple.*[69]

On the surface, Jesus seems angered about commerce in the Temple precincts. A few interpreters think that Jesus disapproved of the Temple's use

66. Mark 11:9.
67. Mark 11:9–10.
68. Matt 21:10–11.
69. Mark 11:15–17.

of animal sacrifice. Still others believe that his demonstration was against the Temple as a symbol of the Jewish religion itself, as if Jesus was rejecting the religion he was raised in and was replacing it with a new one based on himself as the center of devotion. But most likely, and this is an important point, this demonstration at the Temple was a demonstration against the people who managed it and benefited from it—the Sadducees.

The Sadducees were a small group of affluent aristocratic families that formed the ruling upper class in Judea. They were enormously wealthy and lived in great luxury and splendor. Included in their ranks were the high priests of the Jerusalem Temple and a few families of great political influence. The chief priests lived off a Temple tax and the tithes collected from the peasants. By the first century, the lay nobility in Jerusalem had gained ownership of much of the arable land in Judea and other regions.[70] The debt records that led to peasant land foreclosure were kept by the elites in the Jerusalem Temple, providing us with a clue to Jesus' angry criticism of those who controlled the Temple precincts. The Sadducees also oversaw the Temple treasury—essentially the national bank. Thus, they controlled the entire economy. Members of the elite Sadducee party also formed the *Sanhedrin* (*san-HEE-drin*), the high court and legislative body of the Jewish people. Although Judea was now ruled by a Roman procurator, the day-to-day operations were entrusted to this wealthy oligarchy (ruling few) of the Sadducees.

The Sadducees were given a free hand to rule the local population, if they were loyal to Rome, maintained order, and collected the tribute due to the emperor. They cooperated closely with the Roman governor and kept a tight lid on any potential liberation movements in the country that might threaten the status quo and their own privileged positions. There is no question that the Temple was an instrument of the state as was the case in any other ancient temple-state where priest and king or emperor are allied.

All the objects of Jesus' anger in his demonstration were legitimate operations in the huge Court of the Gentiles that surrounded the central areas reserved for Israelite women, men, and priests in smaller but increasing holiness boundaries. The Temple required bird and animal sellers on site so that pilgrims would be able to offer sacrifices that were ritually acceptable. Money changers were required to change foreign currencies into the approved coinage (shekels) for payment of the Temple tax. Jesus upset these operations by driving out those who were selling and buying. But the real

70. Nolan, *Jesus before Christianity*, 27. Also, Jeremias, *Jerusalem in the Time*, 147–232.

objects of his protest were not low-level functionaries. We are told that Jesus addressed the crowds in the Temple precincts with these words:

> *Don't the scriptures say, "My house is to be regarded as a house of prayer for all peoples?" But you have turned it into a hideout for crooks.*[71]

Jesus was not condemning the Temple as a place of robbery, but as a hideout or den for the robbers. A den is not where the robbers rob, it is the place where they count their ill-gotten gains. It was not a few moneychangers or dove sellers who were the target of Jesus anger, but the thieves, robbers, and brigands at the top levels of society who perpetuated a system of economic injustice, who robbed people of their land, their wealth, and their livelihoods. But the governing Sadducees understood his message clearly. The Sadducees had decided that they needed to shut Jesus up before he instigated a rebellion, either violent or nonviolent.

> *So, the chief priests and the Pharisees called a meeting of the council, and said, "What are we to do? This man is performing many signs. If we let him go on like this, everyone will believe in him, and the Romans will come and destroy both our holy place and our nation." But one of them, Caiaphas, who was high priest that year, said to them, "You know nothing at all! You do not understand that it is better for you to have one man die for the people than to have the whole nation destroyed." . . . So, from that day on they planned to put him to death.*[72]

Jesus taught in the Temple precincts for another three days. During that time, the chief priests and the elders along with the scribes and the Pharisees questioned him as he taught and healed.

> *Jesus said, 'What do you think? A man had two sons; he went to the first and said, "Son, go and work in the vineyard today." He answered, "I will not"; but later he changed his mind and went. The father went to the second and said the same; and he answered, "I go, sir"; but he did not go. Which of the two did the will of his father?' The chief priests and elders said, 'The first.' Jesus said to them, 'Truly I tell you, the tax-collectors and the prostitutes are going into the kingdom of God ahead of you . . . The kingdom of God will be taken away from you and given to a people that produce the fruits of the kingdom.*[73]

71. Mark 11:17. (Funk and Hoover, *Five Gospels*, 97).

72. John 11:47–53.

73. Matt 21:28–31, 43.

Jesus said, 'Woe to you, scribes and Pharisees, hypocrites! For you tithe mint, dill, and cumin, and have neglected the weightier matters of the law: justice and mercy and faith. It is these you ought to have practiced without neglecting the others.[74]

When Jesus was arrested late on Thursday night and brought before the chief priest on Friday morning, the Sadducees sought evidence for a capital crime. The chief priest asked Jesus if he was the messiah, meaning a warrior king intending a violent revolution. When brought before Pilate, Jesus was asked if he claimed to be king of the Jews, meaning a contender to the throne. In both cases, Jesus is recorded as having turned the accusations back on the accusers and did not answer directly. He was charged by the Sadducees with blasphemy, but Rome executed him for sedition. On the cross was a sign that listed his anti-government crime—king of the Jews. The cruelty of his crucifixion revealed what imperial authorities do to one who attempts to subvert the domination system. For those who witnessed this event, the cross was not a symbol of divine sacrifice or the taking on of unmerited suffering—it was the price of resistance to the social and economic devastation of empire.

Six agonizing hours after his crucifixion began, on a spring afternoon in the year 33 CE, Jesus died. His heart stopped beating and his brainwave activity ceased. The spirit of life that had animated him at birth, left his body. The biblical tradition says that the body was then removed from the cross and placed in a tomb, sealed with a large stone. But the Roman practice of crucifixion did not usually allow for burial. The corpses of lower-class criminals or revolutionaries were not buried. Instead, the naked bodies of crucified victims were left hanging on the cross to rot as they were exposed to the elements, and be eaten by carrion, a meal for crows and hungry dogs. In any event—whether he was left to rot on the cross or buried in a tomb—we simply do not know what eventually became of Jesus' corpse. In the gospel accounts, the women who went to the tomb on Easter morning were unable to find it. It was never seen again. The earthly Jesus, the pre-Easter Jesus, was gone from history. But he was not to be forgotten.

RESURRECTION AS AN UPRISING

The wealthy and powerful thought that the execution of Jesus would eliminate the threat he posed. Momentarily, the disciples hid in fear. But the

74. Matt 23:23.

movement he created did not end with his death. In a very real sense, Jesus was resurrected in the people who believed in his message of hope and justice and who followed his example. They felt his presence among them, and this presence gave them the courage to transform their lives with passion, zeal, and courage. They began a small but passionate uprising in the confident hope that they could create a better world.

The political nature of the Jesus movement and its threat to the status quo of empire is unmistakable. Blasphemy and sedition were frequent charges aimed at the followers of Jesus in the first three centuries after his death, and capital punishment was the fate of many of the key leaders of the early movement. According to tradition, Peter was crucified in Rome and Paul was beheaded there by the emperor Nero (37–68). The Jewish historian Josephus (37–100) reports that Jesus' brother James (the Just) was stoned to death by Temple authorities in Jerusalem. Legends reported by Christian historians Hippolytus of Rome (170–235) and Eusebius (263–339) say that four other disciples met similar fates: Andrew and Bartholomew were crucified, Stephen was stoned, and James, the son of Zebedee was beheaded. Something was going on in the early Jesus movement that clearly threatened authorities of the domination system.

Jesus died as he lived, leading a movement for justice. It is wrong to simply view Jesus as a spiritual savior with a heavenly goal. He was concerned about lives in the here and now, not in the hereafter. He had a political vision for how society should be structured and what values it should embody. He taught about the coming new reality, and he modeled it in his own life. He created a movement to carry it on after his death, and the early church continued to live out his vision of communities of sharing and equity for many decades, perhaps even centuries, after his crucifixion.

Biblical scholar Burton Mack (1931–2022) believed that much of what is commonly called the resurrection of Jesus was really a process of remembering and retelling the life and message of Jesus—a process that kept him alive within the people of the movement that he created.

> *Jesus' life did not end with his death. That, of course, is the message of Easter. In these early communities of Jesus' followers, his life continued in his ideas and teachings. The resurrection occurred in the activity of a group who sought to understand and then live out the message of Jesus. The spirit of his teachings was kept alive, but, as with all life, these teachings grew and changed with time.*[75]

75. Mack, (original source not found).

In and through our struggles against threatening powers and principalities, whenever we rise to challenge their dominion, Jesus rises. Through our struggles with war, injustice, and suffering, he rises again and again. Only when we stand up, speak out, and act with passion, zeal, and courage can we boldly proclaim to the world: "He is risen! He is risen indeed!"

PART 2

from living to believing

Chapter 4

the Jesus movement

It only takes one person to mobilize a community and inspire change.
—Teyonah Parris (b. 1987)

All who believed were together and had all things in common; they would sell their possessions and goods and distribute the proceeds to all, as any had need.

—Acts of the Apostles (written sometime between 90–150 CE)

After Jesus' death, a small movement in the cities, towns, and villages of Palestine and Syria carried on his ideas. His followers claimed that his spirit had not died, but instead remained alive and permeated their lives, empowering them to live without fear of repressive authorities or the threat of death. These men and women were filled with the revolutionary and compassionate spirit of Jesus and a dedication to an exciting new way of communal life. They continued to live out Jesus' vision of a compassionate community, committed to the welfare of one another. But beyond their own community, widows, orphans, the sick, the destitute, and the disabled were cared for. Shared community meals insured that no one would go hungry. Financial resources were pooled and distributed. This was a working model of the kingdom of God—the conspiracy of love—operating at the margins of empire.

Those early communities were not Christian churches, they were not even Christian. They were simply Jewish followers of a way of living, not a community gathered for worship with clergy, rites, and doctrines. Their movement was simply known as "the Way."[1] We are introduced to these followers of Jesus in the New Testament book called the *Acts of the Apostles*, or more simply as *Acts*. Their first mention is when Saul of Tarsus—later to be the Apostle Paul—desires to go to Damascus in Syria to weed out the unorthodox members of this new Jewish sect.

> *Meanwhile Saul, still breathing threats and murder against the disciples of the Lord, went to the high priest and asked him for letters to the synagogues at Damascus, so that if he found any who belonged to the Way, men or women, he might bring them bound to Jerusalem.*[2]

But he did not bring them back to Jerusalem; instead, he joined them. Later, as a convert to the Way, we are told that Paul spread the message about the kingdom of God in the Greek trading city of Ephesus, starting as he usually did with the Jewish community in their local synagogue, and then after countering resistance, hiring the lecture hall of a local philosopher or teacher named Tyrannus.

> *He [Paul] entered the synagogue and for three months spoke out boldly and argued persuasively about the kingdom of God. When some stubbornly refused to believe and spoke evil of the Way before the congregation, he left them, taking the disciples with him, and argued daily in the lecture hall of Tyrannus. This continued for two years, so that all the residents of Asia, both Jews and Greeks, heard the word of the Lord.*[3]

FOLLOWERS OF THE WAY

The first-century followers of the Way displayed a conspicuous stance within their culture based on the gospel they learned from Jesus. Their love, compassion, and care for one another made them a distinctive community in their societies. Their small communities provided a social safety net for their members at a time when others were totally on their own. Of course, Jewish and Greek families provided care for their kin, but these new communities formed what are known as *fictive families*—meaning they were not blood or marriage related—calling each other brothers and sisters and providing mutual support and care for the poor.

1. See references to "the Way" in Acts 9:2 / 19:9, 23 / 22:4 / 24:14, 22.
2. Acts 9:1–2.
3. Acts 19:8–10.

Early in the book of *Acts*, we are given a glimpse of the Jesus movement in the city of Jerusalem in the weeks, months, and years after his execution. Their life together reflected the contours of the ministry Jesus proclaimed among the peasants of Galilee: to love, care, share, and support one another. The disciples now had become *apostles*, meaning they were no longer simply followers of Jesus, but individuals who were sent forth to act and proclaim.

> *Awe came upon everyone because many wonders and signs were being done by the apostles. All who believed were together and had all things in common; they would sell their possessions and goods and distribute the proceeds to all, as any had need. Day by day, as they spent much time together in the Temple, they broke bread at one house after another and ate their food with glad and generous hearts, praising God and having the goodwill of all the people. And day by day the Lord added to their number those who were being saved.*[4]

Later, we read this similar account:

> *Now the whole group of those who believed were of one heart and soul, and no one said that any of the possessions belonging to him was his own, but everything they owned was held in common. With great power the apostles gave their testimony to the resurrection of the Lord Jesus, and great grace was upon them all. There was not a needy person among them, for as many as owned lands or houses sold them and brought the proceeds of what was sold. They laid it at the apostles' feet, and it was distributed to each as any had need.*[5]

It appears from these texts that community members were not required to sell everything and become homeless. They met and ate in one another's homes, indicating that they still maintained private home ownership, but sold excess possessions, goods, land, and income property to contribute to a common purse to help clothe, feed, and house the less fortunate in the community and those strangers who fell on hard times. The followers of Jesus could do this because they were surrounded by a new family of brothers and sisters who would willingly support them in difficult times. The paradigm of Jesus only works within the context of a close, caring community.

For several hundred years after the death of Jesus, it was their distinctive behavior—the sharing of goods, the welfare of the destitute, a radical social equality, and a commitment to nonviolence—that set Christian

---

4. Acts 2:43–47.

5. Acts 4:32–37.

communities apart from mainstream culture. The early Jesus movement consisted of countercultural groups existing on the margins of society. In the beginning, they were composed of marginalized people—tenant farmers, fishermen, day laborers, slaves, and social outcasts—although soon they attracted artisans, merchants, and a few wealthy elites, especially wealthy women, to their ranks. They became communities of radical equality that cut across class differences, economic status, ethnic backgrounds, and gender roles. These communities developed a lifestyle outside of accepted Roman norms that offered their members security in an insecure world without social safety nets. Each tight-knit community of compassion provided its members with food, shelter, and material support when necessary.

COMMUNITY MEALS AND FUNDS

As they spread, the early communities of the Way varied in their gatherings, but a shared weekly meal seems to be a common element. The late second-century Christian writer and theologian Quintus Septimius Florens Tertullianus, known as Tertullian (160–220), writing from Carthage in North Africa about 190 years after the death of Jesus, described their weekly gathering.

> *We are a body knit together as such by a common religious profession, by unity of discipline, and by the bond of a common hope . . . We assemble to read our sacred writings, if any peculiarity of the times makes either forewarning or reminiscence needful . . . Our feast explains itself by its name. The Greeks call it agapē [ag-AH-pay]. Whatever it costs, our outlay in the name of piety is gain, since with the good things of the feast we benefit the needy . . . As it is with God himself, a peculiar respect is shown to the lowly . . . The participants, before reclining [to eat], taste first of prayer to God. As much is eaten as satisfies the cravings of hunger, as much is drunk as befits the chaste. After manual ablution [washing of hands], and the bringing in of lights, each is asked to stand forth and sing, as he can, a hymn to God, either one from the holy scriptures or one of his own composing . . . As the feast commenced with prayer, so with prayer it is closed.*[6]

These *agape* feasts, or love feasts, seemed to be a way for Christian communities to ensure that at least once a week the poorer members shared a good meal in mutual fellowship. Sometimes—but not always—a ritual

6. Tertullian, *Apology,* ch. 39.

Eucharist was celebrated as part of the meal or after the communal dinner had ended.

The practice of these love feasts probably derives from a common practice of religious fellowship meals on the weekly sabbath and periodic festival days among first-century Jews. Similar social gatherings occurred in the larger Greco-Roman world among pagans. In Judaism, small groups of friends would gather weekly in a home, or another suitable gathering place, before sundown. The host, giving thanks to God, would break a loaf of bread, and distribute it among the participants. This marked the beginning of the meal. Mealtime would often be a festive occasion. As darkness set in, lamps were lighted, and thanks was given to God for the creation of light. When the meal was over, hands were washed, and a prayer of thanksgiving was said over a cup of wine—the cup of blessing—acknowledging God as the giver of all good gifts. The singing of a Psalm concluded the meal. This tradition spread across the Mediterranean world in Jewish communities and was continued as the early Christian communities with a Jewish heritage took root in new locations.[7]

A common fund was also customary in the early Christian movement. The very earliest communities were *communalistic* (even *communistic* in the truest sense), composed of persons who were willing to risk their economic future—income, wealth, and possessions—in a common venture. At first, they did not just make contributions at their comfortable discretion, but radically put everything they had into a pool to maintain the common welfare. That is a risky way of living, relying on the community to respond generously in turn when one's own needs are on the line.

Titus Flavius Clemens, also known as Clement of Alexandria (150–c. 215), served as a leader and teacher at the catechetical School of Alexandria. He described the motivation of the early Christian movement in the first century in this way:

> He impoverishes himself out of love, so that he is certain he may never overlook a brother in need, especially if he knows he can bear poverty better than his brother. He likewise considers the pain of another as his own pain. And if he suffers any hardship because of having given out of his own poverty, he does not complain.[8]

An early manual of Christian living, the *Didaché* (*dee-dah-KAY*), written sometime in the mid to late first century, stated that a Christian must

---

7. Hulitt Gloer, "Love Feast."

8. Clement, *Stromata,* bk. 7, ch. 12.

never claim that anything is their own property, but must share all things communally with their brothers and sisters.

> *You shall not turn away from anyone that is in need, but you shall share all things with your brother and sister, and do not claim that anything is your own.*[9]

These fictive families were simply kindred spirits who were to be as close as or closer than any biological family. The *Didaché* (Greek for "The Teaching") was a brief overview of the lifestyle of the Way—just sixteen concise chapters (really, no more than sixteen short paragraphs or lists)—that was most likely used as a catechism for those who sought membership in the fledgling communities. It did not include a set of beliefs, but instead a compilation of behaviors and actions that were the essence of the Jesus movement. Topics included humility, compassion for others, radical generosity, helping the poor, welcoming strangers, loving and praying for one's enemies, control of anger and jealousy, and nonviolent resistance to oppression. It is reported that the adult catechumens often studied for two years before being admitted to the ritual mysteries of Christianity, indicating that becoming part of the movement was nothing to be taken lightly and that there would be significant expectations and demands once one entered fully into fellowship. The Way was not about accepting a set of beliefs, but about embracing a radical lifestyle. Completion of catechumenal study led to adult baptism and inclusion in the Eucharistic rite (commonly known as the Lord's Supper or Holy Communion).

Justin Martyr (100–165), a second-century apologist (meaning he was a vocal advocate of the faith to Roman authorities), described the Christian lifestyle this way:

> *We who used to value the acquisition of wealth and possessions more than anything else now bring what we have into a common fund and share it with anyone who needs it. We used to hate and destroy one another and refused to associate with people of another race or country. Now, because of Christ, we live together with such people and pray for our enemies.*[10]

Irenaeus (130–202), a second-century bishop in what is now Lyon, France wrote:

> *Instead of the tithes which the* [Hebrew] *law commanded, the Lord* [Jesus] *said to divide everything we have with the poor. And*

---

9. Didache 4:8. (Lumpkin, *Didache*, 87).

10. Martyr, *First Apology*, ch. 14.

he said to love not only our neighbors but also our enemies, and to be givers and sharers not only with the good but also to be liberal givers toward those who take away our possessions.[11]

In the late second century, Tertullian explained that members of early Christian communities contributed to a common fund to aid their work with the poor in their town or city. It is in marked contrast to the radical economic sharing of the Jerusalem community as recounted in *Acts* a century earlier, yet it still shows a commitment to provide funds for the common good and care for the needy.

On the monthly day, if he likes, each puts in a small donation; but only if it be his pleasure, and only if he be able: for there is no compulsion; all is voluntary. These gifts are, as it were, piety's deposit fund. For they are not taken thence and spent on feasts, and drinking-bouts, and eating-houses, but to support and bury poor people, to supply the wants of boys and girls destitute of means and parents, and of old persons confined now to the house; such, too, as have suffered shipwreck; and if there happen to be any in the mines, or banished to the islands, or shut up in the prisons . . . One in mind and soul, we do not hesitate to share our earthly goods with one another.[12]

Basil of Caesarea (330–379), a fourth-century bishop of Cappadocia in what is now Turkey, spent his family inheritance to benefit the poor of his diocese. He bought grain from wealthy landowners and then organized a soup kitchen, hospital, and shelter, distributing food to the poor during a famine that followed a drought. He wrote passionately that:

The bread in your cupboard belongs to the hungry man; the coat hanging in your closet belongs to the man who needs it; the shoes rotting in your closet belong to the man who has no shoes; the money which you put into the bank belongs to the poor. You do wrong to everyone you could help but fail to help.[13]

Throughout the first three centuries of the Jesus movement in its many forms, people were more attracted to the early church communities for how they lived than for what they preached. It was compassionate service to those in need, not a theology of personal salvation leading to a heavenly afterlife that attracted people to the faith. Tertullian wrote:

11. Irenaeus, *Against Heresies*, bk. 4, ch. 13.

12. Tertullian, *Apology*, ch. 39.

13. Excerpt from a sermon by Basil of Caesarea based on Luke 12:18.

What marks us in the eyes of our enemies is our loving kindness. "Only look," they say, "look how they love one another."[14]

CONTRASTING WORLDVIEWS

At the heart of any domination system, then or now, is a fundamental view of reality. It is a mental model of how the world works. In this paradigm, the ultimate reality of the universe is indifferent to human needs. People perceive the world as a cruel and harsh place, and realize that in a largely selfish world, others will normally be unconcerned and unmoved by a yearning for mutual welfare. In this worldview, one's personal well-being will take precedence over any concern for the common good of society.

As humans, we all naturally become anxious about the future, which fills our hearts with fear, insecurity, and self-concern. By and large, most of us find we cannot trust God or others to care for our needs and realize that we are ultimately alone and on our own in an uncaring and hostile dog-eat-dog world. At the root of this paradigm is the belief that we are ultimately separate from one another. If we see ourselves as mutually exclusive beings, we must then prioritize self-reliance and self-sufficiency. In a world of scarce resources, we become hardhearted competitors and ultimately become enemies. As a result, we strive to care for ourselves first and provide for our future security. We grasp all that we can get and hoard it for tomorrow. We look to wealth, possessions, status, pleasure, power, and dominance over others to make ourselves feel better. But it does not work, because it never works, and it's never enough. Our greed, selfishness, and indifference to the needs of others simply confirm and perpetuate this paradigm. The perception becomes a reality and is transmitted through our domination system cultures from generation to generation.

Jesus offered a different paradigm, a different worldview, a different perception of reality. He believed that the foundational reality of the universe is a God of abundant love. For Jesus, it was important that our lives and relationships reflect God's lavish love. He taught that God's love dwells within the lives of caring individuals who extend themselves for others and within a compassionate community that concerns itself with the welfare of all. The essential nature of love calls forth responses of empathy and compassion, generosity and forgiveness, inclusion and acceptance. In a community based on love and compassion, the basic needs of all are satisfied.

---

14. Tertullian, *Apology*, ch. 39.

Jesus believed that if one can trust in the generosity of God's spirit in others, one no longer must trust in oneself alone. Communities of compassion can alleviate fear and insecurity about the future. Indeed, they are the only thing that can. This assurance frees us to share our resources with others in mutuality and partnership. Loving, caring relationships give our lives a meaning and satisfaction that reliance on power, wealth, and status cannot provide. This is the fundamental paradigm of the reign of God that Jesus proclaimed. It stands in sharp contrast to the domination system of individual self-concern and the politics of selfishness that governs most societies.

But because the paradigm of the domination system is so pervasive, it takes an act of radical faith to believe in Jesus' contrasting vision. We cannot enter this new paradigm if we do not learn to trust the spirit of God in others. We must learn to trust the love, compassion, and generosity that dwells deep within the hearts of others and is expressed when they are no longer governed by fear and anxiety.

For over 300 years, these innovative small groups, based on the teachings of Jesus, remained as distinctive communities of generosity, justice, nonviolence, and hope in an oppressive world. Then, in the fourth century, the Roman emperor Constantine invited the church to participate in the power of global empire and everything changed.

Chapter 5

imperial Christianity

Jesus came preaching the kingdom, and what arrived was the church.[1]
—ALFRED LOISY (1857–1940)

FOR NEARLY FOUR DECADES after the execution of Jesus, a close community of goods and livelihood was the predominant form of the Jesus movement in Roman Palestine. These followers of Jesus did not see themselves as anything other than observant Jews inspired by a new way of living. Some scholars refer to the movement as Jesus Judaism to differentiate it from Pharisaic Judaism that emerged after the destruction of the Jerusalem Temple, but it was fully a part of the Jewish religious tradition, inspired by Jesus' interpretation of the Torah covenant and the social message of the ancient prophets. Then, in 70 CE, the Jerusalem community came to a sudden end when Jewish insurrections against oppressive social conditions brought ranks of Roman armies into the city to suppress the Great Jewish Rebellion (66–73), leaving widespread destruction in their wake.[2] Those followers of the Way who lived in Jerusalem abandoned the city and fled to the countryside for safety. The massive Temple complex in Jerusalem was destroyed and every Jewish sect was shaken to its foundation. The members of the Jerusalem community were never heard from again.

Prior to the destruction of Jerusalem, other small communities of the Way had developed in the rural areas and small towns of Roman Palestine, especially in Galilee, the center of Jesus' activity. All these groups were invested in the concept of the kingdom of God as articulated in Jesus'

1. Loisy, *Gospel and Church*, 166.
2. Also known as the First Roman–Jewish War.

teaching. Each small group or network of groups began to work out the details of how to live together in a new way. According to scholar Burton Mack (1931–2022), they had three things in common. The first was the notion of a more perfect human society conceptualized as a realm in which a God of love ruled. It was to be a society in which self-giving love overcomes human selfishness. The second was the idea that any individual, despite ancestry, status, or innate capacity, was fit for and would be fully accepted as a member of this inclusive society. The third concept was the novel notion that a mixture of people was exactly what the kingdom of God should look like.[3]

The earliest communities of the Jesus movement shared stories and teachings of Jesus orally, retelling them in ever more encapsulated forms that biblical scholars today call aphorisms—short, pithy nuggets that are easy to memorize and repeat. Later, they were crafted into written collections that included the Sayings Gospel Q and the Gospel of Thomas, and also into various miracle and pronouncement stories that would later be used as sources for the gospel of Mark, the earliest story of Jesus.

Burton Mack believes that for these early followers, the teachings of Jesus were more important than his life story. The first followers of Jesus were not interested in preserving accurate memories of the historical Jesus. They found his teachings—a subversive wisdom of personal and social transformation—to be much more important. As a result, they left us no record of his appearance and few details of his life.

Many different ideas about Jesus' identity, mission, and message were developing within the diverse communities of his followers. Who was Jesus really? They knew he was a teacher of profound wisdom, a proponent of a radical lifestyle, and an advocate of the poor, but did he have a larger role to play in Jewish history? Was he a new prophetic voice like the Hebrew prophets of old who spoke truth to power with a message from God? Was he a new Moses, presenting people with a new law—an ethic of love and forgiveness? Was he the long-awaited Messiah, anointed to restore the greatness of the Hebrew people? Was he the first of the martyrs to be raised in the coming resurrection of the dead? Many very different ideas about Jesus emerged within these communities.

THE CHRIST CULT

In some Hellenistic cities of the Roman Empire outside of Palestine, a dramatic transformation of Jesus began within a few years after his crucifixion or execution. Greek-speaking Jewish communities of the Jesus movement

3. Mack, *Who Wrote New Testament?* 43.

began shifting their attention away from the teachings of Jesus and focused instead on the significance of his death. Spreading quickly through the Mediterranean trading cities of the empire among Jews and Gentiles who were attracted to Judaism, this Hellenistic Christ cult ultimately became the predominant form of the growing faith.

Beginning just a few years after the death of Jesus—most likely in Antioch in northern Syria—a Hellenistic religious cult began to develop around the figure of Jesus as "the Christ." The book of Acts records:

> *It was in Antioch that the disciples were first called "Christians."*[4]

The term *Christ* comes from the Greek *christos* (*kris-TOHS*) that means *anointed*. The English word *messiah*, from the Hebrew word *mashiach* (*mah-SHEE-akh*), means the same thing. In Jewish history, this was term for a person who was anointed with oil to perform a special office, originally a king or a high priest. Later the term was also used for oil-anointed prophets who spoke about the restoration of a just society. But as Hellenistic Christianity developed, the term *Christ* took on new dimensions. These communities were convinced that Jesus had been transformed at death into a divine spiritual presence—the Christ. The Greek-speaking followers of the Way developed rudimentary theological formulas, rituals, prayers, and hymns that they shared when they gathered in the name of Jesus, the Christ.

"Church" has been translated from the word ekklēsia (ek-klay-SEE-ah) in the Greek New Testament. It refers to "a gathering of those summoned." In ancient Greece, it meant a gathering of citizens called out from their homes into some public place such as a civic assembly.

In the Greco-Roman city of Damascus in the southern part of Syria, a young Hellenistic Jew named Saul of Tarsus—soon to be known as the Apostle Paul—was introduced to this strain of Christianity. He later shared what he had learned from these communities in his letter to the small house church at Corinth in Greece:

> *For I handed on to you as of first importance what I in turn had received: that Christ died for our sins in accordance with the scriptures, and that he was buried, and that he was raised on the third day in accordance with the scriptures, and that he appeared to Cephas [Peter], then to the twelve. Then he appeared to more than five hundred brothers and sisters at one time, most of whom are still alive, though some have fallen asleep. Then he appeared to*

4. Acts 11:26.

> *James* [the brother of Jesus], *then to all the apostles. Last of all, as
> to someone untimely born, he appeared also to me.*[5]

Scholars are uncertain as to which passages in the Hebrew Bible that Paul was referencing when he mentioned Christ having "died for our sins in accordance with the scriptures" and being "raised on the third day in accordance with the scriptures." Possible passages are extremely obscure, but this formula of "accordance with the scriptures" was part of the tradition that was handed on to Paul and clearly accepted by him. Today, we can find little evidence of what he was talking about.

The Jewish followers of the Way in Palestine had focused on applying the teachings of Jesus to their lives, but the Hellenistic Christians in Syria began to praise him in worship. It was here that the first creed, "Jesus is Lord" was proclaimed—a countercultural and insurrectionist statement within the Roman Empire where all citizens were required to confess that "Caesar is Lord."[6] As a result, these Christian communities were viewed with suspicion as both atheists and traitors by Roman authorities. For the high priest in Jerusalem—a Roman political appointee—the Hellenistic leaders of the Way needed to be weeded out to suppress potential rebellion and keep the peace. Saul had been one of those appointed to the task of arresting the ringleaders. Instead, he became fascinated by the possibilities of their beliefs, especially their image of a dying and rising messiah.

MYSTERY RELIGIONS

Paul spent three years immersed in learning and contemplating the ideas of this cult, first in Damascus and later in the Arabian Desert. During this period, he reflected on the implications of a mythological and spiritualized Christ figure in the context of the popular Greek mystery religions that attracted many people throughout the Roman Empire. They included cults from Greece, Asia Minor, Egypt, and Persia that focused on the death and rebirth myths of Demeter, Orpheus, Dionysus, Adonis, Cybele, Osiris, and Mithras. Central to each of these mystery religions was a symbolic reenactment of the natural cycle of growth, death, decay, and rebirth, experienced when plant life dies every fall and is renewed every spring. Each cult

5. 1 Cor 15:3–8.

6. In Greek, "Jesus is lord" is *Iésous kurios (ee-ay-SOOCE KOO-ree-os)*. "Caesar is lord" is *Kaisar kurios (KAH-ee-sar KOO-ree-os)*. In antiquity, the term "lord" (*kurios*) was a courtesy title for social superiors, but its root meaning was "ruler." Claiming that "Jesus is lord" is a rebellious statement of shifting political allegiances within the Roman empire.

was centered in a similar myth in which a deity returns to life after death or descends to the underworld and returns with the arrival of the vernal equinox. They were called "mystery" religions because they involved secret ceremonies, often in connection with an initiation rite that imparted secret knowledge. Only initiates were allowed to observe and participate in rituals. The rites were structured to lead worshippers toward heightened feelings and emotions, sometimes guiding them to a religious ecstasy that expressed the beginning of a new life through the mystical experience of dying and being reborn with the deity. More importantly, the mystery religions offered redemption or salvation in the present life and the promise of immortality in an afterlife—a very pagan concept.

Paul was a product of two vastly contrasting cultures—the ancient Hebraic tradition of Israel and the Greek-speaking Hellenistic civilization of the Roman Empire that had far greater dominion, power, and prominence. He spent his adult life trying to find a way to bring these different traditions together in some new fashion. Judaism held an ethical appeal for many Gentiles—known as "God fearers"—who were attracted by the morality taught in Jewish synagogues. Judaism was a faith that drew people in yet held them apart with requirements of strict dietary laws and male circumcision. Paul envisioned a new religion that could bridge these ancient biblically mandated ethnic and cultural divisions, creating a united community for the future of humanity. But first, the age-old Torah requirements would have to be abandoned. In the dying and rising of the spiritualized Christ figure, Paul found a metaphor for dying to his old life centered in the Hebrew law and rising to a new life in a radically new community no longer based on racial heritage or religious practice, but simply on love and compassion for one another. Paul believed that the Hebrew Torah was now replaced by love.

> *For the whole law* [Torah] *is summed up in a single commandment, "You shall love your neighbor as yourself."*[7]
>
> *Owe no one anything, except to love one another; for the one who loves another has fulfilled the law* [Torah]. *The commandments, "You shall not commit adultery; You shall not murder; You shall not steal; You shall not covet;" and any other commandment, are summed up in this word, "Love your neighbor as yourself." Love does no wrong to a neighbor; therefore, love is the fulfilling of the law.*[8]

For Paul, love for one another replaced the restrictive dietary requirements and genital mutilation of the Torah as signs of common group

7. Gal 5:14.

8. Rom 13:8–10.

identity. He believed that the crucifixion and resurrection of the Christ changed the ancient religious rules and, in his words, "justified" (meaning vindicated and validated) their life together as a multi-cultural community despite restrictive Jewish law codes. For Paul, the old law of the Hebrew Bible was now fulfilled and supplanted by concrete acts of love in a groundbreaking, inclusive group. The artificial barriers of the past were torn down and replaced by a new community centered in mutual love.

> *There is no longer Jew or Greek, there is no longer slave or free, there is no longer male and female; for all of you are one in Christ Jesus.*[9]

For Paul—a Pharisee—the resurrection of Jesus also meant that the general resurrection of the dead was about to commence. Paul believed that Jesus had simply been the first of many martyrs that the Pharisees had long imagined would be restored from death to a renewed life among the living. Paul thought that the faithful dead would soon be raised from their graves and would be judged on the quality of their lives and sacrifices. In the new Pauline communities, he preached that this promise of restoration would be available to everyone. Paul believed that the future was rapidly heading toward an end point when the cosmic Christ—an apocalyptic judge—would return to vindicate his death, reward the faithful martyrs, punish their oppressors, and set things right in the world. The physical resurrection anticipated by Paul was never about a heavenly afterlife but was instead focused on the transformation of human life on earth into a new reality.

AN APOCALYPTIC MYSTERY RELIGION

Through Paul's evangelistic efforts over the next three decades, the emerging Christ cult that he encountered in Damascus and embellished with his own ideas began to spread throughout the major trading cities of Asia Minor, Greece, and Rome. As the Christ cult grew and spread, the Palestinian-centered communities of the Way declined as the primary form of the faith. This always happens when easy belief is contrasted with demanding practice. Thus, the Hellenistic apocalyptic mystery religion developed and proclaimed by Paul became the foundation of orthodox Christianity. Soon, these ideas began to dominate, obscuring the kingdom of God at the heart of Jesus' message and mission, and transforming his identity with mythological images.

9. Gal 3:28.

For the next century in the evolving Christ cult, Greek concepts about the dualism of body and soul as distinct entities eventually replaced the Jewish idea of an integrated, inseparable personhood that ended at death. The Pharisaic belief in an earthly resurrection of the dead became incorporated with the Greek idea of an eternal soul existing beyond death. The combination of the two eventually became a belief in an afterlife in heaven—something that would have been very foreign and strange to Jesus and probably to Paul as well.

The story of Jesus as a martyr who was raised by God from the dead had resonance with the popular mystery religions of a dying and rising god. Like these mystery religions, a rite of initiation (in this case, baptism) became part of the Christ-cult observances. The shared common meal of the early Christian communities also took on the aspects of a ritual meal, the Eucharist—from the Greek *eucharistia* (*yoo-khar-is-TEE-ah*), that means "thanksgiving"—a meal that commemorated the death of Jesus and recalled his last supper with the disciples. Pagan spiritual practices like ecstatic speech (speaking in tongues) were sometimes incorporated. The trappings of a real Greco-Roman religion began to develop around the cult of the mystical Christ.

As time went on, mythical stories grew up around Jesus. He was known in Palestine as a healer and exorcist, but new stories gave Jesus miraculous power over the elements of nature. For a century after the death of Jesus, his teachings were blended with Jewish apocalyptic and Greek Gnostic thought. Words that Jesus never spoke were attributed to him by later generations seeking his word for their specific social context and life situation.[10] He was rapidly transformed from a teacher of wisdom, a radical social critic, and a voice for justice into an apocalyptic preacher who proclaimed the end times.

10. Biblical scholars have written scores of volumes that demonstrate that the gospel writers were second or third generation Christians who combined and edited previous materials and those of their communities in ways to present a distinctive story of Jesus. Mark presents Jesus as a wide-eyed apocalyptic preacher. Matthew views Jesus as a new Moses who gives a new law on a mountain. Luke sees Jesus as a prophet like Elijah concerned about the sick and the poor. Both Matthew and Luke shared a document of Jesus' teachings now known as the "Q Sayings Gospel" that sought to remember his words. But each of these creative editors amplified these words with other stories that spoke to their present circumstances half a century or more after Jesus' death. John's later gospel reflects a more sophisticated Greek theology that presents Jesus as a manifestation of the *logos*, the word or creative intelligence of God that was expressed at creation. The further the gospels were written from the time of Jesus' life, the more the authors promoted the evolving ideas *about* Jesus over the authentic words *of* Jesus. These writers and their communities saw divine revelation as an ongoing process, and they freely put words into the mouth of Jesus, which spoke to their current situation in life (German: *Sitz im Leben*).

His obvious failure as a militaristic and nationalist messiah was corrected by the claim that he would soon return in great power and authority to rid the earth of evil and violently destroy the persecutors of the new faith. The nonviolent prophet was transformed into an avenging warrior king.

THE CONSTANTINIAN SHIFT

Flavius Valerius Aurelius Constantinus (272–337), more commonly known as Constantine or Constantine the Great, became emperor of the western half of the Roman Empire upon his father's death in 306 CE. In 312, he began suppressing challenges to his authority and sought to gain control of the eastern half of the empire as well. While preparing for a battle near Rome against a superior force, Constantine reportedly saw a vision of a flaming cross in the sky inscribed with the Latin words, "*In hoc signo vinces*" (*in hohk SIN-nyoh VIN-chees*), "*In this sign, you shall conquer.*" He led his troops into battle bearing a cross-like standard fashioned from a gold-encrusted spear with the monogram of the Greek word *christos*—the letters *chi* (*kai*) and *rho* (*roh*)—superimposed in a gold wreath. He was victorious. By 324, Constantine finally achieved full control over an undivided empire. In 330, he relocated the imperial headquarters from Rome to the eastern capital of Byzantium and changed the name of the city to Constantinopolis (the city of Constantine), known to us today as Constantinople.

Constantine recognized the strength of Christianity in the cities across the Roman empire and saw that even while it was a prohibited religion—because Christians refused to make offerings to the Roman gods and to the emperor—it was growing increasingly popular. In the major urban centers, unemployment and dissension among the poor was a growing social and political problem. Constantine found that the Christian bishops, who had initiated feeding programs for impoverished people, were gaining the trust and respect of the lower classes. It is reported that by the year 250, they were feeding more than 1,500 hungry and destitute people in Rome every day. This was a religion that could help Constantine maintain his rule and keep the masses subdued and under control. He believed he could harness the power of the Christian movement and the compassionate practices of its adherents for the benefit of the state.

As early as 313, he issued the Edict of Milan that established toleration of Christian worship throughout the empire. The edict made Christianity a lawful religion but did not make it the official state religion. Constantine continued to tolerate paganism and encourage the imperial cult begun three centuries earlier in the time of Augustus (63 BCE–14 CE). At the same time, however, he endeavored to unify and strengthen Christianity for his benefit.

In 314, Constantine convened a meeting of church leaders at Arles (in modern France) to regulate the church in the western part of the empire centered in Rome, and in 325 he convened and presided over a council in the eastern part of the empire at his palace in Nicaea (in modern Turkey) to arbitrate theological disputes about the nature of Jesus. The resulting Nicene Creed and related doctrines established the first official orthodoxy of the imperial church.

Under Constantine's leadership, the church was carefully and craftily co-opted by the state. Christianity moved from a position of state persecution to state protection. Five decades later, in 380, the emperor Theodosius (347–395) declared Christianity as the official religion of the empire, replacing the cult of the emperor. As state support for the old pantheon of Roman gods declined, they dwindled in importance. The small autonomous Christian communities throughout the empire were soon organized into a clerical hierarchy based on the structure of Roman government. The church as a powerful, centralized institution allied with the state rapidly took form.

In the early days of the Christ cult, membership in a community followed a period of preparatory training in which catechumens were taught the subversive wisdom of Jesus—limitless love and compassion, boundless forgiveness and generosity, and radical sharing of worldly goods in mutual support. Now, as an imperial church, the net was cast much wider to bring in as many people as possible. As a result, people were admitted to membership first and were later instructed in the faith. And the essential part of the faith was now concentrated on creedal statements, not on a countercultural lifestyle. From the fourth century onward, becoming a Christian became an increasingly popular trend within the empire. As the upper classes entered the church, the church became progressively more wealthy and powerful. But wealth and numbers transformed the original forms of the church. The very communal life that distinguished early Christianity began to gradually disappear. The extreme differences between social strata made that increasingly impossible.

French philosopher and theologian Jacques Ellul (1912–1994) proposed that as the church grew, the previous forms of small, intimate communities became gradually unworkable.

> *Success and the alliance with social categories of power initiated a process whereby the church became an affair of the masses. Jesus told his disciples that they were a little flock. All his comparisons tend to show that the disciples will necessarily be small in number*

and weak: the leaven in the dough, the salt in the soup, the sheep among wolves, and many other metaphors. Jesus does not seem to have had a vision of a triumphal church encircling the globe. He always depicts a secret force that modifies things from within, that acts spiritually, that shows us community, unable to be anything else but community.

The kingdom of heaven [the kingdom of God] is the little grain, the seed buried in the soil, the treasure hidden in a field . . . But the situation is now the very opposite. It is no longer possible to live in community because of the numbers involved. How can masses of this kind conceivably be organized as a community?[11]

Ellul further believed that the role of women in the church became degraded after Constantine. He did not think this had to do with two or three texts about the subordination of women that have been (mistakenly) attributed to Paul in Colossians and Ephesians, non-authentic Pauline books.[12] Rather, Christianity was moving away from its compassionate beginnings to a virile lust for worldly success and political power that had no place for feminine values.

After a period of independence that came with the spread of Christianity, they [women] were relegated to a lower order. This is all the more interesting because the gospel and the first church were never hostile to women nor treated them as minors, and the situation of women in the Roman empire (particularly in the East) was relatively favorable. In spite of this, when Christianity became a power or authority, this worked against women. A strange perversion, yet fully understandable when we allow that women represent precisely the most innovative elements in Christianity: grace, love, charity, a concern for living creatures, nonviolence, an interest in little things, the hope of new beginnings—the very elements that Christianity was setting aside in favor of glory and success.[13]

11. Ellul, *Subversion of Christianity*, 35.

12. Parallel sayings about the required subordination of women, children, and slaves to their male husbands, fathers and masters are found in two letters formerly attributed to Paul. Known to German scholars as "haustafeln" or household codes, they are recorded in Col 3:18–4:1 and Eph 5:21–6:9, along with an additional variation of the theme in 1 Pet 2:13–3:7. Biblical scholars Marcus Borg and John Dominic Crossan dispute Colossians and Ephesians as authentic Pauline letters. They believe that the mind of Paul is more evident in Gal 3:28: "There is no longer Jew or Greek, there is no longer slave or free, there is no longer male and female; for all of you are one in Christ Jesus." See Borg and Crossan, *The First Paul*, ch. 1.

13. Ellul, *Subversion of Christianity*, 33–34.

Seduced by wealth and power, the church willingly became the servant of the Roman Empire. Where once its role was prophetic—calling the economic elites and ruling powers to create a just society—it now became a chaplain to powerful and wealthy elites, accommodating Christian values to the needs of politics and blessing the very domination system that oppressed the poor. To support the socially conservative politics of the emperor and the economic elites, the church became theologically conservative as well. Jesus and his teachings were spiritualized, because the political and social elements of the reign of God were too threatening to concentrated wealth and power.

The creeds and the doctrine of the Holy Trinity elevated Jesus to the godhead. As his divinity increased, his humanity diminished. He became sinless and perfect, well beyond the ability of anyone to follow his lead. With the establishment of creeds, uniform church dogma was mandated and enforced. Those who dared to deviate were called heretics. In the centuries that followed, both books and people were burned to root out heresy. The church, once a victim of persecution, had now become a persecutor.

Through all of this, Jesus was efficiently and effectively domesticated. His vision of the reign of God was twisted and distorted into a harmless description of an inner personal state, a coming apocalypse, a heavenly afterlife, or even of the church of empire itself. The revolutionary reign of God was spiritualized to the extent that it was no longer a threat to the status quo of the rich and powerful. First, the elites of the empire killed Jesus; now, the elites of the imperial church effectively killed his vision.

Where once the church was completely nonviolent and opposed to military service, Constantine declared that *only* Christians could now serve in the military. This created a theological dilemma resolved by the invention of the idea of a "just war." For the first time, Christians willingly went to war.

It has been thought that, starting with Constantine, the church transformed an empire, but the reality is that the empire transformed the church. The church became supporters, maintainers, and guardians of the status quo of imperial rule. Jesus clearly taught his followers a Way, but the way of the church wedded to empire was not what he intended. Many people think of Christianity as a religion of peace. But our history belies that claim. Since the time of Constantine, Christians have waged war, engaged in human slavery, tortured and burned heretics, and committed unspeakable acts of terror upon those they deemed enemies of the church.

Throughout the Middle Ages, the church was a powerful force in international power politics and a champion of the domination system. The Protestant Reformation of the fifteenth century created a stir in the system, but it didn't restore the countercultural role of the church in opposition to the state. Reformers like Martin Luther challenged the doctrines of the church, but in the end, they needed the support of the princes and emperors to survive. The church continued to be the servant of the state supporting exploitation, domination, and militarism. Then, near the end of the eighteenth century, Christendom (the wedding of church and state) began to show the first signs of disintegration. Revolutions in France and North America created nations in which the church no longer played a significant role. Anti-clericism was very strong in revolutionary France and the First Amendment of the Constitution in the United States prohibited the government from establishing a state religion.

During the early twentieth century, the role of the church as state chaplain got it into further trouble, particularly in Europe. The Protestant churches in Germany had enthusiastically supported German aggression in World War I. German soldiers wore belt buckles with the inscription "*Gott mit uns*" (God with us). In fact, so many nations—on both sides of the war—claimed that God was on their side that the God of the Constantinian church became absurdly separated into many private national Gods. Every side claimed God's support for their unrestrained violence. In 1933, when Adolf Hitler (1889–1945) united the Reformed and Lutheran churches under a state-appointed Reichsbishop and invited the German churches to play a supporting role in his proposed new world order, most German pastors and bishops gladly accepted the offer. The new German Evangelical Church (*Deutsche Evangelische Kirche*), commonly known as the *Reichskirche*, became a hand maiden to horrific evil.

The situation of the German church in the first half of the twentieth century was not unique in history. Churches in the United States have had a long tradition of supporting our nation's wars, at least until they become unpopular with the public. The presence of an American flag in the sanctuary demonstrates that the state has an equal claim to one's loyalty as does the reign of God. The flag and the cross are competing symbols of allegiance, but for some Christians, the two are indistinguishable.

AN IRRELEVANT FAITH

Today, throughout Europe, the church is increasingly seen as an irrelevant force. On both sides of the Atlantic, churches have repeatedly failed to oppose evil in the political realm and have instead focused their message on personal sin—frequently confined to the private realm of mostly sexual behavior. Increasingly, people are demonstrating no real need of the church unless they experience trouble in life. With each new generation, more and more people relate to the church only at significant events in life's journey: birth, marriage, and death, or as some pastors say: "hatching, matching, and dispatching." The church of Jesus has become irrelevant to younger generations because it is intent on focusing its own comfort and security and not on changing the world through a countercultural community with a radical ethic and vision.

Many people believe that the Christian church was founded by Jesus. Still others see the Apostle Paul as the originator of the faith. Neither of these ideas is true. The real creator of Christianity as we know it today was the Roman emperor Constantine. And the faith he brought into being is now falling apart.

Chapter 6

the declining church

If the fifties ever come back, the church will be ready.

—SOURCE UNKNOWN

I should like to save the Shire, if I could—though there have been times when I thought the inhabitants too stupid and dull for words, and have felt that an earthquake or an invasion of dragons might be good for them.

—J. R. R. TOLKIEN (1892–1973)

FOR MANY BABY BOOMERS, church was a second-hand religious experience—participating in a belief and practice that was embraced by their parents and grandparents and passed down from one generation to the next. As children in the 1950s and 1960s, they followed their parents to church for Sunday school, worship, and eventually to catechism classes. At some point they started to realize that the faith they practiced—all the dos and don'ts, the rites, and the religious and cultural assumptions—were their parents' and not their own. Unless they found the religious experience compelling enough to make a personal commitment on their own, their faith became just a set of rituals and practices that had little impact on their lives.

The Boomers grew up in a time when the American church had reached a pinnacle of success in terms of membership, finances, and new construction. It was a major influence in American society. Yet something was wrong; something was missing. Numerical and financial success in mainstream society is often predicated on not rocking the boat of the current situation, of not critiquing social norms, and remaining silent on the need for fundamental social reform, even reform in the church. My contention is that whenever the church is popular and prosperous, the teachings and spirit of Jesus are most likely being disregarded and discounted.

NORMATIVE AMERICA

In the 1940s and 1950s, a cluster of powerful conservative norms set the parameters of American life and culture. In *A War for the Soul of America: A History of the Culture Wars*, historian Andrew Hartman (b. 1973) states that these cultural standards are best described by the phrase "normative America." It consisted of a group of assumptions, aspirations, and values shared by most middle-class white Americans—especially after the Second World War. Normative Americans prized hard work, personal responsibility, individual merit, delayed gratification, and social mobility. Many of these assumptions were derived from the stern Calvinist theology of the early Pilgrim and Puritan settlers. Post-war Americans had strict expectations for sex and gender roles: sex was contained within the parameters of heterosexual marriage, and in this context, men worked outside the home, and women cared for children inside it. Normative Americans believed their nation was the best in history—a shining city on a hill whose light would bring freedom to the rest of the world. Any aspects of American history that cast an unfavorable light on the nation, such as the genocide of Native Americans or the evils of slavery, were ignored or explained away as aberrations. During the 1950s, an unprecedented number of white, heterosexual, Protestant Americans conformed to these norms. Hartman states that even those Americans barred from normative America by virtue of their race, sexuality, or religion felt compelled to demonstrate compliance. And clearly, the church reinforced these values among its members. Social norms were seldom challenged with the radical values of the way of Jesus; instead, the church wholeheartedly reflected the conservative social norms of the American Way. Regardless of creed or doctrine, the American Way of Life was the real religion of the white Protestants who represented the dominant faith in America. Catholics and Jews were all accepted, or tolerated, if their religious practice propped up the American Way.

In his 1955 book, *Protestant–Catholic–Jew*, theologian and sociologist Will Herberg (1901–1977) wrote:

> *The Christian and Jewish faiths tend to be prized because they help promote ideals and standards that all Americans are expected to share on a deeper level than merely "official" religion. Insofar as*

*any reference is made to the God in whom all Americans "be-
lieve" and of whom the "official" religions speak, it is primarily
as sanction and underpinning for the supreme values of the faith
embodied in the American Way of Life.*[1]

Herberg suggested that to grow, the major religious groups in the
1950s had allowed people of minimal faith and understanding to join their
fellowship, and apparently did not try to transform their ideas and behavior
to any great degree. He said that,

*Americans practiced religiousness without religion, a religiousness
with almost any kind of content or none, a way of sociability or
"belonging" rather than a way of reorienting life to God. It is thus
frequently religiousness without serious commitment, without
real inner conviction, without genuine existential decision."*[2]

Moreover, by mid-century, Protestantism had turned its back on the
Social Gospel movement of the late nineteenth and early twentieth century
and had become focused on a personal and private religious expression that
blessed the privileged status quo for upwardly mobile middle-class white
Protestants. The Social Gospel movement had been a social reform movement in the United States from about 1870 to 1920 that tied salvation and
good works together. Now, personal salvation took the forefront and did
not look back.

THE COMFORTABLE PEW

In the mid-1960s, the Anglican Church of Canada asked writer Pierre
Berton (1920–2004) to investigate and report on the state of the Anglican
church in North America. Only a few years earlier, in 1958, church membership in Canada and the United States had reached an historic highpoint.
Yet cracks in the edifice of the institutional church were beginning to show.
Berton asked his Anglican sponsors to widen the report to cover all Protestant denominations, since all were facing similar problems. The result was
The Comfortable Pew (1965), a scathing report of the church as an increasingly irrelevant influence in society. When Berton characterized the church
as a comfortable pew, he meant it as a critique and not a complement. He
saw a church that was interested primarily in its own comfort and was not
committed to making a real difference in the world.

1. Herberg, *Protestant-Catholic-Jew*, 82–83.
2. Herberg, *Protestant-Catholic-Jew*, 260.

> *In the great issues of our time, the voice of the church, when it has been heard at all, has been weak, tardy, equivocal, and irrelevant. In those basic conflicts, which ought to be tormenting every Christian conscience—questions of war and peace, of racial brotherhood, of justice versus revenge, to name three—the church has trailed far behind the atheists, the agnostics, the free thinkers, the journalists, the scientists, the social workers, and even, on occasion, the politicians. In other areas, the church has simply stood aloof.[3]*

LETTER FROM BIRMINGHAM JAIL

Just a few years earlier, in April 1963, American black civil rights leaders initiated the "Birmingham Campaign," marches and sit-ins protesting racial discrimination in the racist center of the American South: Birmingham, Alabama. On Good Friday, April 12th, Dr. Martin Luther King Jr (1929–1968) was arrested along with Ralph Abernathy (1926–1990) and fifty other protestors organized by the Southern Christian Leadership Conference (SCLC) for violating a judge's injunction against "parading, demonstrating, boycotting, trespassing, and picketing." A friend of King's later snuck in a newspaper published on the day of his arrest, which contained "A Call for Unity," a statement made by eight moderate white Alabama Christian and Jewish clergy directed against King and his methods of nonviolent direct action. They agreed that social injustices existed in the South but argued that the battle against racial segregation should be fought solely in the courts, not in the streets. They argued that King and the SCLC needed to slow down and moderate their demands for an end to unequal treatment under the law.

In response, King wrote his famous "Letter from Birmingham Jail" in the margins of the newspaper and on scraps of paper that he smuggled out of the jail. He expressed his disappointment that the church was being driven more by a fear of cultural rejection than by a vision of Jesus. The white Protestant clergy had asked King to lighten up on his nonviolent tactics and to let time make the changes that they were simply too afraid to demand. But in the process, they forfeited something crucial—the ability to speak with passion and integrity on behalf of the radical and inclusive gospel of Jesus. The white church in the early 1960s lacked a prophetic voice, often remaining silent in the face of evil. As King said:

> *So often the contemporary church is a weak, ineffectual voice with an uncertain sound. So often it is an arch-defender of the status quo.*

3. Berton, *Comfortable Pew*, 16.

> *Far from being disturbed by the presence of the church, the power structure of the average community is consoled by the church's silent—and often even vocal—sanction of things as they are.*
>
> *But the judgment of God is upon the church as never before. If today's church does not recapture the sacrificial spirit of the early church, it will lose its authenticity, forfeit the loyalty of millions, and be dismissed as an irrelevant social club with no meaning for the twentieth century. Every day I meet young people whose disappointment with the church has turned into outright disgust.*[4]

Yet this "irrelevant social club" was a very successful and influential part of American society. In 1958, 95 percent of the adult American population declared a religious preference (68 percent Protestant, 23 percent Roman Catholic, and 4 percent Jewish). But aside from identifying with a major religious group, only about 63 percent of the population belonged to a specific church or synagogue.[5] Still, that represented the zenith in American religious membership. It's been all downhill since then.

SHALLOW CHRISTIANITY

Religious historian Diana Butler Bass (b. 1959) contends that the subsequent drop-off in church membership and attendance over the next half century may simply signify a return to more historic levels before the dramatic midcentury religious boom. Although reliable figures are not available, religious historians suggest that at the beginning of the nineteenth century (1800) only about 10 to 15 percent of the American population were church members. At the beginning of the twentieth century (1900) about 36 percent of Americans held church membership thanks to the success of the evangelical movement that spread Christianity on the American frontier and due to the arrival of large numbers of Roman Catholic immigrants to our shores. Over the next quarter century (by 1925), American church membership rose to 46 percent. Twenty-five years later (in 1950), it rose to 57 percent, and finally capped eight years after that (in 1958) at 63 percent.[6]

My family contributed to that last 6 percent gain. In 1952, my parents, my sister, and I joined our first church home—Mount Calvary English Evangelical Lutheran Church, a congregation of the Lutheran Church–Missouri Synod (LCMS) on the north side of St. Louis. My paternal grandmother was the daughter of a German Evangelical pastor who had emigrated to

4. King, *We Can't Wait*, 107.

5. Herberg, *Protestant-Catholic-Jew*, 47.

6. Herberg, *Protestant-Catholic-Jew*, 48.

the United States in 1891 and had served at least seven German-speaking congregations throughout the country. In the fall of 1952, as I approached school age, my grandmother encouraged my parents to enroll me in a Lutheran parochial school. Mount Calvary Lutheran Church was just a few blocks from our upper flat. The small K–8 school had five teachers with two elementary grades per classroom and was nearby the church sanctuary and office. Students were required to be baptized, and contributing congregational members got a discount on tuition. So, we joined the church. I entered Kindergarten that September. Then, on Sunday, October 5, 1952, my four-year-old sister, and my five-year-old self were baptized.

The neighborhood surrounding the church and our upper flat was "changing." The community was becoming poorer and increasingly black, yet the church and school represented an island of middle-class white Protestant respectability, sanctity, and comfort. Those few black families who desired to worship with us on Sunday morning were met at the door by ushers who suggested that they might be "more comfortable" at a nearby black congregation. This was the white American Protestant church of the 1950s. Jesus Christ, meet Jim Crow.

During the 1940s and 1950s, most Americans attended weekly worship services at Protestant and Roman Catholic churches, as well as Jewish synagogues. People were there for a variety of reasons. They went because they were supposed to; because it was the thing to do; because everyone else did; because religious membership marked your place in the community; because religious attendance was synonymous with being a good person and a good citizen; and because, during the anti-communist hysteria of the Cold War, you were suspect if you did not attend. It was a time of large choirs and church dinners, of overflowing Sunday Schools, of Boy Scout troops and church bowling leagues, of new church construction, expanding seminaries, and prospering denominational structures and associated publishing houses. In the 1950s, Mainline Protestants ruled the roost.[7]

It was also a time of a broad but shallow conventional Christianity, not a deeply committed faith based on the teachings of Jesus. Certainly not passionate or countercultural. During its heyday, the church never required American Christians to embrace peace, justice, nonviolence, acceptance of other faiths, racial equality, gender equality, and most certainly not

---

7. The mainline Protestant churches (sometimes known as "the seven sisters") are the United Methodist Church (UMC), the Evangelical Lutheran Church in America (ELCA), the Presbyterian Church USA (PCUSA), the Episcopal Church USA, the United Church of Christ (UCC), the American Baptist Churches USA, and the Disciples of Christ. Some sources claim that the term "mainline" is derived from a group of wealthy Philadelphia suburbs linked to the city along a main railway line.

LGBTQ+ equality. In fact, the attitudes of the most highly religious people of the mid-twentieth century (as defined by membership, attendance, and giving) were indistinguishable from the worst aspects of American society. They embraced racism, anti-Semitism, misogyny, heterosexism, unquestioning patriotism, and militarism. As German pastor Dietrich Bonhoeffer observed, religion had become a superficial garment and not a radical practice that takes the teaching of Jesus seriously.

AUTHORITARIAN AND PREJUDICED

In a 1950 study called *The Authoritarian Personality*, researchers at the University of California, Berkeley led by Theodor Adorno (1903–1969) examined the latent fascist tendencies of most post-war Americans. Authoritarians are nearly always ethnocentric in that they have a simple and unshakable belief in the superiority of their own racial, cultural, and ethnic group along with a powerful repudiation for those in other groups. The researchers developed what they called the "California F (Fascist) Scale" that attempted to measure prejudice and rigid authoritarian thinking. It evaluated obedience and respect for authority; uncritical acceptance of authority; a tendency to condemn anyone who violates conventional norms; an embrace of toughness and a rejection of weakness; rigid, categorical, and stereotypical thinking; preoccupation with dominance over others; a generalized feeling of hostility, cynicism, and anger; a tendency to project inner emotions and impulses outward; and exaggerated concern for proper sexual conduct. Here is the shocking conclusion of their findings: religious people have more authoritarian and fascist tendencies than nonreligious people.

> *Belonging to or identifying oneself with a religious body in America today certainly does not mean that thereby one takes over the traditional Christian qualities of tolerance, brotherhood, or equality. On the contrary, it appears that these values are more firmly held by people who do not affiliate with any religious group.*[8]

In a 1954 study titled *The Nature of Prejudice*, psychologist Gordon Allport (1897–1967) found that religious people were far more racially and ethnically prejudiced than the nonreligious.[9] The key to this behavior had been previously identified by the Berkeley researchers: church attendance is largely irrelevant in shaping the societal attitudes of members.

8. Berton, *Comfortable Pew*, 69.
9. Berton, *Comfortable Pew*, 69.

> *It may be that religious affiliation or church attendance is of little importance one way or the other in determining social attitudes, that the great majority of Americans identify themselves with some religious denomination as a matter of course, without thinking much about it.*[10]

In contrast to this majority, the authors of *The Authoritarian Personality* stated that "the 'radical' Christian [meaning one who seeks to follow the radical Way of Jesus] is prone to think and act differently."[11] In fact, a radical Christian often has more in common with the values of the nonreligious than with the conservatively religious.

As the majority expression of Christianity, white Mainline Protestants supported and shaped the culture of the 1950s. Seventy years later, conservative white Evangelicals now represent the Christian majority in the twenty-first century. In many ways they want to harken back to the normative American way of life in the 1950s before it was shattered by the youth revolt of the 1960s and the resulting cultural wars.

CONSERVATIVE EVANGELICALS

Conservatives and liberals represent two opposing cultures that have been battling for primacy in the United States since the 1970s. These culture wars remain at the heart of the conservative and liberal divide in the political and religious spheres of American life. Even though Evangelicals like to believe they are now a minority faith persecuted for their strong moral (primarily defined as sexual) beliefs by societal secularists, they are seen by the press and other observers as the dominant form of Christianity today.

Beginning in the nineteenth century, Evangelicals were culturally shaped by the prejudices and injustices of the American South and the violent and individualistic values of the American frontier. They have largely accepted the relationship between white identity and conservative Christianity, the mythic claims and promises of neoliberal economics, the failed foreign policies of neoconservatives, and the selfish political stance of writer Ayn Rand (1905–1982). In other words, they share the cultural beliefs of right-wing politics in American society.

Kristin Kobes Du Mez, a history professor at Calvin College and the author of *Jesus and John Wayne*, says:

10. Berton, *Comfortable Pew*, 69.

11. Berton, *Comfortable Pew*, 71.

> *More than most other Christians, conservative evangelicals insist
> that they are rejecting cultural influences when in fact their faith is
> profoundly shaped by cultural and political values, by their racial
> identity, and their Christian nationalism.*[12]

Evangelical ministers rallied their congregations against the threats of demographic decline, secular humanism, communism, radical Islam, feminism, gay rights, critical race theory, and Democrats in the White House.

> *Evangelical militancy is often depicted as a response to fear. But
> it's important to recognize that in many cases evangelical lead-
> ers actively stoked fear in the hearts of their followers in order to
> consolidate their own power and advance their own interests.*[13]

These cultural influences dominate the politics of conservative Evangelical denominations. In fact, it's difficult to determine which one shaped the other—the religious beliefs of white Evangelicals or the culture of the empire's domination system. They are tightly intertwined—a wedding of individualized Christianity with American militaristic and capitalistic civil religion.[14]

When the numbers of conservative white Evangelicals, fundamentalists, and Pentecostals are included with white conservatives within the Roman Catholic and Mainline Protestant denominations, they amount to an undeniable majority of all American Christians. When we look at the correlation of church attendance to political stance, most worshippers every Sunday are overwhelmingly conservative—religiously, socially, and politically. Those who attend church frequently are found to favor a Republican political and economic agenda, which means that—unlike the God of the Bible—they have a preferential concern for the bounty of the wealthiest Americans and for corporate profitability over the needs of poor children, the ill, the elderly, low-wage workers, the declining middle class, and the deteriorating environment. For many of us who have made progressive Christianity central to our lives, the pain of this moment is watching those who claim to follow Jesus do so much to distort who he really was.

Writer and religious studies scholar David Bentley Hart (b. 1965)) said in a recent conversation published in Commonweal magazine:

> *I honestly believe that America uniquely is the land where Chris-
> tianity went to die, and that the proof that it died here is that
> it could be so easily supplanted by a completely different religion*

12. Wehner, "Breaking Apart."
13. Wehner, "Breaking Apart."
14. For more on this topic, see my book *Conspiracy of Love*, 144–170.

*called "Christianity," and yet no one noticed the absurdity of it
. . . The American Evangelical religion is simply not the thing
called Christianity, either faithfully or unfaithfully, throughout
Christian history . . . Christians have always betrayed Christianity, and they have always misunderstood it. They've always in a
casual way assumed that it was meant to affirm whatever it was
they wanted to be valued. But I don't think that there's ever been
another culture that could so sublimely corrupt and so sublimely
efface the original Gospel and replace it with something else—with
a counterfeit that's not just a dissemblance, but almost a polar
opposite—in the way that American religious culture did. I don't
know what else to say about America. We're the most religious
country in the developed world, supposedly, but it's definitely not
Christianity that forms our religious consciousness.*[15]

DECLINE AND FALL

The decline and fall of the church in the Global North have been well documented in recent years. Today, many historic cathedrals in Europe, Australia, and Canada are largely tourist destinations, while other houses of
worship have been converted to museums, community centers, restaurants,
or pubs. In the United States, the decrease in attendance and membership
has been less significant than in other industrialized nations, but it has
become serious enough that observers now wonder about the continued
viability of the American congregation. Some suggest that in the next two
decades, two-thirds of American congregations will close their doors due
to lack of members, financial resources, and clergy. With diminishing opportunities in the long term, fewer young people are entering the ministry.
Many newly ordained pastors are older, entering the ministry after pursuing
other career choices. Protestant seminary enrollments are down, and many
are consolidating or closing, especially among Mainline denominations.
Mainline Protestants anxiously compared their membership losses since the
1970s to a growth in Evangelical, Pentecostal, and fundamentalist churches.
These conservative churches have claimed that their expansion came at the
expense of Mainline denominations whose members were uncomfortable
with an increasingly liberal focus on social issues and who took off for more
conservative "Bible-based" territory. Dean Kelley (1926–1997), author of
Why Conservative Churches Are Growing (1972), supported that conclusion
and it has been touted by evangelicals for five decades.

15. Robbins and Hart, "Only God."

But now, because of decreased fertility, increasing loss of youth, graying membership, and other factors, major conservative church bodies have recently reported membership declines as well. The Southern Baptist Convention is the biggest Protestant denomination in the United States, accounting for 5.3 percent of the adult population. Southern Baptists make up about a fifth of all conservative evangelical Protestants in America. The latest report shows that membership has declined for fourteen straight years. Since 2006, they have lost 2.6 million members. The year 2020 marked the largest annual decline with a loss of over 436,000 members, and the downward trend continues unabated. At the same time, baptisms have fallen to a low not seen since 1947. Membership in the much smaller conservative Lutheran Church–Missouri Synod (LCMS) has declined for the past 50 years by a million people to 1.8 million members with hundreds of thousands expected to die off in the next decade or so. Since peaking in the late 1950s, LCMS child baptisms have fallen 70 percent.

At the same time, equally conservative nondenominational churches are growing. In 2010, twelve million Americans worshipped in a nondenominational Evangelical church. If current trends continue, the largest evangelical denomination will soon be "nondenominational." These churches hide their denominational origins, if any, but they espouse the same conservative theology just the same.

What's dramatically declining in America is white Christianity. People of color are preventing a more precipitous drop in overall church participation. The Assemblies of God, a Pentecostal denomination, one of the few denominations showing growth, saw its white membership decrease in the 10 years between 2004 and 2014, but nonwhite members increased by 43 percent, reflecting trends continuing today. One-third of U.S. Catholics are now Hispanic. Without its growing Hispanic members, the Catholic Church would be in free fall instead of remaining at about 22 percent of the U.S. population.

THE RISE OF THE "NONES"

Beginning in 1990, the growing influence of the religious right in public life did lead to a decline in Mainline Protestant membership, but not because the right presented an attractive option; instead, many liberal Christians were so repulsed by this dominant representation of American Christianity that they left the institutional church in disgust. Liberal church members have become tired of explaining "I'm not that kind of Christian." Sometimes referred to as the "church alumni association," those who have left are more generally known as the "dones," Christians who no longer want to participate in a compromised religious institution. In conjunction with growing numbers of younger generations who have little to no interest in the church, they are collectively called the "nones." And their numbers are growing.

According to the American Religious Identification Survey web site, the 1990s was the decade when a "secular boom" occurred in American religion. From 1990 to 2001, those who identified themselves as Christian dropped by one percent a year. An average of 1.3 million adult Americans joined the ranks of the nones every year in that decade. In 2002, two Berkeley sociologists noticed this dramatic increase. In a paper in the *American Sociological Review*, Michael Hout (b. 1950) and Claude Fischer (b. 1948) announced the startling fact that the percentage of Americans who said they had "no religious preference" had doubled in less than 10 years, rising from 7 percent in 1992 to 14 percent of the population by 2000. The researchers explained that this unexpected spike was not the result of growing atheism; rather, Americans were distancing themselves from organized religion as "a symbolic statement" against the religious right. As the public face of Christianity achieved greater notoriety in the public square, conservative Evangelicals cast a negative attitude toward all American Christians in the public eye and it caused a corresponding drop in those who personally identified as a Christian. It's not just the religious right in conservative evangelicalism, it is also the conservatives within Mainline Protestant and Roman Catholic churches that are driving members away.

Churches have lost their prophetic voices. Pastors especially have lost their prophetic voices. Many feel captive to churches where there is a fifty-fifty split among members, half espousing rightwing politics and half espousing liberal values. And so, many pastors remain silent about issues that matter and try to go on ministering to people on both sides.

People began distancing themselves from a faith that no longer reflected their religious values. As the Christian right gained national influence by espousing a conservative social agenda, liberals and young people who already had weak attachment to organized religion, began to drop their affiliation and their identification with Christianity. As younger generations began moving to the left on social issues (particularly on abortion and homosexuality), the church remained firmly anchored on the right. In June 2015, the U.S. Supreme Court struck down all state bans on same-sex marriage, legalized it in all fifty states, and required states to honor out-of-state same-sex marriage licenses. While gay marriage is now law, in the church it continues to be in dispute. Even today, as Mainline denominations squabble over the issue of homosexuality, many young people view the church as homophobic, intolerant, and unaccepting of their friends who are gay, lesbian, and transgender. Yet, although they dislike what the church has become, younger generations are still attracted to Jesus. And they see a clear difference between the way of Jesus and the church of the conservative status quo.

As the twentieth century came to an end, the exodus of the nones only accelerated. From 14 percent in 2000, it skyrocketed. According to the Gallup poll, by 2011, nones represented 19 percent of the population and then increased again to 29 percent in 2021. The nones are now the largest religious/nonreligious group in the United States with slightly larger numbers than Evangelicals and Roman Catholics.

The future is post-denominational as well. In 2000, half of all Protestants identified with a denomination. That number shrank to 30 percent in 2016.[16] The decrease is partly due to the rise in nondenominational churches, but mostly can be attributed to the rejection of organized religion and the increasing secularization of the nones.

FEWER MEMBERS

The impact on congregations is noteworthy. Americans are abandoning the pews. In 2000, according to the Gallup Poll, church membership among adult Americans was at about 70 percent, about the level that it had consistently reported since 1937. (It likely was much lower than that, by about 10 percent, according to Will Herberg's report in 1955, which used self-reporting from churches on membership, but that's what American individuals reported in 2000.) In 2010, it dropped to 61 percent, probably a bit more accurate number. But by 2020, only 47 percent reported being members of a church, synagogue, or mosque, the first time that self-reported membership dropped below half of the population.

Today, our best estimate is there are about 350,000 congregations of all faith traditions within the nation. The vast majority of the country's congregations are very small, but most worshipers are in larger congregations. For instance, in 2020, the median congregation had only 70 regular participants, counting both adults and children, and an annual budget of $100,000. At the same time, the average attendee worshipped in a congregation with 360 regular participants and a budget of $450,000. The key to understanding this apparent paradox is that there are relatively few large congregations, but these large congregations are big enough that they contain most of the churchgoers in the country.

16. Newport, "No Specific Identity."

A study titled "Twenty Years of Congregational Change"[17] found that in 2020 about 70 percent of all congregations (about 245,000) had attendance of less than a hundred people and nearly 45 percent (157,500) had fewer than 50 people in worship. Twenty percent of churches (70,000) having between 101 to 250 members, attract 15 percent of the worshiping population. Only 10 percent of churches (35,000) have more than 250 folks in weekly services. However, far more people attend these larger congregations—roughly 70 percent of all attendees—than the many smaller ones. Those smallest communities of 100 or less are home to only 14 percent of all weekly attendees. So, 70 percent of congregations attract just 14 percent of the attendees while 10 percent of congregations attract 70 percent of the people. But the larger the congregation gets, and the faster it grows, the greater the decline in per capita giving. Growth and large size also correlate to smaller percentages of the congregation willing to volunteer and a lower overall level of participant commitment generally.

Nearly half of the country's congregations are divided between rural areas (25 percent or 87,500) and small towns (22 percent or 77,000), while the 2020 census found that only six percent of Americans live in rural areas and eight percent in small towns. Additionally, half of the nation's congregations are in the South, even though only 38 percent of the American population lives there. The result is that regions outside of metropolitan areas have too many congregations for the population living there to adequately sustain. In part, this situation is due to the dramatic migration of Americans, especially young adults, out of smaller towns and rural areas since the mid-1950s. A large percentage of Americans no longer live where they did seventy years ago.

These rural and small-town congregations used to anchor and support their communities. But church buildings were built for much larger congregations than they have now. When members and their offspring leave the town, many of the congregations and their facilities remain mostly empty. Half of all congregations (175,000) have no more than 38 percent of their seating capacity occupied during weekend services. Maintaining a church building can be a costly burden. Although financial giving has remained relatively high—even during a pandemic—a quarter of all churches (87,500) operate in a deficit.

On the other hand, the number of megachurches has doubled in the last decade. Ten percent of worshipers attend churches that draw in more than 2,000 people, totaling nearly six million attendees each weekend in 1,600 megachurches (or approximately one half of one percent of all

17. Roozen, "Twenty Years of Change."

congregations). While these large churches are considerably outnumbered by smaller churches in the country, their influence is undeniable.

It is not just a changing culture outside that is harming the churches in America. Internal strife is also taking its toll. In the past five years, almost two of every three congregations had experienced conflict in at least one of four key areas—worship, finances, leadership, and priorities. In a third of the congregations, the conflict was serious enough that members left or withheld contributions, or a clergy leader left.[18]

GRAYING CONGREGATIONS

Youth losses are a significant factor in congregational decline. Every year, the percentage of people over the age of 60 increases in American churches and the percentage of those between the ages of 18 to 34 continues to drop. For churches with a preponderance of members over age 60, their future is in peril as members die off. In seventy-five percent of Mainline Protestant congregations, less than ten percent of their regular participants are between 18 and 34. Younger generations are becoming increasingly secular and more liberal in their social views, but many churches remain mired in the past.

Only 35 percent of young people from the Millennial Generation (1981–1996)—(ages 27 to 42 in 2023)—attend church once or twice a month. And Generation Z (1997–2012)—(ages 11 to 26 in 2023)—are at about 25 percent, although that is expected to go up as they mature. Many of these generations have never been involved in a church or even a Sunday school because their parents stopped attending church when they were young adults from the 1970s on. The younger generations are interested in spirituality but have no background and little interest in formal religion. They are clearly becoming more secular and less religious, and the institutional church is increasingly seen as an irrelevant factor in their lives.

PANDEMIC SURVIVAL

The COVID-19 pandemic has accelerated the decline facing most congregations in America, but the effects are not evenly distributed among all churches.[19] One key finding of a 2021 study is that congregations that were the least cautious and were the most likely to experience infections and deaths of members through the pandemic also were the most likely to

18. Roozen, "Twenty Years of Change."
19. Winfield, "Study of COVID's Impact."

report growth. On the other hand, congregations that were the most cautious and least likely to return to in-person worship are the most likely to report decline.

The real factor related to growth is hybrid worship, the study reported. Eighty percent of U.S. congregations were found to offer a hybrid of in-person and online services, while only 15 percent of churches offered in-person worship only and 5 percent offered online only. Regardless of church size, adapting to hybrid services was a key to survival during the pandemic, the study found. The steepest decline in attendance was reported among the 15 percent of congregations that said they offered only in-person worship. These churches on average experienced a 16 percent drop in attendance. These congregations tend to be smaller in size with older clergy, are the least willing to change, and had the most struggle to adapt to the internet.

But now we are finding that many people got used to life with less church. Or, perhaps, even life without church. It's not even that people aren't returning—they might never have been strongly connected in the first place. People have experienced how easy it is to live without their church. Some discovered that the church isn't a necessary part of their lives. Regular attenders are now becoming semi-regular, fringe members are fading away, and super volunteers are now looking to do just one or two things. As much as churches miss people, people just aren't missing back. We are a traumatized people because of COVID-19. For each of us, all at once, our whole world stopped. And now, every single person is recovering from the shared trauma.

PASTORAL FATIGUE

Melissa Florer-Bixler (b. 1980), writing in Sojourners magazine, commented on why pastors are joining the Great Resignation:

> *Church ministry isn't glamorous . . . But what we gain as pastors—and why we continue in low-to-middle pay work—is the opportunity to help forge communities held by common commitments to the gospel. We learn to get along with people with whom we disagree. We carve out new ways for conflict, repair, and restoration . . . But in the wreckage of Trumpian politics and a never-ending-pandemic, our jobs have been reduced to negotiating skirmishes over mask-wearing and vaccination status. Former and current pastors have shared with me that their denominations and powerful congregants have pushed for a false unity that tolerates homophobia, racism, and conspiracy theories . . . When*

we name the need to repent of sexism and racism, powerful church members withhold their giving and muster factions to oust us. Our compassion fatigue is real.[20]

Recent polling data collected by Barna Group, a research firm that studies faith and culture, reported that about 38 percent of Protestant senior pastors surveyed have considered leaving ministry over the past year. Among pastors under age 45, that number rose to 46 percent.

Florer-Bixler concluded:

It was never our job as pastors to keep the institutional church from dissolving . . . The institutional church is an experiment and like all experiments, it can fail. When it does, we wait in hope to see what good work God is up to next.

THE SECULAR WORLD

The real problem we are all facing of course is an increasing secular postmodern world. The word *secular* comes from the Latin *saecularis* (*say-KOO-lah-ris*). It is usually defined as worldly, temporal, or profane—standing in opposition to the sacred or the religious. But in Latin it refers to a *saeculum* (*say-KOO-loom*), an age or time in history. Specifically, it refers to the present age, or the here and now. There is a hard form of secularism which is found in atheism, or in the denial of the divine and the supernatural. In its softer form, it means the rejection of the primacy of the church or religion in society. Religious institutions are no longer able to call the shots.

Canadian philosopher Charles Taylor (b. 1931), author of *A Secular Age* (2007), has proposed a way of speaking to our secular crisis. He uses the term *the immanent frame*, referring to the frame or lens through which we see the world around us. The term *immanent* means existing within something; existing within humanity or the world. It is a secular way of imagining the world which does not look to a supernatural God to explain the way the world works. The immanent frame sees everything around us as entirely part of natural existence and is totally understandable without any reference to the supernatural. A *transcendent frame*, on the other hand, sees God as necessary to the way the world works. Transcendence is the belief that an existence may be found beyond the normal or physical world. A transcendent God is beyond human perception, independent of the universe, and wholly "other" when compared to us. Still the divine may be experienced

20. Florer-Bixler, "Joining Great Resignation."

within the immanent frame; it is just not a supernatural, all-knowing, all-powerful God—a God who answers prayer and performs miracles. An immanent God is one which exists within each of us and is very much a part of our existence. It is found in the form of transformative love. I described selfless love—or agape love—as God earlier in chapter three. It fits nicely in the immanent frame.

Taylor says we should think of four stages of secularism—zero through three. If we could go back five or six hundred years, we would encounter a time when there was no secularism, when virtually everyone was a believer in a transcendent God. Taylor calls this stage *secular 0*. Secularism simply did not exist. In the pre-modern world, a transcendent frame was the only way of seeing reality. People looked to religion to explain the way things worked. It was an age of enchantment, a world of magic, of miraculous healings and exorcisms, of the power of holy relics, of supernatural demons and devils.

But in the modern era, there has been a progressive disenchantment with the transcendent. Today, fewer people declare themselves believers, religion has lost most of its public role, and rational thought and the scientific method have replaced religion as the basis for authoritative knowledge. That is the story of secular stages 1, 2, and 3.

Now, Charles Taylor's *A Secular Age* is nearly 900 pages long and is a very dense read, so I sought help from the writings and videos by Andrew Root, a youth and family ministry professor at Luther Seminary in St. Paul, Minnesota. Root has written five books in his "Ministry in a Secular Age" series. He analyzes Taylor's book in relation to the modern church and simplified things a bit for me.[21]

Root explains that the arrival of the *secular 1* stage occurs when there is a divide between the public and the private spheres of life. In particular, it is when religious belief is viewed as a very private matter. For instance, America was founded as a secular society in which there is a separation between church and state. There is no official state religion. All belief in America is thus found in the private realm. And that has led to a plethora of denominations found nowhere else in the world.

In a *secular 2* stage, the private religious space begins to be countered by an "a-religious" space, which is unconcerned with or indifferent to religious matters. In a secular 2 world, fewer and fewer people are going to church. The church's reaction to that is to try to win people back. Churches assume this is just a temporary blip and so they develop marketing strategies to attract people. They attempt to innovate, to entertain, to try to be relevant.

21. Root, "Ministry Inside Immanent Frame."

If only the pastor could present more dynamic sermons designed to appeal to younger people. Perhaps we could make church more accessible by replacing robes in favor of casual clothing. Maybe we could update the church experience by installing projectors and large screens, so people don't have to flip pages in a hymnal. Perhaps we could attract younger people by singing praise songs taken from Christian radio, accompanied by amplified guitars and drums. Or maybe a coffee bar would make people feel more welcome, et cetera, et cetera. Those things, in general, may appeal to some segment of Baby Boomers and possibly some Gen X members (all over age 43 in 2023), but they largely fail to attract the Millennial generation and Gen Z (age 42 and younger). Younger people are simply not interested. In fact, they think that the church is largely irrelevant. Why would they waste their time there. Belief in a transcendent reality, of a God somewhere out there who is active and interested in our daily lives, is becoming more and more unbelievable to people. And so, they do not come.

HUMANISM

When Taylor Talks about a "secular age," he means that we are moving to a society where religious belief is understood to be one option among many, and frequently not the easiest to embrace. In Taylor's words, in the secular 3 stage, an "exclusive humanism" emerges—a vision of life in which anything beyond the immanent is hidden. Humanism is the epitome of seeing life through an immanent frame. It is a way of constructing meaning and significance without any reference to God as divine or transcendent. Humanism has been widely seen as antithetical to religion, as humanists prefer critical thinking and evidence over acceptance of dogma or superstition. It is a philosophy, or a way of thinking, about the world. The motivation is a desire to live a good, authentic, and meaningful life. Humanists believe this is the only life we have, and so we need to make the most of it.

It is difficult to attribute any set of beliefs to a widely diverse group, but many people who ascribe to humanism stand for the building of a more humane, just, compassionate, and democratic society, as well as an ethical stance based on human reason, experience, and knowledge. According to the American Humanist Association website, many humanists are committed to social justice as essential to peace and happiness for the greatest number and see it as a moral failing to stand by while others are denied their civil and human rights. Humanistic social justice advocacy involves respect for the equality of all people, compassion for their dignity and welfare, and a conviction that positive change will only come through human intervention. This means disrupting he forces of dehumanization like white supremacy, patriarchy, and heterosexism through every dimension of society. In doing so, they join people of faith who are also pursuing these ends.

THE SPIRITUAL QUEST

But in a secular 3 world, most people are still searching for some kind of meaning and purpose in their lives. This usually involves a kind of spiritual quest. If spirituality is the quest for meaning, then religion—especially institutional religion—is a sanctioned set of answers. The religious life is a pilgrimage to a known destination. The end is given as well as the means. God is the goal of the search; the church, the Bible, creeds, clergy, and religious rites are the means. The spiritual quest, on the other hand, is the opposite of the religious pilgrimage. It is an experiential search for meaning, an exploration of a country not yet mapped, whose boundaries are not yet known. Spirituality is often the name for a longing—for more meaning, more feeling, more connection, more life, more passion—than postmodern people have found in church. When it comes to matters of faith, they are embracing spirituality, but largely rejecting traditional organized religion. Growing numbers now claim to be "spiritual, but not religious."

The secular 3 world, in Taylor's terminology, is one in which all spirituality and belief becomes *fragilized* or uncertain. The fragility of belief can go both ways. If you believe in a transcendent God, if you recite the creeds of the church, if you say your prayers, from time to time you will call them all into question. You will occasionally doubt if any of it is true. Similarly, if you reject the existence of God, you will occasionally experience some sense of the transcendent in your life. It is often found in feelings of awe and wonder. It is a reverence of the majesty and beauty we encounter in many aspects of life—the Webb space telescope images of our vast universe, a glorious sunset, the deep quiet of a forest, the lights of the aurora borealis, a moving piece of music, a tender moment, the face of a new-born child, or the death of a loved one. It is the sense that in the midst of everyday life, we are standing on holy ground. In Marcus Borg's terminology, we find ourselves in "thin spaces"—places where the veil that hides the reality of the sacred momentarily lifts, and we have a sense of something more. Both positions, belief and unbelief, are very fragile. Everyone, at some point, finds themselves moving in and out of either frame of reference.

MY JOURNEY WITH THE CHURCH

These days, I find myself, at a somewhat advanced age, able to see the dissolution of the church with painful but inevitable clarity. I am a person who has had an intense love-hate affair with the church all throughout my life. In my youth, I worshiped in a conservative Missouri Synod congregation in St. Louis where I met my future wife. After marriage and college, we moved to Michigan and joined a small congregation of the more liberal American Lutheran Church (ALC). The ALC eventually merged with two other denominations to form the Evangelical Lutheran Church in America (ELCA). Throughout my faith journey, I have been at times a very active church member, frequently teaching high school and adult Bible classes from a progressive perspective and participating in church councils and synodical activities. I suppose somewhere along the way—and I suspect it was very early—I became a humanist. God had simply ceased to function in my life. I intuitively knew from my youth that neither God nor an eternal life in heaven existed. However, I not only stayed in the church but embraced it, because I sincerely believed that the church is the only place one could speak about things that really mattered. And people I loved and cared for were there. Moreover, I continued to be an avid student of Jesus and of his Way. I saw the historical Jesus—the fully human Jesus—as a model and guide to true humanity. I saw his life, not as a call to be more religious, but to be more human. I suppose I considered myself to be a Jesus humanist.

I took the words of Walter Wink (1935–2012) to heart:

> *We are not required to become divine: flawless, perfect, without blemish. We are invited simply to become human, which means growing through our sins and mistakes, learning by trial and error, being redeemed over and over from compulsive behavior—becoming ourselves, scars and all. It means embracing and transforming those elements in us that we find unacceptable. It means giving up pretending to be good and, instead, becoming real.*[22]

I continued along this path for many years. Then one day, I realized that I could no longer recite the creeds with any authenticity. The prayers of the church had lost all meaning for me, calling as they did on a God of power that I knew was powerless to act. Newly-minted praise songs declared the glory of a God I no longer believed in. My church never said I was unwelcome. I simply felt that there was no longer anything there that was calling to me. So, I just stopped going. Years before, I found a spiritual practice in writing. And so, I continue to write for others who may be experiencing

22. Wink, *The Human Being*, 29.

a similar journey of deconstruction and painful separation. And I watch with sadness and pain as my friends see the churches they love—and have devoted their lives to—dissolve around them.

People are not coming back to the churches of America. That I can say with some confidence. If the church is to exist, it must find a new way forward. It must somehow transform itself to address secular people. The future remains, at this point, highly speculative and largely unknown. But if I had to guess, I would say that a church that gives up trying to be the star of its own show, might be able to see some possibilities for renewed ministry outside their doors in the secular world. And they might finally recover their prophetic voices for the sake of all the oppressed people that we share our lives with on this planet.

PART 3

a pact with evil

Chapter 7

the banality of evil

We must be really grieved that things are as they are. Those people are not real mourners who say, "Sure, the world is in a mess, and I guess maybe I'm a bit guilty like everybody else, but what can I do about it?" What they're really saying is that they are not concerned enough about themselves or the world to look for anything to do. No great burden hangs on their hearts. They aren't grieved. They don't mourn.

—Clarence Jordan (1912–1969), *The Sermon on the Mount*

If only there were evil people somewhere insidiously committing evil deeds, and it were necessary only to separate them from the rest of us and destroy them. But the line dividing good and evil cuts through the heart of every human being.

—Alexander Solzhenitsyn (1918–2008), *The Gulag Archipelago*

Solzhenitsyn contends that all people are capable of evil and can fluctuate between good and evil at different times in their lives—at different ages or under different circumstances. It is a commonly held myth that evil acts are committed by fundamentally "evil" people with purely evil intent. And yet, if "good" people exist, can they be complicit in evil as well?

I had a conversation some years ago about a horrific crime in which a man had kidnapped, imprisoned, and repeatedly raped a young woman in an underground bunker for years until her escape. There have been many of these crimes in the last several decades. In the moment, my friend claimed that the perpetrator was the epitome of evil. If so, I thought, he was just one of many. This crime was only the most recent example of incredible evil in the news, one that captured our momentary attention. Serial killings and mass shootings are seemingly endless daily events. Throughout the twentieth century, the genocides of Hitler, Stalin, and Pol Pot reached unbelievable magnitudes of death.[1] With many of these horrific crimes we can name the individuals responsible and will readily describe them as truly evil people.

Yet something kept nagging at me: a feeling that many seemingly good people in America and in many other countries are regularly complicit with evil—evil acts, evil policies, evil laws, evil systems, and evil events. I immediately began to think of the history of slavery, racism, and Jim Crow in the American South and wondered about the evil intent not only of those who crafted these systems, but the seemingly good people who actively or tacitly supported them as well.

In an article in Psychology Today, author Elliot Cohen (b. 1951) asked the question, "So what does it mean to be evil?"

> *People are not evil because they have done bad things or else we'd all be evil. As Aristotle maintained, being evil portends a persistent habit of doing bad things. Moreover, evil people know that what they are doing is bad but choose to do so anyway. They therefore act with malicious intent. Moreover, evil people typically care little or not at all that what they are doing is or may be harmful to others; and some evil people even derive sadistic pleasure from it. Moreover, some evil people are very cunning and can disguise their evil intentions and lack of regard for others. These individuals may be con artists or even charming rapists or murderers. Of course, there are degrees of evil and some evil people are not as evil as others. For example, it is arguable that a person willing to kill you and be amused by it, is more evil than a person who is only willing to steal your money.*
>
> *Indeed, there are some evil people, so-called "sociopaths," who have Antisocial Personality Disorder and are therefore mentally ill according to current psychiatric standards. For example, the Ted Bundys and Jeffrey Dahmers of the world can commit brutal murders with little or no remorse. But these cases are rare, and the vast majority of sociopaths are not mass murderers.[2]*

---

1. Adolf Hitler's holocaust in Europe murdered at least 11,000,000 people; Joseph Stalin's Great Purge in the Soviet Union killed at least 700,000 and Stalin's agricultural policies caused the great Ukrainian famine—known as the Holodomor—killing 3,900,000 people, Pol Pot's Cambodian genocide may have murdered almost 2,000,000 people.

2. Cohen, "Are Evil People Crazy?" Theodore Robert Bundy was an American serial killer who kidnapped, raped, and murdered numerous young women and girls during

So, evil people are those who persistently act with malicious intent and fully understand the immorality of their actions yet choose to do it anyway. But what of people who believe that what they are doing is not evil at all; rather, they are engaging in a behavior that is normalized by the society in which they reside. Can people perpetrate supremely evil acts even when they are obeying a set of laws or rules—even biblical injunctions—and when their hearts are not filled with unconceivable malice? Their hearts may still demonstrate a lack of empathy and a moral indifference to the fate of others. Philosopher and political theorist Hannah Arendt called the first kind of evil behavior "radical evil." She termed the second as "banal evil."

THE BANALITY OF EICHMANN'S EVIL

Hannah Arendt (1906–1975) was born in Germany to a secular Jewish family. Having studied with prominent German philosophers, she obtained a doctorate in philosophy in 1929. She fled Germany in 1933 during Adolf Hitler's rise to power, living for a time in Paris until it was overrun by Nazi forces, and later, in the United States. In 1963, she published *Eichmann in Jerusalem: A Report on the Banality of Evil*. The book resulted from Arendt's reporting for *The New Yorker* on the trial in Israel of Nazi official Adolf Eichmann (1906–1962). The noun *banality*, like the adjective *banal*, refers to something that is typically ordinary, commonplace, familiar, and unexceptional. How did Eichmann's evil qualify as banal?

Adolf Eichmann, who had escaped from Germany at the end of the Second World War, was captured in Argentina in 1960 by agents of Mossad, the Israeli Secret Service. They brought him to Israel to stand trial on 15 criminal charges, including war crimes, crimes against humanity, and crimes against the Jewish people. He was found guilty on all charges and was executed by hanging in June 1962.

During the trial, Eichmann did not deny the Holocaust or his role in organizing it but claimed that he was simply following orders in the totalitarian system of Germany's Third Reich. The *Führerprinzip* (leader principle) held that "the *Führer's* word is above all written law" and that all governmental policies, decisions, and offices ought to work toward the realization of the ends he desired.

---

the 1970s and possibly earlier. After more than a decade of denials, he confessed to thirty murders he committed in seven states between 1974 and 1978. Jeffrey Lionel Dahmer, also known as the Milwaukee Cannibal or the Milwaukee Monster, was an American serial killer and sex offender who committed the murder and dismemberment of seventeen men and boys between 1978 and 1991.

Eichmann thought of himself as very intelligent. However, as Arendt observed, he had been unable to complete either high school or vocational training, and only found his first significant job as a salesclerk and later district agent for an oil company through family connections. A few months after the Nazi seizure of power in Germany in January 1933, Eichmann lost his job due to staffing cutbacks at Vacuum Oil.

Adolf Eichmann had been a "joiner" his entire life, constantly joining organizations to define himself. In the early 1930s, he was attracted to antisemitic and anti-Bolshevist right-wing political groups, especially the National Socialist (Nazi) party. He joined the SS or Schutzstaffel (meaning "protective squad"), and eventually rose to the rank of Lt. Colonel.

Eichmann was assigned to study and prepare reports on the Zionist movement and various Jewish organizations. He even learned a smattering of Hebrew and Yiddish, gaining a reputation as a specialist in Zionist and Jewish matters. He went to Palestine to investigate the Zionist movement, but Nazi leaders eventually concluded that the creation of a Jewish state was counter to their objectives.

In 1939, Eichmann was given command of the Central Office for Jewish Emigration. Initially, Nazi policy was to compel all Jews and other undesirables to emigrate to other countries, but that soon shifted to forced deportation to areas under German control, first to Poland, and later—if Germany defeated the Soviet Army—to Siberia. After using the deportees as slave laborers, they would be exterminated.

Eichmann was charged with arranging all deportations into occupied Poland, which entailed coordinating with police agencies for the physical removal of the Jews, dealing with their confiscated property, and arranging financing and transport. Within a few days of his appointment, Eichmann formulated a plan to deport 600,000 Jews from Germany and Austria into Poland. On many of the trains, up to a third of the deportees died in transit. While Eichmann claimed at his trial to be upset by the appalling conditions on the trains and in the transit camps, his correspondence and documents of the period show that his primary concern was to achieve the deportations economically and with minimal disruption to Germany's ongoing military operations. The deportation plan was eventually halted because Nazi leaders wanted to divert the trains for military purposes and because it was interfering with their plans to have occupied Polish territories settled by German families.

In mid-September 1941, Adolf Hitler (1889–1945) ordered that all Jews in German-controlled Europe were to be killed. With the entry of the United States into the war in December and the German failure in the Battle of Moscow, Hitler decided that the Jews of Europe were to be annihilated immediately rather than after the war, which now had no assured end in sight.

On January 20, 1942, Reinhold Heydrich (1904–1942), the chief architect of the Holocaust, hosted the Wannsee Conference in a villa outside Berlin, which brought together fifteen administrative leaders of the Nazi regime to co-ordinate planning for the proposed genocide. In preparation, Eichmann drafted a list of the numbers of Jews in various European countries and prepared statistics on emigration. Then he attended the conference to record the decisions. Heydrich appointed Eichmann as his liaison with each of the departments involved. Under Eichmann's supervision, large-scale deportations began almost immediately to extermination camps. The Holocaust lasted two and a half years.

In her book, Hannah Arendt argued that Eichmann witnessed the elite of the German civil service heartily endorse Reinhard Heydrich's program for the extermination of millions of Jewish men, women, and children. Upon seeing members of "respectable society" endorsing mass murder and enthusiastically participating in the planning of the "final solution," Eichmann felt that his moral responsibility could be relaxed, as if he were Pontius Pilate. He consoled himself with the thoughts that he no longer "was master of his own deeds," and that he was unable "to change anything." So, he went along with enthusiastic and efficient participation in the horrific slaughter.

Eichmann had been born to Lutheran parents, so perhaps the injunctions of Paul's Letter to the Romans gave him a religious foundation for obeying the directives of governing authorities without misgivings.

> *Let every person be subject to the governing authorities; for there is no authority except from God, and those authorities that exist have been instituted by God. Therefore, whoever resists authority resists what God has appointed, and those who resist will incur judgement.*[3]

Eichmann later wrote, "There is a need to draw a line between the leaders responsible and the people like me forced to serve as mere instruments in the hands of the leaders. I was not a responsible leader, and as such do not feel myself guilty."

This was a commonly accepted moral argument, particularly for military service during wartime. In 1969, when I became a conscientious objector to the war in Viet Nam, my Lutheran pastor argued that fighting in combat was not a sinful or moral issue, or at least one I would be held personally accountable for by men or God. He declared that I could serve in the military without any responsibility or blame for the inevitable death and destruction, because God would hold only political and military leaders

---

3. Rom 13:1–2.

accountable for doing what was right and wrong. In other words, obey the authorities and follow orders. A "good" soldier or citizen should not question the morality of the legal system in which they participate.

Arendt wrote that while Eichmann certainly had antisemitic beliefs, at the trial he showed "no case of insane hatred of Jews, of fanatical antisemitism, or indoctrination of any kind. He personally never had anything whatever against Jews." They just stood in the way of Germany's greatness and had to be eliminated. He was energized because he was part of making history and the Nazi party accepted him and made him feel truly important.

I recently read a statement by Chuck DeGroat (b. 1970), a professor at Western Theological Seminary. He was speaking of a different subject, but his words made sense to me.

> What we're seeing in our world today is people gather around particular people, particular movements, and attach themselves to it for a sense of power: I feel small, I feel insignificant, I feel like I'm lacking, I don't feel like people are taking me seriously, I feel like I'm the forgotten man. But when I attach myself to the movement, to the figure, now I feel strong, I feel large, I feel important.[4]

Arendt observed that at the end of the Second World War, Eichmann found himself depressed because "it then dawned on him that thenceforward he would have to live without being a member of something or other." Not just any something, but something truly great. In the spirit of the Führer, he was trying to make Germany great again. And he wanted to play a central role in that objective.

During his imprisonment before his trial, the Israeli government had no fewer than six psychologists examine Eichmann. They found no trace of mental illness, including personality disorder. One doctor remarked that his overall attitude towards other people, especially his family and friends, was "highly desirable," while another remarked that the only unusual trait Eichmann displayed was being more "normal" in his habits and speech than the average person. Arendt suggests that this most strikingly discredits the idea that all Nazi criminals were manifestly psychopathic monsters and different from "normal" people. While the prosecution again and again attempted to paint Eichmann as a man who was radically evil, Arendt became convinced that the man truly was as banal as he said he was but was no less responsible for his actions that led to enormous evil.

Hannah Arendt's book introduced the expression and concept of "the banality of evil." Her thesis was that Eichmann was not a fanatic or sociopath, but an extremely average person who relied on cliché defenses ("I was

4. Cosper, "Aftermath."

just following orders") rather than thinking for himself and was motivated more by professional self-promotion than ideology. Banality, in this sense, is not that Eichmann's actions were ordinary, or that there is a potential Eichmann in all of us, but that his actions were motivated by a lack of ethical introspection and empathy toward others that was wholly unexceptional. It was very normal. A moral indifference to the fate of others outside of one's personal sphere marks a significant segment of the population in every country. Arendt thought that Eichmann, like many others, was a superficial person and she declared that the more superficial someone is, the more likely they will yield to evil.

Writings discovered after the publication of Arendt's book revealed Eichmann was in fact a vile and deeply antisemitic ethno-nationalist, who sought a Germany dedicated to pure Aryan ethnicity. Years earlier, at the Nuremberg trials after the war, one of the key Nazi executioners testified that Eichmann told him he would "leap laughing into the grave because the feeling that he had five million people on his conscience would be for him a source of extraordinary satisfaction." Hanna Arendt got it wrong. Eichmann embodied a radical evil, not a banal one. He was just very good at hiding it.

In the end, however, it doesn't matter whether Eichmann was acting from some wicked motive; what matters is that he helped facilitate, with murderous efficiency, one of the greatest evil events of the twentieth century. Eleven million people died in the Nazi genocide: six million Jews and five million others, including Poles and other Slavic peoples, Gypsies, homosexuals, people with mental or physical disabilities, Communists, and Jehovah's Witnesses.

But this still begs the question. Who is evil in society? Do common people bear some responsibility for the existence of evil in their midst? What happens when good people close their eyes to the immorality of legal systems that benefit them? What if entire races of people are involved? Let us explore further.

NAZIS IN AMERICA

In 1933, after Adolf Hitler became the chancellor of Germany, pro-Hitler groups popped up across the United States. They often targeted German Americans for recruitment and encouraged them to intimidate Jewish communities. By 1939, the German American Bund—one of the largest pro-Hitler groups in the country—had grown big enough to pack Madison Square Garden with 20,000 supporters. During the economic turmoil and social disorientation of the Great Depression, they recruited a vocal minority of disaffected Americans by appealing to ethnic pride and exploiting both their insecurities and their racial superiority. Its members defined themselves as quintessentially American while dehumanizing Roman Catholics, Jews, blacks, and immigrants. The Bund was organized into chapters and claimed a total membership of 200,000. In 1940, 1,237,000 people of German birth lived in the United States.

As I have researched my family history in St. Louis, Missouri, I came across this letter to the editor in the *St. Louis Star and Times* from August 11, 1937. It was written by a man named Fritz Brandt to protest picnics run by the German American Bund. The letter was titled "Stars and Stripes and Swastika."

> *As the danger of a new world war increases, a number of German businessmen deriving substantial profits from the fruits of American labor jointly with fascist American friends of the "New Germany" are throwing bait to their crowds of political dupes to swell the ranks of the believers in a fascist dictatorship in the United States. The new method consists in staging "very innocent picnics" and the establishment of camps, just for the sake of beer-drinking, Bratwurst eating and what is called "Gemütlichkeit" [warmth, friendliness, and good cheer]. At the same time the Gemütlichkeit consists in Jew-baiting, red-baiting, and the extolling of der Fuehrer and his wonderful system of government. And all that is done under the shield of the Nazi flag marching side by side with the American flag, the symbol of democratic liberties and civil rights which are given the death penalty in Nazi Germany. As an American citizen of German extraction, I hereby lodge my most energetic protest against the effrontery and insult against the defiling of the American flag and all it stands for . . . Do the Nazis really believe the American people to be stupid enough to overlook the fact that the carrying of the American flag next to the black flag of Nazi piracy is mere sham to make converts in the name of patriotism to their devious plans of killing every vestige of freedom and democracy when "der Tag" [the day] has come, when the American flag is torn to shreds and the Hakenkreuz [hooked cross, or swastika] hoisted on the White House?*

In response, my paternal grandfather, Charles W. Struckmeyer (1886–1979), wrote a letter that was published a week later, on August 18, 1937. It was titled "American Nazis Good Citizens."

> *Fritz Brandt, who claims to be of German extraction, says: "when der Tag has come when the American flag is torn to shreds and the Hakenkreuz (Swastika to you) hoisted on the White House." From*

the bitterness of his Nazi hate, I judge that Fritz is all hot and bothered. Why not go down to the German House garden [Das Deutsche Haus] tonight and over a few seidels [large glasses] of beer study these terrible American Nazis at first hand? He will see the same type of people I saw last night. Quiet gemütliche [friendly and festive] papas and mamas with a big stein in their right hand. Fifty years ago, we found these same hard-working artisans and small businesspeople in our many turnvereins [gymnastic associations]. Time has marched on and today instead of a gym suit he chooses to wear breeches and boots. Don't be alarmed, Fritz, because underneath he is the same steady if not stodgy guy who will be a credit to the community if given a chance and will bring his children up the same way. Fritz speaks of Jew-baiting. It is true we find it in all European countries: in Russia with its pogroms, in Poland, in Rumania and even in Arabia. Is that any reason why we should have German-baiting here?

It was clear from this letter that my grandfather participated in these Bund gatherings and was proud to consider himself a good American Nazi. He exposed the banality of evil in himself and the "quiet gemütliche papas and mamas" who were attracted to the Nazi beliefs of white German supremacy.

My grandfather had grown up in a small Southern Illinois farming community that had been settled by German immigrants from Westphalia. Church services were conducted in German, the local newspaper was printed in German, and the one-room school was taught in both German and English. Later, his family moved to St. Louis where he graduated from dental school. Throughout his life, he had an intense dislike for Jews, Roman Catholics, people of color, and southern and eastern Europeans. He saw German and Nordic people and their culture as vastly superior. He was an ideal candidate for German American Bund picnics. This was 1937, but the roots of evil in which the average American participated go back much further and have made an indelible stain on the nation's history.

BLACK AFRICAN ENSLAVEMENT

Racism is a perpetually insidious cultural myth in America, despite those who would have us believe that we live in a post-racial society. Racism is rooted in the belief that some people are superior to others because they belong to a particular racial, ethnic, or national group. American white racial superiority is very similar to the Nazi ideology of the "master race," in which the hypothetical Nordic or Aryan races are deemed the highest in racial hierarchy. It was all based on an absurd nineteenth-century racial theory, which imagined a hierarchy of races based on lightness and darkness of skin color.

In the United States, the concept of master race arose early in our history within the context a white European master race ruling over black African enslaved peoples in the Southern colonies and states of the seventeenth, eighteenth, and nineteenth centuries. To justify the institution of black enslavement, an ideology of white supremacy was developed, asserting a natural inferiority of dark-skinned people, even alleging that black Africans were subhuman. Although the American Revolution of 1776—and later the French Revolution of 1789—popularized the ideas of liberty and the rights of all human beings, asserting a natural inferiority to blacks was the way that the leading intellectual figures of the time reconciled their ideals with slave economics.

Slavery in the United States probably began in 1619 with the arrival of a small group of enslaved Africans to the British colony of Jamestown, Virginia. This was a year before the arrival of the Mayflower in Cape Cod and a century after the start of the African slave trade in the Caribbean and Latin America. It became a legal institution in America for the next 250 years. Let me repeat that: slavery was legal in America for 250 years. In 1750 there were approximately 250,000 African slaves in the colonies and by 1860 a census counted 4,441,830 in the United States.

A Virginia law in 1662 created the status of "chattel property" for black Africans, stating that they were to be slaves for life and that their condition as slaves would be transmitted to their children. A South Carolina law in 1696 introduced the basic guidelines for slavery in British North America. It said that enslaved Africans, Native Americans, and mulattoes could be bought and sold like any property, and their children would become enslaved at birth.

Enslaved people were considered chattel property—a type of personal property that is movable between locations, as opposed to real estate and houses. As chattel property, they were dehumanized, and regularly included in inventories of cattle and hogs. They were not paid for their labor because they were simply regarded as *things*, not people. The enslaver had absolute control over their lives and absolute ownership from birth until death. Families were separated and sold at will. Black women were raped by white masters without consequences. And they kept having babies: black babies and mixed-race babies. Chattel kept producing more chattel. Thomas Jefferson calculated that he was making a four percent profit every year on the births of black children. To an acquaintance he advised if he had any money, "every farthing of it [should be] laid out in land and negroes." Land was the only thing of value greater than enslaved people.

Delegates to the Constitutional Convention of 1787 hotly debated the issue of slavery in the country they were creating. The resulting Constitution of the United States of America was deliberately ambiguous about the topic, but it was operationally proslavery, counting enslaved people as 3/5ths of a white person for the purpose of representation. Some states were rightly horrified by the practice, and they outlawed slavery within their boundaries. Pennsylvania abolished slavery in 1780, followed by the New England states, and those that were created out of the Northwest Territories. Yet it was flourishing in the American South. For the next six decades, increasing animosity between free and slave states led to the American Civil War. In 1861, there were 19 free states in the North and on the Pacific Coast, and 15 slave states across the South.

After the war's conclusion and the abolition of slavery in 1865, the ideology of white supremacy did not diminish, but instead found new life in legalized racial segregation and the denial of civil rights, resulting in another century of discrimination and oppression for blacks. Even after the Civil Rights Act of 1965, the ideology of white superiority over people of color remains a factor in the American conscience and a theme of conservative politics.

NATIVE AMERICAN GENOCIDE

The same thinking of white European superiority was applied to Native Americans when white Americans wanted to expropriate their land. By the time Christopher Columbus (1451–1506) reached the Caribbean in 1492, historians estimate that there were 10 to 15 million indigenous peoples living in the future territory of the United States. Over the next 400 years—by 1890—the number had reduced to less than a quarter of a million. Disease was a major killer, rapidly wiping out an estimated 90 percent of the population. But racism was a major factor as well.

In the northeast British colonies, edicts to create "redskins"—or scalps of Native Americans—were common. According to a 1775 proclamation in Massachusetts, King George II of Britain called for "subjects to embrace all opportunities of pursuing, captivating, killing, and destroying all and every of the aforesaid Indians." Colonists were paid for each Penobscot native they killed—fifty pounds for adult male scalps, twenty-five for adult female scalps, and twenty for scalps of boys and girls under age twelve.

As settlers moved to the south and west into Native American territory, cotton growers and white settlers pressured the federal government to remove indigenous people from their ancestral homelands. At the beginning of the 1830s, nearly 125,000 Native Americans lived on millions of acres of land in Georgia, Tennessee, Alabama, North Carolina, and Florida. By the end of the decade, very few natives remained anywhere in the southeastern United States.

Andrew Jackson (1767–1845) had advocated the removal of Native Americans for a decade before his election as president in 1829, and it became his highest priority during his two terms in office. As an Army general, Jackson had spent years leading brutal campaigns against the Creeks in Georgia and Alabama and the Seminoles in Florida—campaigns that resulted in the transfer of hundreds of thousands of acres of land from Native Americans to white farmers. In his campaigns, Jackson recommended that troops systematically kill indigenous women and children after massacres to complete the extermination. As president, Jackson continued this crusade on a wider scale: complete removal of Native Americans from the Southeast.

Following the passage of the Indian Removal Act of 1830, Native Americans in the southeastern United States were forcibly removed from their ancestral homelands to areas west of the Mississippi River that had been designated as Indian Territory (later, Oklahoma). This relocation affected a group of indigenous people collectively referred to as the Five Civilized Tribes (the Cherokee, Chickasaw, Choctaw, Muscogee, and Seminole) who had assimilated to European culture while living as autonomous nations in the Southeast.

The relocated peoples suffered from exposure, disease, and starvation while en route to their new designated reserve in Indian Territory, and many died before reaching their enforced destinations. In 1831, the Choctaw became the first indigenous nation to be removed from the future states of Alabama, Mississippi, and Louisiana, and their removal (12,500 people) served as the model for all future relocations. After two wars, many Seminoles (3,600) were removed from Florida in 1832. The Creek removal (19,600) from Georgia followed in 1834, the Chickasaw (4,000) from the woodlands of Alabama, Mississippi, and Tennessee in 1837, and lastly the Cherokee (20,000) from Georgia in 1838. That winter, forcible removals of the Cherokee resulted in the deaths of 4,000 people in the 1,000-mile trek from Georgia to Oklahoma. We know it today as "the trail of tears."

From the country's establishment in 1789, the U.S. government authorized over 1,500 wars, attacks, and raids on Native Americans, the most of any country in the world against its indigenous people. The series of conflicts west of the Mississippi River between Native Americans, white settlers, and the United States Army are generally known as the Indian Wars. Beginning in 1823, battles were fought in Texas, the Southwest, California, and the Northwest. Then after the Civil War, the conflicts shifted to the Great Plains.

On December 26, 1862, six days before signing the Emancipation Proclamation, President Abraham Lincoln ordered the hanging of 38 Dakota men—the largest mass execution in U.S. history. These men had taken part in the Sioux Uprising of 1862 in response to broken treaties. The United States government allowed the treaties to be violated, and punished resistance, all while pushing Native Americans out of their homes and into smaller areas of land.

After several successful indigenous uprisings led by warriors such as Red Cloud, Sitting Bull, and Crazy Horse, the federal government responded with a new method of legal land theft. The Dawes Act of 1887 divided Native American reservations into individual allotments (capped at 160 acres per head of family, 80 acres per adult single person) and sold the "excess" to white homesteaders. Tribes lost 90 million acres, nearly two-thirds of their land. Later amendments to the law removed federal recognition of tribal governments. The legal destruction of Native American tribes was complete, but white supremacy demanded the destruction of indigenous culture as well.

Boarding schools for Native American children, often run by Christian organizations, were created to remove their identities. Native children were required to cut their hair, wear uniforms, speak only English, and take Anglicized names. Until 1978, Native American children could legally be kidnapped from their families by the U.S. government and forced to attend these boarding schools.

The Snyder Act of 1924 finally granted Native Americans full U.S. citizenship. Even with the passing of this bill, Native Americans were still prevented from participating in elections because the Constitution left it up to the states to decide who had the right to vote. It took over forty years for all fifty states to grant them this right. In 1965, the Voting Rights Act was passed by Congress, finally granting suffrage to Native Americans.

JIM CROW SEGREGATION

The enslavement of black Americans was officially abolished in 1865 with the ratification of the Thirteenth Amendment. In 1868, the Fourteenth Amendment gave black people full citizenship and promised them equal protection under the law. To further protect blacks from substandard treatment, the Civil Rights Act of 1875 made it illegal to segregate schools, places of public accommodation, modes of transportation, and juries.

In 1866, one year after the war ended, the Ku Klux Klan emerged as an organized resistance to the Reconstruction of the South, and the era of intimidation, lynching, and burnings began. Klan members saw themselves as protectors of white Protestant supremacy and demonstrated particular concern about keeping black men from mixing with white women. Through fear, brutality, and murder, this terrorist group helped to overthrow local reform-minded governments and restore white supremacy. Their activities did not last long, however.

During the administration of President Ulysses S. Grant (1822–1885), the Department of Justice was established in 1870. It's first job was to vigorously prosecute Ku Klux Klan members. In 1870, there were 1,000 indictments against Klan members with over 550 convictions. By 1871, a total of 3,000 indictments and 600 convictions were made, and while most Klan members served only brief sentences, the ringleaders were imprisoned for up to five years. The result was a dramatic decrease in violence in the South.

By 1872, the Klan was largely finished. (However, it would return with a vengeance in 1915.) But the regular intimidation of black Americans in the South was by no means diminished. Lynching fever soon gripped the Southern states. Between 1882 and 1968, over 3,000 black men were lynched in the South, sometimes for alleged crimes, and at other times for merely looking at or speaking to a white woman. Lynchings were often advertised in newspapers and drew large crowds of white families.

In 1877, federal troops largely withdrew from the South, ending the short-lived era of Reconstruction (1865–1877) and returning power to local white rule. Most states of the former Confederacy quickly adopted "Black Codes," modeled on former slave laws, intended to limit the freedom of emancipated African Americans by restricting their movement and by forcing them into a labor economy based on low wages and debt. In 1883, the Supreme Court nullified the 1875 Civil Rights Act because of white Southern backlash. By the 1890s, Black Codes were expanded into broader "Jim Crow" laws that mandated racial segregation in all public facilities, establishing different rules for blacks and whites. These laws established a formal, codified system of racial apartheid that dominated the American South for three quarters of a century. The segregation laws were upheld in 1896 by the U.S. Supreme Court's "separate but equal" legal doctrine for facilities for African Americans in *Plessy v. Ferguson*. The facilities for blacks and whites were decidedly separate, but they were never equal.

The term "Jim Crow" derives from "Jump Jim Crow," an 1832 minstrel show caricature of an old black man in ragged clothes performed by a white performer in black face. As a result, Jim Crow soon became a pejorative expression for African Americans. It created a stereotypical negative view of African Americans as uneducated, lazy, and dishonest. Jim Crow laws mandated the segregation of public schools, public places, and public transportation, and the segregation of restrooms, restaurants, and drinking fountains for whites and blacks. The U.S. military was already segregated. President Woodrow Wilson (1856–1924), a racist Southern Democrat from Virginia, initiated segregation of federal workplaces in 1913.

In November 1898, a coup d'état—a violent overthrow of a duly elected government—was carried out by white supremacists in Wilmington, North Carolina. Before the coup, black and white working-class people lived side-by-side in the city. They had elected a slate of biracial local leaders two days prior to the attack. The coup was the result of a backlash of white Democrats from the state government leading a mob of 2,000 white racists to expel black and white political leaders from the city and destroy the property and businesses of black citizens, including the only black-owned newspaper in the city. White supremacists killed anywhere between 60 and 300 black citizens. Over 2,100 black people fled the city and never returned. In 1900, the North Carolina legislature effectively stripped black Americans of the vote through a "grandfather clause" and ushered in the worst of the Jim Crow laws.

The Race Riot of 1908 in Springfield, Illinois, between August 14 and 16, consisted of events of racial violence committed against black Americans by a mob of about 5,000 white racists. Two black men had been arrested as suspects in a rape and murder. When a mob seeking to lynch the men discovered the sheriff had transferred them out of the city, the whites furiously spread out to attack black neighborhoods, murdered black citizens on the streets, and destroyed black businesses and homes. The fact that it took place in a Northern state, specifically in Springfield, a state capital and hometown of Abraham Lincoln, demonstrated that blacks were mistreated across the country, not just in the South.

The riot was a catalyst showing the urgent need for an effective civil rights organization in the U.S. On February 12, 1909, journalist Ida B. Wells (1862–1931) and other civil rights activists, including W. E. B. DuBois (1868–1963) and Mary Church Terrell (1863–1954), formed the National Association for the Advancement of Colored People (NAACP), which fought lynching, segregation, and other forms of racial injustice.

In 1915, a landmark silent film, *The Birth of a Nation*—originally called *The Clansman*—was the longest film up to that point, at nearly three hours, and was lauded for its technical virtuosity that had a profound influence on the film industry. The racist film portrayed black men (many of whom were played by white actors in blackface) as unintelligent and sexually aggressive toward white women. The Ku Klux Klan was portrayed as a heroic force to preserve so-called white American values, protect white women, and maintain white supremacy. It was shown in the White House to President Woodrow Wilson, his family, and members of his cabinet. By 1930, it was seen by an estimated ninety percent of white southerners. Black leaders tried to have it banned on the basis that it inflamed racial tensions and could incite violence. Despite its divisiveness, *The Birth of a Nation* was a huge commercial success and has been acknowledged as an inspiration for the rebirth of the Ku Klux Klan, which took place only a few months after its release.

The early twentieth century witnessed "The Great Migration," as hundreds of thousands of African Americans moved from the South to the Northeast, Midwest, and West. One of the main causes was the continuing racial violence, including lynching and massacres, as well as the return of the Ku Klux Klan. The post-World War I period was marked by a spike in racial violence, much of it directed toward African American veterans returning from Europe, where they were often treated much better there than by white Americans.

The summer of 1919 was known as Red Summer because of the white-on-black violence that occurred throughout the United States. The bloodiest incident occurred in Elaine, Arkansas, where it is estimated that over 100 black Americans were killed. The racial violence of the Red Summer erupted in many Southern locations, but it occurred in the North as well, most notably in Washington DC; Chicago, Illinois; Knoxville, Tennessee; and Indianapolis, Indiana.

Over the Memorial Day weekend of 1921, mobs of white racists attacked black residents and businesses of the Greenwood District in Tulsa, Oklahoma over an incident in which a black man entered an elevator operated by a young white woman. This is considered one of the worst incidents of racial violence in the history of the United States. The attack, carried out on the ground and by air with private aircraft, destroyed more than 35 blocks of the district, at the time the wealthiest black community in the United States. It is estimated that between 100 to 300 African Americans were killed in the rioting and about 10,000 black people were left homeless.

In the mid-1920s, the Ku Klux Klan became a powerful political force in both the South and the North, boasting over five million members, including many members of Congress. In addition to hating African Americans, its growth was based on a new anti-immigrant, anti-Catholic, and antisemitic agenda, which reflected contemporary social tensions. Demographic shifts, including immigration, urbanization, and the migrations of African Americans from the South to the North gave urgency and legitimacy to the Klan's fears that the nation was in danger of losing white supremacy and control. The influx of immigrants was seen as a menace that threatened America as a so-called white civilization. Klan leaders vowed to "make America great again" and return it to its former glory. The Ku Klux Klan was at the height of its popularity in August 1925 when more than 30,000 members paraded down Pennsylvania Avenue in Washington, DC. The Klan eventually declined in power, but it had succeeded in inflaming racial hatred and strengthening the political power of white supremacists in many parts of the country.

The Congress of Racial Equality (CORE) was founded in 1942 by an interracial group of students in Chicago. In the 1940s, CORE used sit-ins and other nonviolent direct actions to integrate Chicago restaurants and businesses. In 1947, CORE organized the Journey of Reconciliation, a multi-state integrated bus ride through the upper South to test the previous year's Supreme Court ruling against segregation in interstate travel. It was a precursor to the 1961 Freedom Rides.

A race riot took place in Harlem, New York City, on August 1 and 2 of 1943, after a white police officer, James Collins, shot and wounded Robert Bandy, an African American soldier; and rumors circulated that the soldier had been killed. The riot was chiefly directed by black residents against white-owned property in Harlem. It was one of five riots in the nation that year related to black and white tensions during World War II. The others took place in Detroit; Beaumont, Texas; Mobile, Alabama; and Los Angeles.

Legalized racial segregation existed primarily in the South, while Northern racial segregation was "de facto" (meaning "in practice"), enforced in housing with discriminatory bank lending-practices, red-lining, private covenants, and unspoken agreements among whites, kept black people out of certain neighborhoods and prevented most African Americans from buying their own homes. Employment discrimination was bolstered by bigoted labor-union hiring practices.

In a landmark May 1954 U.S. Supreme Court decision, *Brown v. Board of Education of Topeka*, the Court ruled in a unanimous 9–0 decision, that state laws establishing racial segregation in public schools were unconstitutional. The decision partially overruled the Court's 1896 decision of *Plessy v. Ferguson*, which had held that racial segregation laws did not violate the U.S. Constitution if the facilities for each race were equal in quality. However, in the face of entrenched Southern opposition, progress on integrating American schools moved slowly. Governors in Texas, Arkansas, Florida, Mississippi, and Alabama all attempted to obstruct the order. For several decades after the decision, African American teachers, principals, and other school staff who worked in segregated black schools were fired or laid off as Southerners sought to create a system of integrated schools with all-white leadership.

During the 1950s and 1960s, the Civil Rights Movement eventually secured new protections in federal law for the civil rights of all Americans. It was characterized by nonviolent protests and civil disobedience following a series of highly publicized events such as the murder of Emmett Till (1941–1955). In August 1955, Till, a 14-year-old African American from Chicago was abducted, tortured, and lynched by two white men in Mississippi after being accused of offending a white woman in her family's grocery store. The picture of Till's brutally beaten body in the open-casket funeral requested by his mother was widely publicized in much of the black community in the North. Nonviolent protests began to spring up throughout the South. These included boycotts such as the Montgomery bus boycott, sit-ins such as the Greensboro and Nashville sit-ins, and marches such as the Selma to Montgomery marches.

The Montgomery bus boycott campaign lasted from December 1955 to December 1956, after Rosa Parks (1913–2005), an African American woman, was arrested for her refusal to surrender her seat to a white man on a city bus. A one-day boycott of buses, eventually stretched to 381 days. A young minister, Dr. Martin Luther King Jr (1929–1968), was chosen to lead the boycott. King was only twenty-six and had just become pastor of the Dexter Avenue Baptist Church in Montgomery a year earlier. He was asked to take a leadership role simply because his relative newness to community leadership made it easier for him to speak out. Ralph Abernathy (1926–1990) served as Program Director. As the boycott progressed, boycotters organized a system of carpools instead of riding buses. Black taxi drivers charged ten cents per ride—a fare equal to the cost of riding the bus. Boycotters walked when they could and used other means of transportation such as bicycles or horse-drawn buggies. The boycott proved extremely effective, with enough riders lost to the city transit system to cause serious economic distress. It led to a United States District Court decision that declared the Alabama and Montgomery laws that segregated buses were unconstitutional. More importantly, it stimulated activism and participation in a national Civil Rights Movement and gave King national attention as a rising leader and the best-known spokesman of the movement.

In 1957, King, Ralph Abernathy, Fred Shuttlesworth (1922–2011), Joseph Lowery (1921–2020), and other civil rights activists founded the Southern Christian Leadership Conference (SCLC). The group was created to harness the moral authority and organizing power of black churches to conduct nonviolent protests in the service of civil rights reform. Another group, the Student Nonviolent Coordinating Committee (SNCC, pronounced "snick"), was founded in April 1960 by young people dedicated to nonviolent, direct-action tactics. Although King and others had hoped that SNCC would serve as the youth wing of the SCLC, the students remained fiercely independent of King and SCLC, generating their own projects and strategies.

The Greensboro, North Carolina sit-ins lasted from February to July 1960, and were directed at the lunch counter of a local Woolworth's store. Four black college students sat at the lunch counter and asked to be served. When they were inevitably denied service, they would not leave. They vowed to repeat this process every day for as long as it would take. The next day the number of protestors grew to 20, then 300, and finally more than 1,000 protesters and counter-protesters packed themselves into the store. Students then began a far-reaching boycott of other stores in Greensboro with segregated lunch counters. Sales at the stores dropped by a third, leading their owners to finally abandon their segregation policies. The negative national publicity led the F. W. Woolworth Company department store chain to remove its policy of racial segregation throughout the South. Simultaneously, the Nashville, Tennessee sit-ins lasted from February to May 1960 and were directed at the lunch counters of various stores in the central business district. Inspired by the Greensboro sit-ins, over 150 students were eventually arrested for refusing to vacate store lunch counters when ordered to do so by police. On May 10, six downtown stores began serving black customers at their lunch counters for the first time. These sit-ins became a catalyst for the subsequent sit-in movement across the South in which over 70,000 people participated.

CORE organized the Freedom Rides in the spring of 1961. Modeled after the earlier Journey of Reconciliation, the rides took an integrated group through the Deep South. In Anniston, Alabama, one bus was firebombed, and its fleeing passengers were forced into an angry white mob. As the violence against the Freedom Rides increased, CORE considered halting the project. However, a Freedom Ride Coordinating Committee was formed by representatives of the SNCC, CORE, and SCLC to sustain the rides.

In April 1963, King and the SCLC began a campaign against racial segregation and economic injustice in Birmingham, Alabama. During the protests, the Birmingham Police Department, led by Eugene "Bull" Connor (1897–1973), used high-pressure water jets and police dogs against protesters, including children. Footage of the police response was broadcast on national television news and dominated the nation's attention, shocking many white Americans and consolidating black Americans behind the movement. King was arrested and jailed early in the campaign, From his cell, he composed the now-famous "Letter from Birmingham Jail" that responds to calls on the movement to pursue legal channels for social change.

Dr. Martin Luther King Jr, representing the SCLC, was among the leaders of civil rights organizations who were instrumental in the organization of the March on Washington for Jobs and Freedom, which took place on August 28, 1963. The march made specific demands: an end to racial segregation in public schools; meaningful civil rights legislation, including a law prohibiting racial discrimination in employment; protection of civil rights workers from police brutality; a $2 minimum wage for all workers (equivalent to $20 in 2023); and self-government for Washington, DC. More than a quarter of a million people of diverse ethnicities attended the event, sprawling from the steps of the Lincoln Memorial onto the National Mall and around the reflecting pool. At the time, it was the largest gathering of protesters in Washington, DC's history. King delivered a 17-minute speech, one part of which was later known as "I Have a Dream."

In the summer of 1964, known as Freedom Summer, nearly 1,000 activists came to Mississippi—most of them white college students from the North and West—to join with local black activists to register voters and teach in "Freedom Schools." On June 21, three civil rights workers disappeared: James Chaney (1943–1964) who was black, Andrew Goodman (1943–1964), and Michael Schwerner (1939–1964) who were both Jewish. They were found weeks later, murdered. Many white Christian residents deeply resented the outsiders and their attempts to change their society. State and local governments, police, the White Citizens' Council, and the Ku Klux Klan used arrests, beatings, arson, murder, spying, firing, evictions, and other forms of intimidation and harassment to oppose the project and prevent black people from registering to vote or achieving social equality.

The legal apartheid system in the South came to an end after almost 90 years of segregation when President Lyndon Johnson (1908–1973) signed the Civil Rights Act of 1964. Then, on October 14, 1964, Dr. Martin Luther King Jr was awarded the Nobel Peace Prize for combating racial inequality through nonviolent resistance.

But voting rights were not yet secured. The Selma to Montgomery marches were three protest marches, held in 1965, along the 54-mile highway from Selma, Alabama to the state capital of Montgomery. The marches were organized by nonviolent activists to demonstrate the desire of African American citizens to exercise their constitutional right to vote in defiance of segregationist repression. On February 18, white segregationists attacked a group of peaceful demonstrators in the town of Marion, Alabama. In the ensuing chaos, an Alabama state trooper fatally shot Jimmie Lee Jackson, a young African American demonstrator. In response to Jackson's death, Martin Luther King and the Southern Christian leadership Conference (SCLC) planned a massive protest march from Selma to the state capitol of Montgomery.

A group of 600 people, including activists John Lewis (1940–2020) and Hosea Williams (1926–2000), set out from Selma on Sunday, March 7, a day that would come to be known as "Bloody Sunday." When the marchers passed over the county line at the Edmund Pettus Bridge, state troopers attacked the unarmed marchers with whips, nightsticks, and tear gas, leaving many of them injured and bloodied. The brutal scene was captured on television, enraging many Americans and drawing civil rights and religious leaders of all faiths to Selma in protest. The second march took place on March 9, when Dr. Martin Luther King led roughly 2,500 people, both black and white, to the Pettus Bridge where troopers, police, and marchers confronted each other. King paused the marchers and led them in prayer, whereupon the troopers stepped aside to let them pass. Instead, King turned the marchers around and returned to the church where they had begun—obeying a court order that prevented them from making the full march. The protesters demanded protection from President Lyndon Johnson, whose administration had been working on a voting rights law. He complied. The third march started on March 21, protected by 1,900 members of the Alabama National Guard under federal command, and many FBI agents and federal marshals. The marchers grew in number over four days until 25,000 people entered the capital city of Montgomery on March 25.

Only a few months later, Congress passed the Voting Rights Act, which President Johnson signed into law on August 6, 1965. Still, many states continued to ban interracial marriages through anti-miscegenation laws until they were finally invalidated by the 1967 Supreme Court decision in *Loving v. Virginia*.

ONGOING AFRICAN AMERICAN DISCRIMINATION

However, discrimination did not end. Many black Americans still faced discrimination in jobs, housing, education and politics. And urban tensions grew high between white police officers and black communities.

Major race riots have occurred in the United States since the Harlem Riots of 1943, but the 1960s surpassed anything previously experienced. The six-day Watts riots in August 1965, sometimes referred to as the Watts Rebellion, was a series of violent confrontations between Los Angeles police and residents of Watts and other predominantly African American neighborhoods of South-Central Los Angeles. A total of 34 people died and a thousand were injured. In mid-July 1967, the city of Newark, New Jersey, erupted in violence as black residents battled police following the beating of a black taxi driver, leaving 26 people dead. A few days later, the 1967 Detroit Riot, also known as the Detroit Rebellion, was the bloodiest of the urban riots in the United States during the "long, hot summer of 1967."

The precipitating event was a police raid of an unlicensed, after-hours bar, known as a "blind pig," on the city's Near West Side. By the time the bloodshed, burning, and looting ended after five days, 43 people were dead and 1,189 were injured. Nearly 1,400 buildings had been burned and some 7,000 National Guard and U.S. Army troops had been called into service. A year later, following Martin Luther King's assassination in 1968, rioting broke out in over 120 cities including Chicago and Washington.

I am now going to fast forward to the twenty-first century skipping past four decades. On the night of February 26, 2012, in Sanford, Florida, George Zimmerman (b. 1983) fatally shot Trayvon Martin (1995–2012), a 17-year-old African American boy who was walking back to the home of his father's fiancée after buying a pack of Skittles from a nearby convenience store. Zimmerman, the neighborhood watch coordinator for his gated community, shot Martin, who was unarmed, during a physical altercation between the two. Zimmerman, slightly injured during the encounter, told police he shot Martin in self-defense. Initially not charged, following widespread protests Zimmerman was eventually charged with murder for Martin's death, but was acquitted in July 2013 after claiming self-defense. Martin's death inspired a new generation of protests against police and vigilante violence toward black people, one that would go on to highlight systemic racism in nearly every aspect of American life.

In 2013, in response to the acquittal of Trayvon Martin's murderer, three female black organizers—Alicia Garza (b. 1981), Patrisse Cullors (b. 1983), and Ayọ Tometi (b. 1984)—created a project with the hashtag #BlackLivesMatter on social media. It became nationally recognized for street demonstrations following the 2014 deaths of two more African Americans, Michael Brown (1996–2014)—resulting in protests and unrest in Ferguson, Missouri, a city near St. Louis—and Eric Garner (1970–2014) in New York City. Both were killed by police officers. Since then, participants in the movement have demonstrated against the deaths of numerous other African Americans by police actions or while in police custody. The movement returned to national headlines and gained further international attention in 2020 during the George Floyd (1973–2020) protests following his murder by Minneapolis police officer Derek Chauvin (b. 1976). An estimated 15 million to 26 million people participated in the 2020 Black Lives Matter protests in the United States, making it one of the largest movements in the country's history. It comprised many views and a broad array of demands, but they centered on criminal justice reform.

On June 17, 2015, a mass shooting occurred in Charleston, South Carolina, in which nine African Americans were killed during a Bible study at the Emanuel African Methodist Episcopal Church. The morning after the attack, police arrested Dylann Roof in Shelby, North Carolina, a 21-year-old white supremacist who had attended the Bible study before he committed the shooting. Founded in 1816, this church is one of the oldest black churches in the United States, and it has long been a center for organizing events which are related to civil rights. In the wake of the shooting, efforts were made across the South to remove Confederate monuments from public spaces and rename streets honoring notable figures from the Confederacy.

Finally, I want to address the problem of police bias, the unjustified arrests and killings of black men by white police officers, and mass prison incarceration of people of color. Racial bias keeps more people of color in prisons and on probation than ever before. The origins of modern-day policing can be traced back to the use of white "slave patrols" to keep black slaves in line. The earliest formal slave patrol was created in the Carolinas in the early 1700s with one mission: to establish a system of terror and squash slave uprisings with the capacity to pursue, apprehend, and return runaway slaves to their owners. Tactics included the use of excessive force to control and produce desired slave behavior. State militias were formed to back up these slave patrols. For instance, the militia was called upon in 1739 to put down a massive slave uprising in Stono, South Carolina, called the Stono Rebellion.

Then in August 1791, enslaved people began a successful insurrection against French colonial rule in Saint-Domingue. It ended in 1804 with the former colony's independence under black rule, now the state of Haiti. This sent shock waves among slave holders in the United States who had long feared a similar uprising of enslaved people. Professor Carol Anderson (b. 1959) of Emory University claims that the language of the Second Amendment to the Constitution, ratified on December 15, 1791, was crafted to ensure militias backed by slave owners could quickly crush any rebellion or resistance from those they had enslaved. And she says the right to bear arms, presumably guaranteed to all citizens, was repeatedly denied to African Americans with brutal consequences.[5]

For the next 75 years, slave patrols stepped up their oppression and continued until the end of the Civil War. Then during Reconstruction, slave patrols were no longer needed to suppress rebellions. Their function in the South was replaced by state and local militias who were empowered to control freed slaves who they feared would extract revenge for the previous 250 years. They relentlessly, systematically, and violently enforced the Black Codes of the Jim Crow South. Over the next century these militias began transitioning to local police departments who took over the suppression of blacks in the South, and as they migrated North, there as well.

5. Anderson, *The Second: Race And Guns*, 5.

Throughout the United States and continuing to this day, white police officers began patrolling black neighborhoods and disproportionately arresting black people; prosecutors disproportionately indicted black people; juries disproportionately found black people guilty; judges disproportionately gave black people long sentences; and, then, after all this, some social scientists, observing the number of black people in jail, decided that, as a matter of biology, black people were disproportionately inclined to criminality. The default position among many police officers is that the black man is a threat. And when they feel threatened, they react violently. Today, one out of every three black boys can expect to go to prison in his lifetime, as can one of every six Latino boys—compared with one of every 17 white boys.

Mass incarceration in prisons began in the 1970s, when politicians from both parties used fear and thinly veiled racial rhetoric to push increasingly punitive policies. President Richard Nixon (1913–1994) started this trend, declaring a "war on drugs" and justifying it with speeches about being "tough on crime." But the prison population truly exploded during the administration of President Ronald Reagan (1911–2004). When Reagan took office in 1980, the total prison population was 329,000, and when he left office eight years later, the prison population had essentially doubled, to 627,000. This staggering rise in incarceration hit communities of color hardest: They were disproportionately incarcerated then and remain so today. In 1950, 70 percent of those behind bars were white; by 1990, the ratio had flipped: 70 percent were African American and Latino. Blacks are incarcerated for drug offenses at a rate 10 times greater than that of whites, even though blacks and whites use drugs at roughly the same rates.

Incarceration grew both at the federal and state level, but most of the growth was in the states that house the vast majority of the nation's prisoners. In Texas, for example, the state incarceration rate has quadrupled. In 1978, the state incarcerated 182 people for every 100,000 residents. By 2003, that figure was 710. These changes were spurred in part by laws like the 1994 Crime Bill, signed by President Bill Clinton (b. 1946), that created tough new criminal sentences and incentivized states to build more prisons. It was the largest crime bill in the history of the United States. Among other things, it instituted the death penalty for nearly 60 crimes, and encouraged the prosecution of young people as adults. The era of mass incarceration has seen the U.S. prison population grow by 500 percent in 40 years, peaking in 2008. Including those in local jails, more than 2.3 million Americans are incarcerated today, the highest incarceration rate in the world. It costs anywhere from $20,000 to $50,000 annually to keep an individual behind bars, causing the United States to spend over $80 billion each year.

IMMIGRATION RESTRICTIONS

Throughout our history, the theory of white racial superiority clearly affected U.S. immigration, favoring Northern Europeans until the mid-1960s. In the eighteenth and nineteenth centuries, America encouraged relatively open immigration to settle its empty lands. There were no visas, no quotas, no barriers to immigration. Between 1790 and 1820, an estimated 5,000 to 6,000 people freely immigrated to the United States each year. Through its open borders, anyone could move into the United States, start a new life, pay taxes, participate in military service, and conduct business. However, anyone who wanted to vote or hold elective office had to become a naturalized citizen. That required five years of residency. In addition, the Fourteenth Amendment specified that anyone born in the United States was automatically considered a citizen.

In 1855, the Emigrant Landing Depot at Castle Garden opened in New York City to provide a safe experience for immigrants, but it was not intended to restrict immigration. During the next 37 years, until it was replaced by Ellis Island in 1892, more than eight million people passed through Castle Garden, especially from Germany and Ireland, and later from Italy and Eastern Europe. Following the Civil War, a few states passed the first immigration laws, but in 1876 the Supreme Court declared the regulation of immigration should be a federal responsibility.

Immigration first became a political issue in the mid-1850s, primarily due to the arrival of large numbers of Irish and German Catholics in the 1840s. The American Party, commonly known as the "Know Nothing" movement, was primarily anti-Catholic and hostile to immigration. Starting originally as a secret society, adherents to the movement replied "I know nothing" when asked about its specifics by outsiders. These nativists believed a "Romanist" (Roman Catholic) conspiracy was trying to subvert civil and religious liberty in the United States and they sought to politically organize native-born Protestants in what they described as a defense of their traditional religious and political values. Nativism has always sought to protect the interests of native-born or established inhabitants against those of newly arrived immigrants.

By the 1870s, nativist Americans on the West Coast became increasingly hostile to a rise in Chinese immigration to the United States. The racially prejudiced press coined the term "Yellow Peril" to stir fears that Asians would invade the continent and endanger democracy and Christianity. Working-class Americans worried that Chinese immigrants would compete unfairly for their jobs by working for lower wages. Illiterate Irish immigrant railroad laborers found themselves in direct competition with

Chinese workers, as both groups struggled at the lower end of the wage scale. In 1882, the Chinese Exclusion Act was passed by Congress to create a ten-year moratorium on Chinese labor immigration. The law was renewed in 1892 and 1902.

The year 1882 saw the arrival of the largest number of immigrants in American history to that point—nearly one million. The Immigration Act of that year continued to welcome unrestricted immigration of Europeans, rejecting only Asian and African immigrants who were considered racially undesirable. From 1900 to 1920, nearly 24 million immigrants arrived during what is known as the "Great Wave." Italians, Greeks, Hungarians, Poles, and other Slavic-speaking immigrants made up the bulk of this migration.

White racial superiority was emboldened by the eugenics movement that was sweeping the United States in the twenties. A 1916 book, *The Passing of the Great Race* by amateur anthropologist Madison Grant (1865–1937), argued that the American racial stock was being diluted by the influx of new immigrants from the Mediterranean, the Balkans, and European ghettos. He expounded a theory of Nordic superiority and argued for a strong eugenics program that would improve the genetic quality of a human population by excluding (through selective breeding and forced sterilization) certain genetic groups judged to be less desirable and promoting other genetic groups judged to be superior. Adolf Hitler wrote to Grant to personally thank him for his ideas, referring to the book as "my Bible."

The Passing of the Great Race reached wide popularity among Americans and influenced immigration policy in the twenties when a broad national consensus sharply limited the overall inflow of immigrants from southern and eastern Europe. Congress responded with a new restrictive immigration policy—the national-origins quota system of 1921 and 1924. Immigration was limited by assigning each nationality a quota based on its representation in the 1890 census. This quota favored immigrants from Northwestern Europe, especially from Germany, England, and Ireland. The law banned Arab and Asian immigration outright and made immigration from Africa close to impossible. It was this restrictive law that served as the legal basis for the State Department not accepting Jewish refugees from Nazi Germany and Austria in the years before the Holocaust.

In 1928, Adolf Hitler praised the American immigration quotas:

> *The American Union feels itself to be a Nordic-German state and by no means an international porridge of peoples. This is revealed by its immigration quotas. Scandinavians, then Englishmen, and finally Germans have been accorded the largest contingent.*

In Hitler's 1926 manifesto, *Mein Kampf* (*My Struggle*), he praised America as "the one state" that was making progress toward becoming a racially healthy order. And when the Nazis came to power in the 1930s, Nazi lawyers carefully studied the long history of U.S. policies to close its doors to non-whites.

It was not until the 1965 Immigration and Nationality Act that the U.S. began to separate itself from the worst aspects of its racist past. Entry was opened to immigrants other than the traditional Northern European groups, and significantly altered the demographic mix in the U.S. as a result. Most applicants for immigration visas in the following decades started coming from Asia and Latin America rather than Europe.

JAPANESE AMERICAN DISCRIMINATION

After 1900, the 1882 Chinese Exclusion Act was interpreted to exclude all Asian immigrants, including the Japanese Issei who had been born in Japan. The Immigration Act of 1924 solidified that prejudice into law, banning all immigrants from "undesirable" Asian countries. In addition, U.S. law prohibited Japanese immigrants from becoming naturalized citizens, making them dependent on their native-born American children to rent or purchase property. They were also not allowed to operate businesses in white communities.

During one of the most atrocious violations of American civil rights in the 20th century, Japanese Americans were incarcerated in isolated concentration camps from 1942 to 1945. On February 19, 1942, just months after the Japanese attack on Pearl Harbor, President Franklin D. Roosevelt signed Executive Order 9066, ordering the arrest and internment of 117,000 Japanese Americans on the West Coast of the United States, 62 percent of whom were native-born American citizens. Yet, during the Second World War there was no wholesale incarceration of U.S. residents who traced their ancestry to Germany or Italy, America's other enemies. The internment is considered to have resulted more from racism than from any security risk posed by Japanese Americans. In January 1942, a naval intelligence officer in Los Angeles had reported that Japanese Americans were being perceived as a threat almost entirely "because of the physical characteristics of the people." Fewer than three percent of them might be inclined toward sabotage or spying, he wrote, and the Navy and the FBI already knew who most of those individuals were, having investigated Japanese Americans since the rise of Japanese power in the 1930s. Still, the government took the position summed up by John DeWitt, the Army general in command of the

West Coast: "A Jap's a Jap. They are a dangerous element, whether loyal or not." After the Executive order was written, DeWitt issued orders to empty declared military exclusion zones in California, Oregon, Washington, and Arizona of Issei (*EE-say*), immigrants born in Japan, and Nisei (*NEE-say*), their children, who were U.S. citizens by birth.

The Japanese Americans were forced to leave their houses, shops, farms, and fishing boats. For months they stayed at "assembly centers," living in racetrack barns or on fairgrounds. Then they were shipped to ten "relocation centers," primitive concentration camps in the western interior of the country. The system was severe, degrading, and humiliating with armed guards, barbed wire, and daily roll call.

In a 6–3 decision, the Supreme Court affirmed the constitutionality of Executive Order 9066 in *Korematsu v. United States* (1944). Later that year, the exclusion orders were rescinded, after the war had turned in the Allies' favor. By then the Army was enlisting Nisei soldiers to fight in Africa and Europe. After the war, President Harry Truman told the much-decorated, all-Nisei 442nd Regimental Combat Team: "You fought not only the enemy, but you fought prejudice—and you have won." Unfortunately, that was not the case. Japanese Americans met waves of hostility when they tried to resume their former lives. Many found that their properties had been seized for nonpayment of taxes or otherwise appropriated by local authorities.

JEWISH AMERICAN DISCRIMINATION

Antisemitism is hostility to, prejudice towards, or discrimination against Jewish people. It is a form of racism and has existed for centuries in the United States nourished by deeply ingrained, centuries-old anti-Jewish bias that began in Europe in the Middle Ages. The most persistent form of antisemitism has been a series of widely circulating stereotypes that portray Jews as being socially, religiously, and economically unacceptable to American life.

There have been Jewish communities in the United States since colonial times. A population of 1,000–2,000 Jewish residents in 1790 of mostly Sephardic Jews of Spanish and Portuguese descent, was composed of immigrants from Brazil who settled in American cities. Until the 1830s, the Jewish community of Charleston, South Carolina, was the largest in North America. The American Jewish community grew to about 15,000 by 1840, and to about 250,000 by 1880. Many Jewish immigrants arrived from Germany in the 1850s. They established stores in towns across the country, formed Reform synagogues, and were active in banking in New York. After

1881, approximately three million Ashkenazi Jews, whose ancestors lived in Central and Eastern Europe, immigrated to America, many of them fleeing pogroms, particularly in Russia, and the difficult economic conditions that were widespread in much of Eastern Europe during this time. Many Americans distrusted these Jewish immigrants. Whereas before 1900, American Jews never amounted even to one percent of America's total population, by 1930, Jews formed about 3.5 percent. This dramatic increase, combined with the upward mobility of some Jews, contributed to a resurgence of antisemitism. As immigration swelled the Jewish population of the United States, there developed a growing sense of the Jew as different and hated.

During the first half of the 20th century, Jewish Americans were discriminated against in some areas of employment, and blocked from certain properties, social clubs, and resort areas. Restaurants, hotels, and other establishments that barred Jews from entry were called "restricted." Furthermore, the Jewish Americans encountered quotas on enrollment and teaching positions in colleges and universities.

In 1913, Max Leo Frank (1884–1915), a Jewish businessman who moved to Atlanta, Georgia to manage his family's pencil factory, was convicted of the rape and murder of a 13-year-old female white Christian employee, following a trial that was defined by antisemitism. When the governor of Georgia reduced his death sentence to life in prison, a hate-filled mob—including many influential community leaders—dragged Frank from his prison cell and lynched him. In response to the lynching of Leo Frank, an attorney from Chicago, Sigmund Livingston (1872–1946), founded the Anti-Defamation League in September 1913. The ADL became the leading Jewish group fighting antisemitism in the United States. But moreover, the ADL's original charter calls on the organization to secure justice and fair treatment for all citizens. They want to put an end forever to unjust discrimination toward any sect or body of citizens.

Antisemitic fervor and scapegoating of Jews reached a peak during the interwar period with the rise of the Ku Klux Klan in the 1920s, along with antisemitic publications in *The Dearborn Independent* between 1919 and 1927, and incendiary radio speeches by Father Charles Coughlin (pronounced *COG-lin*) in the late 1930s.

Industrialist Henry Ford (1863–1947)—a pacifist who opposed World War I—used his newspaper, *The Dearborn Independent*, to spew antisemitic hatred. He believed that Jews were responsible for starting wars in order to profit from them. The paper was exposed for circulating *The International Jew, the World's Foremost Problem*, based on the antisemitic forgery, *The Protocols of the Learned Elders of Zion*, a hoax that described a Jewish plan for global domination. Adolf Hitler reportedly revered Ford for his work. The

Anti-Defamation League organized a boycott of Ford products, which was supported not only by Jews, but also by several liberal Christian groups. In December 1927, Ford gave in and abolished the paper.

Throughout the 1930s, Father Charles Coughlin (1891–1979), a Roman Catholic priest, was one of the most influential men in the United States. Foreshadowing modern talk radio and televangelism, Coughlin led radio broadcasts that reached an estimated 30 million listeners, over 40 percent of the 128 million Americans, the largest radio audience in the world. He broadcast religious services with political overtones and antisemitic views. He also voiced pro-Nazi opinions that made him a person of interest for the U.S. Federal Bureau of Investigation (FBI) in 1942. Coughlin's newspaper, *Social Justice*, reached a circulation of 800,000 at its peak in 1937.

Originally from Ontario in Canada, in 1926 he was assigned to the newly founded Shrine of the Little Flower in the largely Protestant suburban community of Royal Oak, Michigan. Typical of Coughlin's dramatic excesses, the church he constructed, which was intended to serve a small parish of some two dozen families, could seat about 600. Aware that he was unable to pay back the diocesan loan that had paid for his church structure and disturbed by anti-Catholic cross burnings on his church grounds organized by the Ku Klux Klan, Coughlin began broadcasting his Sunday sermons, *The Hour of Power*, from local radio station WJR in Detroit. He denounced the KKK, while appealing to his Irish Catholic audience. Many of his sermons were rambling, disorganized, repetitious, and as time went by, they became increasingly full of bigoted rhetoric. But as a champion of the poor, a foe of big business, and a critic of federal indifference by the Hoover administration in the face of widespread economic distress, he spoke to the hopes and fears of lower-middle class Americans throughout the country during the early days of the Great Depression. In 1930, the program was picked up by CBS for national broadcast.

After the 1936 election, Coughlin increasingly expressed sympathy for the fascist policies of Hitler and Mussolini, as an antidote to Bolshevism. His weekly radio broadcasts became suffused with hatred and antisemitic falsehoods. He blamed the Depression on an international conspiracy of Jewish bankers and claimed that they were behind the Russian Revolution.

In a 1938 broadcast, Coughlin helped inspire and publicize the creation of a political association called the Christian Front. A militia-like organization, the Front promised to defend the country from communists and Jews. In 1940, the Christian Front was shut down when the FBI discovered the group was arming itself and planning to murder Jews, communists, a dozen members of Congress, overthrow the government of the United

States, and eventually establish, in J. Edgar Hoover's (1895–1972) words, "a dictatorship, similar to the Hitler dictatorship in Germany."

In November 1938, two weeks after Kristallnacht (the "Night of Broken Glass"), when Jews across Germany were attacked and killed, and Jewish businesses, homes, and synagogues burned, Coughlin blamed the Jewish victims. After this speech, and as his programs became more antisemitic, some radio stations began refusing to air his speeches without pre-approved scripts. This made Coughlin a hero in Nazi Germany, where papers ran headlines like: "America is Not Allowed to Hear the Truth." In December 1938, several thousand of Coughlin's followers marched in New York city protesting potential asylum law changes that would allow more Jews (including refugees from Hitler's persecution) into the U.S. After the outbreak of World War II in Europe in 1939, the Roosevelt administration forced the cancellation of his radio program and forbade distribution by mail of his newspaper, *Social Justice*, shutting down his voice.

President Franklin Delano Roosevelt (1882–1945) was inaugurated for his first term in 1933, only five weeks after Adolf Hitler was appointed Chancellor of Germany. He faced immense domestic challenges and struggled to restore an economy shattered by the Great Depression. Roosevelt did not take significant action to aid German Jews, either by ordering a diplomatic protest or by publicly supporting increased immigration quotas. Yet, he did more for them than any other world leader at the time. He responded to the worldwide threat of fascism and moved the nation from isolation to victory in a global war.

In a 1938 poll, approximately 60 percent of Americans held a low opinion of Jews, labeling them greedy, dishonest, and pushy. Forty-one percent of respondents agreed that the Jewish people had "too much power in the United States," and this figure rose to 58 percent by 1945. Several surveys taken from 1940 to 1946 found that Jews were seen as a greater threat to the welfare of the United States than any other national, religious, or racial group.

Roosevelt was a compassionate yet pragmatic man who faced a public that was largely antisemitic. Nevertheless, he did what he could for the Jewish people. In his three-plus terms from 1933 to 1945, he led the war in Europe against Hitler, supported a Jewish homeland in Palestine, and surrounded himself with Jewish advisers who helped shape the laws that revolutionized the role of government in American life—what critics labeled the "Jew Deal."

After the Second World War, publicly expressed antisemitism declined dramatically in the United States. The percentage of Americans who reported hearing recent criticism of Jews plummeted from 64 percent in 1946 to

16 percent in 1951. In postwar public discourse, commentators began to discuss Protestantism, Catholicism, and Judaism as America's three prominent spiritual traditions—a "Judeo-Christian" tradition. As the civil rights era gained momentum in the 1950s, Jews gradually were loosened from the grip of discrimination that had blocked their entry into universities, success in the job market, and access to the housing market. But a 1992 survey by the Anti-Defamation League showed that about 20 percent of Americans still held antisemitic views.

By 2016, the emergence of the so-called "alt-right," a set of far-right groups and individuals, embracing white nationalism, began using online media to disseminate hateful content. This movement gained national attention in August 2017, when white supremacists and neo-Nazis gathered for the "Unite the Right" rally in Charlottesville, Virginia. Their brazen chants of "Jews will not replace us!" evoked the longstanding white supremacist claim that Jews are conspiring to destroy pure, white American society. That year alone, antisemitic incidents rose by 57 percent. Hate crimes in general hit a 27-year high in 2018, with Jews and Jewish institutions constituting the most frequent target of religion-based incidents by a large margin. In 2018, a gunman entered the Tree of Life Synagogue in Pittsburgh at Sabbath services, shouting "All Jews must die," then opened fire upon the congregation, killing 11 people in the deadliest attack on Jews in American history.

In the year after the Pittsburgh shooting, the FBI reportedly acted against at least 12 violent plots or threats planned by white supremacists against Jewish communities. Today, while Jewish people in America represent about four percent of the population, they are victims of 60 percent of the hate crimes. A 2021 report called *The State of Antisemitism in America* found that one in four American Jews say they have been targets of antisemitism in the last 12 months and that 82 percent say antisemitism has risen since 2016.

SUBJUGATION OF WOMEN

Patriarchy is a social system in which positions of dominance and privilege are held by men, and women are oppressed by them through various systemic structures. Male dominance is one of the earliest known and most widespread forms of inequality in human history. Humans probably evolved as an egalitarian species and remained that way for hundreds of thousands of years. But then, about 10,000 years ago, with the transition from the Paleolithic to the Neolithic and the rise of agriculture, patriarchal societies emerged in which men began to control the lives of women and children.

Historically, patriarchy has manifested itself in many ancient and modern cultures through a social structure of political, religious, and economic subjugation of women. Laws, created by men, historically gave men substantial powers over the lives, property, and bodies of their wives and children.

Before the nineteenth century, most families were organized according to patriarchal tradition. Household heads owned and controlled the means of production, and their wives and children were obliged to provide the unpaid labor needed to sustain family enterprises such as farms and shops. Masters of the household had a legal right to command the obedience of their wives and children—as well as any servants or slaves—and to use corporal punishment to correct disobedience. Divorce was possible, but rare. Until the middle of the nineteenth century in the United States, grounds for divorce were pretty much confined to adultery, cruelty, and desertion. The big problem at the time for women, was that they were a legal non-entity in the sense that it was difficult for them to claim ownership of property, including their children, or financial assets which worked against them in the case of a divorce.

Over the past two centuries, this patriarchal family system has begun to collapse in the Global North, as household heads lost control over their children, wives, and servants. But vestiges remain. Consider the widespread practice of a father giving away his daughter at her wedding. He is symbolically transferring ownership of her body to her new husband.

Religion, particularly Christianity, reinforced patriarchy in American society. A male God, repeatedly addressed as "Father," contributed to the idea of male dominance. The Epistles (Letters) in the New Testament contain numerous directives regarding the role of women: Women may learn in silence but are not permitted to teach men.[6] Women are not permitted to speak in church. If they have questions, they must ask their husbands at home.[7] Women are to be subservient to and follow the instructions of their husbands.[8] Women "shall be saved in childbearing, if they continue in faith and charity and holiness with sobriety."[9] The Hebrew Bible includes a clear message to women as well: "Your desire will be for your husband, and he will rule over you."[10]

The American colonies based their laws on the English common law, which said that a husband and wife were considered as one person—"one

6. 1 Tim 2:12.

7. 1 Cor 14:34–36.

8. Eph 5:22–24.

9. 1 Tim 2:15.

10. Gen 3:16.

flesh" per Genesis. The legal existence of the woman was suspended during the marriage, or at least was incorporated into that of her husband under whose protection she existed. Maybe the most basic indicator is the apparently quaint custom of wives assuming their husbands' last names. Prior to the 1970s, women could not get passports, driver's licenses, or register to vote unless they adopted their husband's last name. Among U.S.-born married women, only six percent had a surname that differed from their husbands in 2004.

For the first half of the nineteenth century, only a minority of American children, both girls and boys, spent any meaningful time in a classroom. An even smaller minority received any secondary education. Few girls attended formal schools, but most were able to get some education at home where they were taught rudimentary reading and writing skills by their mothers. There was no higher education for women. Their access to education was considered unnecessary for the performance of domestic tasks and to prepare them for their roles as mothers. Overall, their abilities were not considered equal to those of their male counterparts, so no pressing need to further develop their intellect was acknowledged.

The second half of the nineteenth century, on the other hand, produced relatively rapid gains for women's education in the United States. The Morrill Land-Grant Colleges Act of 1862 founded universities to educate both men and women in practical fields of study, though women's courses were still centered around home economics. The founding of Oberlin (1833), Vassar (1865), Wellesley (1875), Smith (1875), Radcliffe (1879), Bryn Mawr (1885), and Barnard (1889) made the study of the humanities possible. Despite growing numbers of women graduates, many were denied positions in the workplace that they were qualified for in favor of men. The basic assumption was that women should marry and become housewives and mothers. As early as the 1930s, there was also the perception that the college experience deluded them into believing "marriage should be between equals." Today, women have surpassed men in terms of college enrollment and graduation rates. Since the late 1970s and early 1980s, women have surpassed men in number of bachelor's degrees and master's degrees, and since 2005, they have surpassed men in doctorate degrees as well.

Despite their increasing education, until 1920, women were denied the right to vote. The first attempt to organize a national movement for women's rights occurred in Seneca Falls, New York, in July 1848. Led by Elizabeth Cady Stanton (1815–1902), a young mother from upstate New York, and the Quaker abolitionist Lucretia Mott (1793–1880), about 300 people— most of whom were women—attended the Seneca Falls Convention to outline a direction for the women's rights movement. Stanton's call to arms, her "Declaration of Sentiments," echoed the Declaration of Independence: "We hold these truths to be self-evident: that all men and women are created equal." In a list of resolutions, Stanton cataloged economic and educational inequities, restrictive laws on marriage and property rights, and social and cultural norms that prevented women from enjoying "all the rights and privileges that belong to them as citizens of the United States." Stanton also demanded for women the "sacred right to the elective franchise"—despite objections from Mott and others who considered this provision too radical. The convention eventually approved the voting rights resolution after abolitionist Frederick Douglass (c. 1817–1895) spoke in support of it.

It took another 40 years, until in 1890, the state of Wyoming granted women the right to vote in all elections for the first time. Women soon secured the right to vote in three other western states—Colorado (1893), Utah (1896), and Idaho (1896). On March 3, 1913, the day before President-elect Woodrow Wilson's inauguration, suffragist Alice Paul (1885–1977) organized a parade in support of women's suffrage in Washington, DC. Approximately eight thousand women marched with banners and floats down Pennsylvania Avenue from the Capitol to the White House, while a half million spectators watched, both supporting and harassing the marchers. On March 17, Paul and other suffragists met with Wilson, who said it was not yet time for an amendment to the Constitution. Four years later, in January 1917, Alice Paul and over 1,000 "Silent Sentinels" began eighteen months of picketing the White House, standing at the gates with such signs as, "Mr. President, how long must women wait for liberty?" They endured verbal and physical attacks from spectators, which increased after the U.S. entered World War I. Instead of protecting the women's right to free speech and peaceful assembly, the police arrested them on the flimsy charge of obstructing traffic. Paul was sentenced to jail for seven months, where she organized a hunger strike in protest. Doctors threatened to send Paul to an insane asylum and force-fed her, while newspaper accounts of her treatment gathered public sympathy and support for suffrage. By 1918, President Woodrow Wilson announced his support for a suffrage amendment. It took two more years for the Senate, House, and the required 36 states to approve the amendment. In 1920, the Nineteenth Amendment to the U.S. Constitution was finally ratified, giving white women the right to vote. Black women, however, had to wait another 45 years until the Voting Rights Act was passed in 1965.

By 1900, every state had passed legislation modeled after New York's Married Women's Property Act (1848), granting married women some control over their property and earnings. But it was not until 1981, that the

U.S. Supreme Court overturned state laws designating a husband "head and master" with unilateral control of property owned jointly with his wife.

Margaret Sanger (1879–1966) felt that for women to have a more equal footing in society and to lead healthier lives, they needed to be able to determine when to bear children. She also wanted to prevent so-called back-alley abortions, which were common at the time because abortions were illegal in the United States beginning in the 1870s. She believed that, while abortion may be a viable option in life-threatening situations for the pregnant, it should generally be avoided. She considered contraception the only practical way to avoid them. In 1916, Sanger tested the validity of New York's anti-contraception law by establishing the first birth control clinic in the United States in Brooklyn. She was arrested for distributing information on contraception, after an undercover policewoman bought a copy of her pamphlet on family planning. Her subsequent trial and appeal generated significant controversy. Two years later, she won a suit in New York to allow doctors to advise their married patients about birth control for health purposes. But the case only applied to New York and only to married couples. It was not until 1972, over 50 years later, that the Supreme Court ruled that the right to privacy included an unmarried woman's right to use contraceptives.

On September 25, 1921, the National Woman's Party announced its plans to campaign for an amendment to the U.S. Constitution to guarantee women equal rights with men. It read, "Men and women shall have equal rights throughout the United States and every place subject to its jurisdiction. Congress shall have power to enforce this article by appropriate legislation." Proponents asserted it would end legal distinctions between men and women in matters of divorce, property, employment, and other matters. The first version of an Equal Rights Amendment (ERA) was written by Alice Paul and Crystal Eastman (1881–1928) and introduced in Congress in December 1923. It failed to pass. It would take Congress another 50 years to pass the ERA in 1972. In August 1970, over 20,000 American women held a nationwide Women's Strike for Equality protest to demand full social, economic, and political equality. On August 10, 1970, Michigan Democrat Martha Griffiths (1912–2003) successfully brought the Equal Rights Amendment to the House floor, after 15 years of languishing in the House Judiciary Committee. On March 22, 1972, the Equal Rights Amendment finally passed in both houses. That same day, the ERA was placed before the state legislatures, with a seven-year deadline to acquire ratification by three-fourths (38) of the state legislatures. Most states ratified the proposed constitutional amendment within a year. When the 1979 deadline approached and all 38 states had not yet ratified the amendment, Congress voted to extend the deadline to June 30, 1982. But by the 1982 deadline, the ERA was still three states short. The Equal Rights Amendment failed. Women were still not legally equal to men.

In 1963, the Equal Pay Act was passed by Congress, promising equitable wages for the same work, regardless of the race, color, religion, national origin, or sex of the worker. The following year, the Civil Rights Act passed, which included a prohibition against employment discrimination based on race, color, religion, national origin, or sex. But today, women in the U.S. who work full time, year-round are paid only 83 cents for every dollar paid to men—and for women of color, the wage gap is even larger.

In the 1973 case of Roe v. Wade, the U.S. Supreme Court declared that the Constitution protected women's right to terminate an early pregnancy, thus making abortion legal everywhere in the country. However, 50 years later, in June 2022, a reactionary Court reversed that decision, leaving it up to individual states to decide the fate of women's reproductive rights. To date, at least fourteen states have enacted legal abortion bans.

A 1975 Supreme Court decision denied states the right to exclude women from juries. The 1978 Pregnancy Discrimination Act banned employment discrimination against pregnant women. And in 2013, the ban against women in military combat positions was removed.

Women have struggled for equality and against oppression for centuries, and although some battles have been partly won, women are still disproportionally affected by violence within the home and discrimination in every other aspect of life. For many years, women's rights movements have fought hard to address this inequality, campaigning to change laws or taking to the streets to demand their rights are respected. The struggle for legal equality with men continues.

LGTBQ+ DISCRIMINATION

LGBTQ+ or more specifically LGBTQIA (Lesbian, Gay, Bisexual, Transgender, Queer, Intersex, and Asexual) is the contemporary shorthand recognizing the range of diversity of human sexuality and gender identity.

The first mention of legal discrimination against the LGBTQ+ community in the United States were sodomy laws that were inherited from colonial laws in the seventeenth century. These laws generally prohibited oral and anal sex, even between consenting adults. While most of these laws applied to both straight and gay people, they were primarily used against gay men. In the colonies and states, they were enacted over the course of four centuries and varied state by state. Sodomy crimes were a capital offense in some states, while cross-dressing was considered a felony punishable by imprisonment or corporal punishment. Restrictions against loitering and solicitation of sex in public places were established in the late nineteenth century by many states, and increasingly tighter restrictions upon homosexuals were common by the turn of the century. The twentieth and twenty-first centuries brought a slew of additional laws prohibiting gay sex, while lesbian sex remained largely invisible to lawmakers.

The crossdressing laws were challenged by a few individuals in the late nineteenth century. The first person known to describe himself as a "drag queen" was William Dorsey Swann, born enslaved in Hancock, Maryland. During the 1880s and 1890s, Swann organized a series of drag balls in Washington, DC. Swann was arrested in police raids numerous times, and in April 1888 was the first documented case of arrest for female impersonation in the United States. He was the first American on record who pursued legal and political action to defend the LGBTQ+ community's right to assemble.

By the mid-1920s, at the height of the Prohibition era, masquerade balls, more commonly known as "drag balls," were attracting as many as 7,000 people of various races and social classes, straight as well as gay. Harlem's famous drag balls were part of a flourishing, highly visible LGBTQ+ nightlife and culture. Though New York City may have been the epicenter of the so-called "pansy craze" of the 1930s, gay, lesbian, and transgender performers graced the stages of nightspots in cities all over the country. Their audiences included many straight men and women eager to experience the gay culture themselves as well as ordinary LGBTQ+ Americans seeking to expand their social networks or find romantic or sexual partners.

While researching my family history, I discovered a newspaper article about William Gustave Sagner (1894–1959), one of three brothers to my maternal grandfather, Ernest Frederick Sagner (1901–1978). Beginning at age 24, William Sagner served in World War I from July 1918 to November 1919 as a member of the 7th Infantry. He was sent to Europe in September 1918 and arrived in France in October. He was then sent to Germany in November where he served in the Army of Occupation along the Rhine River until May 1919. In November 1919, he was honorably discharged from the Army with a 100-percent disability. William Sagner never recovered from his wartime experiences. In World War I, they called his condition "shell shock." In World War II, it was known as "battle fatigue." Today, we call it "post-traumatic stress disorder." Family members recalled that he was a changed person after the war and was difficult to be around. Later in his life he would have serious mental and nervous problems, finding it difficult to hold down a steady job. He spent some time as an inmate at the Missouri Sanitarium in St. Louis and at Veterans Hospitals in Iowa and Illinois in the 1930 and 1940 census reports.

On September 12, 1927, an article appeared in the *St. Louis Star and Times* about William Sagner. The article was titled "Legs Betray Man in Woman's Dress."

> *Silk hose is poor camouflage for the legs of a veteran which have been developed by hikes over the roads of France. "Those legs don't belong to any woman," said Detective McNiff last night to Detective Sergeant Girard as he pointed out a "woman" at Easton and Hodiamont avenues. "I'm going to talk to that guy." It developed the "woman" was William Sagner, 33 years old, who said he rooms at 1726 North Euclid Avenue. He receives $80 a month from the government as a vocational training student, he told the detectives. "I got this layout to amuse myself at masquerade balls this winter," Sagner explained. He was arrested, charged with masquerading as a woman. He is in jail. It was his first time out in the outfit, which consisted of a blue silk dress, a pink leghorn hat, tan silk hose and tan slippers.*

William Sagner was arrested and spent jail time for dressing as a woman. I don't know his motivation, but he was criminalized for violating the Christian cultural standards of "normative America" after World War I: men shall be men and women shall be women, and none shall cross the line. The St. Louis city council first put a masquerading ordinance on the books in 1843 and it didn't come off until 1986.

A few years earlier, the first documented gay rights organization, The Society for Human Rights (SHR), was founded in 1924 by Henry Gerber, a German immigrant. Police raids forced them to disband in 1925, but not before they had published several issues of their newsletter, "Friendship and Freedom," the country's first gay-interest newsletter.

The 1950s and 1960s in the United States was an extremely repressive legal period for LGBTQ+ people. Gay individuals met in gay bars and clubs, places of refuge where they could express themselves openly and socialize without worry. However, in New York City, the New York State Liquor Authority penalized and shut down establishments that served alcohol to known or suspected LGBTQ+ individuals, arguing that the mere gathering of homosexuals was "disorderly." Thanks to activists' efforts, these regulations were overturned in 1966, and LGBTQ+ patrons could then be served alcohol. But engaging in gay behavior in public—holding hands, kissing, or dancing with someone of the same sex—was still illegal, so police harassment of gay bars continued, and many bars operated without liquor licenses, in part because many were owned by the Mafia. The crime syndicate saw profit in catering to shunned gay clientele, and by the mid-1960s, the Genovese crime family controlled many Greenwich Village gay bars. In 1966, they purchased the Stonewall Inn—a "straight" bar and restaurant—at 43 Christopher Street in Greenwich Village, cheaply renovated it, and re-opened it the next year as a gay bar.

In 1962, consensual sexual relations between same-sex couples were decriminalized in Illinois, the first time that a state legislature took such an action. Over the next several decades, such relations were gradually decriminalized on a state-by-state basis.

But in the early hours of June 28, 1969, New York City police raided the Stonewall Inn and arrested thirteen people. This raid witnessed a new development as some of the patrons in the bar began actively resisting the police arrests. Fed up with constant police harassment and social discrimination, angry patrons and neighborhood residents hung around outside of the bar rather than dispersing, becoming increasingly angry as the events unfolded and people were aggressively manhandled. At one point, an officer hit a lesbian woman over the head as he forced her into the police van—she shouted to onlookers to act, inciting the crowd to begin to throw bottles, cobble stones, and other objects at the police. An insurrection had begun.

For the first time, a large group of LGBTQ+ Americans, who had previously had little or no involvement with the organized gay rights movement, rioted for six days against police harassment and brutality. These new activists, sometimes involving thousands of people, were angry people who confronted the police and the anti-vice laws that allowed the harassment of gay men and gay drinking establishments.

On June 28, 1970, one year after the Stonewall Insurrection, the Christopher Street Liberation Day marked the first anniversary of the Stonewall riots with a march, which was the first Gay Pride parade in New York history. A day earlier, on June 27, the Chicago Gay Liberation organized a march in that city. The next year, Gay Pride parades took place in the cities of Boston, Dallas, Milwaukee, London, Paris, West Berlin, and Stockholm. By 1972, the participating U.S. cities included Atlanta, Buffalo, Detroit, Miami, Philadelphia, San Francisco, and Washington DC.

By the time of Stonewall, there were fifty to sixty gay groups in the country. A year later there were at least fifteen hundred. By two years after that, it was twenty-five hundred. Before 1969, this movement was generally called the homosexual or homophile movement. But now many consider the Stonewall uprising the birth of the gay liberation movement. Certainly, it was the birth of gay pride on a massive scale.

In 1978, the first gay pride flags flew at the Gay Freedom Day Parade in San Francisco. They were designed by Gilbert Baker (1951–2017).

Originally, the flags contained eight colors, but were eventually standardized on six colors (red, orange, yellow, green, blue, and violet) in 1979.

The long-standing prohibition on open homosexuals serving in the United States military was reinforced under "Don't Ask, Don't Tell" Act (DADT), a 1993 Congressional policy that allowed for homosexual people to serve in the military if they did not disclose their sexual orientation. The Defense of Marriage Act (DOMA) of 1996 also barred the federal government from recognizing same-sex couples in any legal manner. Anti-sodomy laws were ruled unconstitutional in 2003, making it legal throughout the nation for consenting adults to have sex with a person of the same gender in private.

The tipping point of activism in favor of same-sex marriage came in 2008, when the California State Supreme Court ruled that the previous state proposition that barred the legalization of same-sex marriage in California was unconstitutional under the United States Constitution. Over 18,000 couples then obtained legal licenses from May until November of the same year, when another statewide proposition reinstated the ban on same-sex marriage. This was received by nationwide protests against the ban and several legal battles that were projected to end up in the Supreme Court of the United States.

The Matthew Shepard and James Byrd Jr Hate Crimes Prevention Act of 2010 recognized gender identity as a protected class. President Barack Obama (b. 1961) signed the "Don't Ask, Don't Tell" Repeal Act of 2010 into law and withdrew the government's legal defense from The Defense of Marriage Act (DOMA) in 2011. In 2015, the U.S. Supreme Court struck down all state bans on same-sex marriage, legalized it in all fifty states, and required states to honor out-of-state same-sex marriage licenses in the case *Obergefell v. Hodges*. In 2016, President Barack Obama designated the site of the riots—the Stonewall Inn, Christopher Park, and the surrounding streets and sidewalks—a national monument in recognition of the area's contribution to gay rights.

Since 2015, as soon as there was a victory on marriage equality, Republicans and Christian conservatives made a pivot to targeting transgender people. Everyone has a gender identity, although most people never think about it because it usually matches their sex at birth. When a person realizes their gender identity is different from the gender they were assigned at birth, they are considered "transgender." So, someone who was formerly a man but lives as a woman today is called a "transgender woman" and prefers the pronouns "she" and "her." Someone who once was a woman but lives as a man today is a "transgender man," and prefers the pronouns "he" and "him." Many transgender people risk social stigma, discrimination, and harassment when they tell other people who they really are. Despite those risks, being open about one's gender identity can be life-affirming and even lifesaving. Some transgender people identify as neither a man nor a woman, or as a combination of male and female, and may use terms like "non-binary" or "genderqueer" to describe their gender identity. Such people often prefer the pronouns "they" and "them."

In 2022 alone, there were over 300 anti-trans bills introduced by 37 state legislatures by Republicans. The bills differ—some ban gender-affirming health care, some ban participation in school sports, and others create barriers to accessing accurate IDs—but they all represent a coordinated effort by Republican state legislators and white Christian conservatives to deny the very existence of transgender people.

Today, there is a seismic shift going on in gender identity and sexual orientation. Recent polling by the Gallup group found that LGBTQ+ self-identification has been doubling with each successive generation. A mere 2.6 percent among Baby Boom Generation (1946–1964) identified as LGBTQ+. That increased to 4.2 percent among Generation X (1965–1980), more than doubled to 10.5 percent among Millennials (1981–1996), and now stands at 20.8 percent among Generation Z (1997–2012).[11] Fully one-fifth of that generation—of those 18 and older—identify as LGBTQ+ people. As a measure of the total adult population, 7.1 percent now identify as LGBTQ+, up from 3.5 percent ten years earlier. We are finally getting a true picture of the real diversity of sexual attractions and gender identities. But Republicans and white Christian conservatives are trying to turn back the clock. Like many autocrats around the world, they call for the reestablishment of traditional family values to try to shove LGBTQ+ people back in the closet.

Hate speech and violence against LGBTQ+ people have continued to increase. In 2016, a mass shooting at the Pulse nightclub in Orlando, Florida, left 49 people dead and another 53 wounded. In 2022, another shooting at Club Q in Colorado Springs, Colorado, left 5 dead and 17 wounded.

Hate is learned, and it is being taught. Those who feed the hate, stoke the vitriol, and profit from our divisions are powerful people who base their power on the ability to frighten. And violence is the result. At the end of 2022, the Department of Homeland Security issued a warning of domestic terror threats to LGBTQ+, Jewish, and migrant communities. Americans motivated by violent ideologies pose a "persistent and lethal threat."

11. Jones, "LGBT Identification in U.S."

WHITE AMERICAN COMPLICITY

So, what do we make of all this? What do we make of the white Christian Americans who legislated and supported racial superiority, subjugation, separation, incarceration, relocation, and exclusion through much of our history? This short history overlooks many, many, many other acts of legalized dominance by a majority over marginalized people. Racist, misogynist, and heterosexist legal systems and corresponding cultural practices can only survive with broad popular support. Perhaps many Americans never questioned the immorality and harmfulness of the domination system that benefitted them, but that would clearly indicate an absence of introspection, a lack of empathy and compassion, and a moral indifference to the daily degradation they witnessed and pretended not to see. After all, these systems and practices had become accepted regional or national laws. A culture of racism, misogyny, and heterosexism blinds people to the humanity and dignity of their victims, viewing them as inferior—even subhuman—allowing those in power to subjugate others without any feelings of compassion or guilt. Like Eichmann, many people probably feel they are unable to change the direction of the situation, so they participate with either resignation or enthusiasm. In any event, white Christian Americans generally benefitted from the status quo of racist systems, even if it made some of them uncomfortable. Their behavior in support of evil practices were ordinary, commonplace, familiar, unexceptional, banal. However, bystanders are always complicit and can never claim to be innocent.

Chapter 8

the continuing civil war

*My mama always said, "You got to put the past behind you before
you can move on."*

—Forrest Gump (fictional character from 1986)

THE COUNTRY IS UNDERGOING a massive religious and social realignment. The Republican Party has become a predominantly white Christian party, while the Democratic Party has become the party of everyone else. This is not to say there are no white Christians in the Democratic Party, rather their size and influence in the Democratic coalition has fallen precipitously. The Democratic party has shifted in response to tectonic religious and social changes—becoming more diverse—while the Republican party has remained fairly static. The two parties are now composed of very different kinds of people, which is why we see debates over fundamental questions of who counts as Americans and what rights they have. We see it expressed in immigration policy and views toward sexual orientation, the role of women, reproductive rights, and gender fluidity, among others. It is expressly seen in divisions between North and South and between urban and rural regions.

The triumph of the civil rights movement in the mid-1960s may have eliminated legal racial segregation and oppression in the South, but in many ways the states of the old Confederacy have never fully rejoined the Union. Since Lyndon Johnson's efforts to obtain civil rights and voting rights, southern states have abandoned the Democratic Party to become a Republican bastion, evolving from the segregationist Democratic "Dixiecrats," after white voters were courted by the "Southern strategies" of Nixon and Reagan that overtly appealed to racism against African Americans. Within a decade, the people of Appalachia and the South went from being solidly Democratic to solidly Republican. This was the beginning of the descent of the Republican Party. Once representing a mainstream conservative movement, the party began a decades-long degeneration as it allied itself with Southern racists. After the election of the first black president, the reactionary Tea Party movement transformed it further into an anti-government party, setting the stage for the Trump presidency.

1965 was a watershed year in racial animosity. The Civil Rights Act of 1964, the Voting Rights Act of 1965, and the Immigration and Nationality Act of 1965, marked the beginning of the end of white domination of American society. In response, we have experienced a nearly 60-year intense backlash. White Christian nationalist groups have flourished, citing these landmark pieces of legislation as the forerunners of white dispossession and so-called "white genocide"—the idea that whites in the United States are being systematically replaced and destroyed. They advocate for policies that would reverse changing demographics and the loss of an absolute white majority. A major influence was the 2001 book, *The Death of the West*, by right-wing commentator Pat Buchanan (b. 1938), which argued that declining white birth rates and an "immigrant invasion" would transform the United States into a Third World nation by 2050. At the August 2017 "Unite the Right" rally in Charlottesville, Virginia, white supremacist marchers chanted "Jews will not replace us!" and "Blood and Soil!" The latter was a Nazi nationalist slogan (*Blut und Boden!*) that declared a single racially defined group (blood) should control the nation (soil).

After the Civil War, Confederate flags (the battle flag of Northern Virginia) were not displayed very frequently until the 1960s when they flourished as an angry response to the civil rights movement. At Charlottesville, Confederate flags were carried alongside Nazi banners, mingling historic symbols of white supremacy representing a hatred for people of color, immigrants, LGBTQ+ people, Jews, and Muslims.

Columnist Rebecca Solnit (b. 1961), writing in The Guardian in November 2018 commented:

> *In the 158th year of the American civil war, also known as 2018, the Confederacy continues its recent resurgence. Its victims include black people, of course, but also immigrants, Jews, Muslims, Latinos, trans people, gay people and women who want to exercise jurisdiction over their bodies. The Confederacy battles in favor of uncontrolled guns and poisons, including toxins in streams, mercury from coal plants, carbon emissions into the upper atmosphere, and oil exploitation in previously protected lands and*

waters. Its premise appears to be that protection of others limits the rights of white men, and those rights should be unlimited . . . You don't have to be oppressed or come from a history of oppression to stand with the oppressed; you just have to have a definition of "we" that includes people of various points of origin and language and religious belief and sexual orientation and gender identity. A lot of us do: many large US cities are places of thriving everyday coexistence across difference. A lot of Americans have married across racial and religious lines, some have devoted themselves to the work of solidarity, and a lot subscribe to a grand inclusive "we, the people." Those who don't are not a majority, but they have an outsized impact, more now than in a very long time. The Confederacy didn't win in the 1860s and it is not going to win in the long run but inflicting as much damage as possible seems to be how they want to go down.[1]

Over the past 25 years, rural areas have increasingly voted Republican, while cities have increasingly voted Democratic—a dividing line that has replaced the North/South divide as the nation's biggest source of political friction. What we are seeing is rural white resentment. Rural voters care about "geographic inequity"—the idea that rural areas receive less than their fair share from the government, are ignored by politicians, and are mocked and derided in popular culture. Without these beliefs, the urban-rural political divide would not be as vast as it is today.

WHITE RESENTMENT

During the presidential campaign of 2016, Amazon noted that one of the most popular non-fiction books was *The Origins of Totalitarianism*, written by Hannah Arendt in 1951. In it, she raises a set of fundamental questions about how tyranny can arise and the dangerous forms of inhumanity to which it can lead. The rise of right-wing racist populism in Europe and the United States, accentuated by the election of Donald Trump, led to growing fears about the possibility of new forms of authoritarianism in the present.

Arendt described the social crisis that sparked the rise of the Nazi party in Germany. Across Europe, she said, large numbers of people felt dispossessed, disenfranchised, and disconnected from dominant social institutions. The political party system, and parliamentary government more generally, were regarded as corrupt and controlled by wealthy oligarchs. Such an environment was fertile ground for a "mob mentality," in which

---

1. Solnit, "American Civil War."

outsiders—Jews, Roma, Slavs, gays, and "cosmopolitan intellectuals"—could be scapegoated for societal issues. There was a hope that a savior would arise. "The mob always will shout for 'the strong man,' the 'great leader.' For the mob hates the society from which it is excluded, as well as the legislature where it is not represented."[2]

And a society inundated with resentment, according to Arendt, is ripe for manipulation by the propaganda of sensationalist demagogues.

> *What convinces masses are not facts, and not even invented facts, but only the consistency of the system of which they are presumably part . . . Totalitarian propaganda thrives on this escape from reality into fiction . . .* [and] *can outrageously insult common sense only where common sense has lost its validity.*

We have clearly witnessed this story in the last several years in the United States. An enormous class of resentful white people who feel ignored and disenfranchised; a government that is largely distrusted by them; ethnic and religious scapegoats; a hatred of intellectuals who look down on them; contempt for the truth; a willingness to accept lies and conspiracy theories; continual right-wing media propaganda; arena-sized personality-cult rallies; and a "strong man" who promised to Make America Great Again.

There is, for many at least, a sense that America is losing its whiteness—what novelist Toni Morrison (1931–2019) once referred to as "the horror of lost status." As immigrant and ethnic minority populations grow and white communities gradually lose their numerical advantage, a sense of white Christian dominance begins to disappear. That a way of life might be receding, or a psychological sense of privilege or prestige might be waning, is enough to cause many to romanticize the past. Various boogeymen, from immigration to affirmative action, are viewed in terms of a theft of white resources. Most white Christian grievance is built on a perceived sense of being under siege. The aggrieved think of themselves as a persecuted people, wronged, and under attack. To cultivate white victimhood, imagined enemies must be fashioned and then be targeted and attacked.

WHITE CHRISTIAN NATIONALISM

White Christian nationalism is the theory that the American nation is defined by Christianity, that it was founded by Christians, and that the government should take active steps to keep it that way. It is a cultural framework that idealizes and advocates a fusion of Christianity with American civic life.

2. Arendt, *Origins of Totalitarianism*, 49.

It's also a mixture of Christianity and racism. Its intention is to assure that national political power will always be controlled by white Christian people. In *The Flag and the Cross: White Christian Nationalism and the Threat to American Democracy*, sociologists Philip Gorski (b. 1963) and Samuel Perry (birthdate unknown) argue that in the years around 1690—when Puritan colonists began envisioning their battles against Native Americans as an apocalyptic holy war to secure a new Promised Land, and when Southern Christians began to formulate a theological justification for chattel slavery— a new national mythology was born.

Today, that Christian nationalist myth has at least four parts. First, that the founding and success of America is part of God's plan, and that the Declaration of Independence and the Constitution are divinely inspired documents. Second, that the government should declare America to be a white Christian nation, and only white Christian Americans should control the destiny of the country, through authoritarian means if necessary. Third, that conservative "family" values—including mandating distinctly different roles for men and women, banning legal abortion, and forbidding gay marriage—are Christian values and should be backed by the force of law. Fourth, America has been given a mission: to spread Christianity, freedom, and civilization—by force, if necessary. But that mission is endangered by the growing presence of non-whites, non-Christians, and non-Americans on American soil. White Christians must therefore "take back the country" to restore it to greatness. Donald Trump echoed white nationalist beliefs when he claimed he would take America back from the outsiders and invaders who had taken control—immigrants and secularists—and then restore it to its rightful white owners.

Tom Van Denburgh, writing in Newsweek, declared:

> *At its very core, Christian nationalism is a hateful, exclusionary ideology. It posits that America was, is, and must remain a Christian conservative nation, even if that means subjugating Jews, progressive Christians, atheists, Muslims, polytheists, and other groups white Christian nationalists place low in their hierarchy: people of color, LGBTQ people, women, and immigrants ... They want to turn America into a theocracy from behind the scenes.*[3]

Manifestations of white Christian nationalism have ebbed and flowed throughout America's history, and usually they rise and fall in response to perceived threats against a white Christian majority. Sometimes the enemies change. Early on it was Native Americans. Throughout our history it has always been black Americans. In the late nineteenth century, it was

3. Van Denburgh, "Christian Nationalists Sound Like KKK."

Asian Americans. In the twentieth century, it was socialists, communists, and Jews. In the twenty-first, it is Hispanics, Muslims, and LGBTQ+ people. So, throughout American history, you see this thread of race and religion in the boundaries of who is and who is not truly American. Who is not varies, but the in-group is almost always the same: conservative white Christians who "belong" here as part of the dominant ethnic group. Christian nationalism wants order in the form of hierarchies. Men on top. Whites on top. Christians on top. Heterosexuals on top. And any threats to that order are met with violence.

White evangelicals—the group most beholden to Christian nationalist ideology—have long been characterized by what sociologist Christian Smith (b. 1960) called the idea of "embattlement." They constantly feel they are at war with a surrounding culture that aims to persecute or marginalize them. It is a battle between good and evil.

Peter Wehner, writing in The Atlantic, commented:

> *The root of the discord lies in the fact that many Christians have embraced the worst aspects of our culture and our politics. When the Christian faith is politicized, churches become repositories not of grace but of grievances, places where tribal identities are reinforced, where fears are nurtured, and where aggression and nastiness are sacralized. The result is not only wounding the nation; it's having a devastating impact on the Christian faith.*[4]

TRUMP VOTER'S DISAFFECTION

Several sociologists have studied the people who voted for Donald Trump in the elections of 2016 and 2020. Gallup reports that Trump supporters are more likely to be white, older males. They are less educated and more likely to work in blue collar occupations; but they earn relatively high household incomes (in 2016, the median annual income of Trump supporters was $72,000) and are less likely to be unemployed or exposed to competition through trade or immigration. They are more likely to be Christian and to say their faith is important to them. But other factors stand out. Key predictors of Trump support come from those who live in racially isolated communities with poor health care, low social mobility, few social networks, more reliance on social security income, and less reliance on capital income from land or investments.

---

4. Wehner, "Evangelical Church Breaking Apart."

In The Great Revolt (2018) by Selena Zito (b. 1959) and Brad Todd (birthdate unknown), the authors describe Trump voters as responsible people who have worked their whole adult lives, not only to support themselves but also to support their families. The importance and dignity of work is a common and recurring theme across the various groups they profiled. They believe hard work has been devalued in America; that elites belittle people who live outside of urban centers; that once-normal opinions have become taboo. Some of these voters moved away from the Democratic Party out of a belief that it no longer supports white working people but instead seeks to win votes by promising to give away things for free to others.

These findings were validated by political scientist Katherine Cramer (b. 1970) in her book *The Politics of Resentment*.

> *In our rural areas what I have learned is that there are many people who feel that neither party represents them, and many have a strong resentment toward the cities and urban elites. They feel as though they are not getting their fair share of power—no one is really listening to them. They are not getting their fair share of taxpayer dollars—the money goes to the cities, and also, they are not getting their fair share of respect—people assume folks in small towns are ignorant and racist. That mix of resentment is pretty fertile ground for a right-leaning candidate.*
>
> *Many times, this resentment comes out as a feeling of, "I'm a deserving person, a hardworking American and the things I deserve are actually going to other people who are less deserving." Donald Trump's message really tapped into that sentiment. What I heard him saying was: You are right, you are not getting your fair share, you should be angry, you are a deserving, hardworking American and what you deserve is going to people who don't deserve it. He pointed his finger at immigrants, the Chinese, bad trade deals, Muslims, uppity women. He gave people concrete targets, and it was a way of sparking anger and mobilizing support.[5]*

Digging deeper, social psychologist Arlie Hochschild (b. 1940) spent five years interviewing people in Calcasieu Parish in the heart of Louisiana's staunchly conservative bayou country. Many of these people are Tea Party and Republican Party loyalists. They see themselves playing by the rules but still getting screwed, disdained by elites above them, and mooched off by freeloaders beneath. In her book *Strangers in Their Own Land*, Hochschild describes lives ripped apart by stagnant wages, a loss of home, an elusive American dream, and political choices and views that make sense in the

5. Wallis, "Trump's Victory and Politics."

context of their lives. The people she talked to feel their cultural beliefs are belittled by the culture at large. They think that they are seen as ignorant rednecks. Many of them are deeply religious and they see American culture becoming increasingly secular. And then they see that an economic trapdoor is opening and gobbling up them and their children that used to only affect black people. So altogether it makes them feel like a forgotten tribe. And the main point is that they feel the federal government has been an instrument of their marginalization.

As Hochschild probed further, what she found most common was a "deep story" the conservative white residents were telling themselves.

> *Think of people waiting in a long line that stretches up a hill. And at the top of that is the American dream. And the people waiting in line felt like they'd worked extremely hard, sacrificed a lot, tried their best, and were waiting for something they deserved. And this line is increasingly not moving or moving more slowly. Then they see people cutting ahead of them in line. Immigrants, blacks, women, refugees, public sector workers. And even an oil-drenched brown pelican getting priority. In their view, people are cutting ahead unfairly. And then in this narrative, there is [President] Barack Obama, to the side, the line supervisor who seems to be waving these people (and the pelican) ahead. So, the government seemed to be on the side of the people who were cutting in line and pushing the people in line back.*[6]

These people felt left behind or even kept down by a federal government that no longer looked out for them and was against their interests at every turn. When Donald Trump entered the scene, he found fertile territory to exploit—a demographic defined by fear, resentment, anxiety, and anger.

THE RISE OF A DEMAGOGUE

The slogan of the Donald Trump presidential campaign in 2016 was to "Make America Great Again." In that phrase lies the essence of his message. Did it symbolize a return to an age when wages were higher and jobs more secure? Or was it coded racial language designed to signal a rollback to a time when people of color, women, and immigrants knew their place? Primarily, it was directed toward blue-collar white men who have experienced a powerful sense of loss. For Trump supporters, this message resonated.

6 Plumer, "Liberal Sociologist Learned."

This used to be a great country for them, but now they feel they are losing their status in society. Yet for most Americans, the good old days weren't all that good. Certainly not for women, people of color, gay men, or religious minorities. In the bygone days that Trump harkens back to, it wasn't so great to be anything but a straight white Christian male. Now, Trump supporters blame the long-oppressed groups who have finally gotten a toehold on the American dream. Trump's promise was that if he was elected, he would put his supporters back on top. In Trump's eyes, making America great requires sowing fear and hatred to create enthusiasm and support for cruel policies of exclusion and intolerance aimed at advancing white supremacy. His tools were dehumanization, slander, and negative stereotyping.

Like demagogues before him, President Trump and his aides first chose two groups for scapegoating and persecution—Hispanic and Muslim immigrants. Trump didn't much seem to like nonwhite newcomers from anywhere, but he displayed an especially vicious antipathy toward men, women, and even children from Mexico and Latin America. Hispanics are by far the biggest minority group in the country, making up nearly 18 percent of the population. By 2060, the Census Bureau estimates that share will rise to nearly 29 percent.

Trump began his campaign for president by calling Mexican people "criminals" and "rapists." He described Central American migrants who arrive at the border lawfully seeking asylum with words such as "invading" and "infesting" and "breeding." He declared that only a border wall would stop the influx. In the meantime, he created immigration policies that were cruel, immoral, destructive, and a violation of the American ideal that our nation is a beacon for oppressed people everywhere. It is unbelievable that the U.S. government would separate more than 2,000 children from their parents just to traumatize children as a cruel deterrent for desperate asylum seekers. The aggressive pace of U.S. Immigration and Customs Enforcement's (ICE) deportations of immigrants, the elimination of the Deferred Action for Childhood Arrivals (DACA) program protecting immigrant children, and other proposals were intended to slow the rapid racial diversification of the United States population.

The Muslim community was another target. Stoking fear and hatred of immigrant and refugee Muslims—many of them fleeing ISIS and the civil war in Syria—was a recurring theme in Trump's political rhetoric. He claimed that he witnessed Muslims cheering as the World Trade towers came down on September 11, 2001. During his campaign, Trump called for a total and complete shutdown of Muslims entering the United States, characterizing refugees as potential terrorists—strong young men who may have been ISIS-affiliated. After three tries, he succeeded in banning travel from six predominantly Muslim nations, none of which had contributed in any way to terrorism, yet leaving in place travel from Saudi Arabia, Egypt, and Lebanon—three countries that did supply terrorists—and Turkey and the United Arab Emirates—with whom the Trump organization did business.

Finally, Trump wanted to restrict immigration by eliminating a process critics call "chain migration." Green card holders and legal residents could petition the Immigration Service to bring over their spouses and their minor children. And once the petitioner got citizenship, they could apply to bring over parents, married children, and adult siblings. Trump proposed a sweeping change: citizens and green-card holders would be able to sponsor only spouses and minor children. He claimed this would prevent terrorists from entering the country, although all immigrants, and especially refugees, must undergo rigorous security screening.

Trump's attempts to make America whiter are doomed to fail because the demographic revolution is now irreversible. The driving force of the browning of America is no longer immigration, but birth and death rates. Most babies being born are of color, and a majority of people dying are white. White children are already a minority of all children under age five, so if all immigration ceased tomorrow, the country is still inexorably on a path to a new multiracial reality.

Recently, opinion columnist Maureen Dowd stated, "Trump, the modern Pandora, released the evil spirits swirling around us—racism, anti-semitism, violence, hatred, conspiracy theories, and Trump mini-Mes who should be nowhere near the levers of power."[7]

Some of Trump's supporters are outright racists who belong to hate groups. Others are not. Unfortunately, they are often followers of right-wing propaganda lies woven by people like Fox TV's Sean Hannity (b. 1961), Tucker Carlson (b. 1969), Ann Coulter (b. 1961), and Laura Ingraham (b. 1963), and talk radio hosts Alex Jones (b. 1974), and Steve Bannon (b. 1953). These pundits of misinformation stoke fear in their audience and manipulate it into support of hateful policies. Their target is anyone who threatens the authoritarian right-wing agenda of Donald Trump's MAGA Republicans.

All the while Donald Trump and his cohorts were riling up conservative Americans, the big winners of his administration were the billionaire class and global corporations. A Republican congress cut the corporate tax rate from 35 percent to 21 percent via the Tax Cuts and Jobs Act of 2017. Republicans claimed that the cuts would boost the average U.S. household income by at least $4,000 a year in a trickle-down fashion. This was the same

7. Dowd, "Greene-ing of America."

old lie we heard in the Reagan years. In the past six years, that promise has failed to materialize. Subsequent studies revealed that just 20 percent of the bonanza was spent on increasing capital expenditures or research and development. The remaining 80 percent of cashflow went to investors through buybacks and dividends. Most corporate stocks are held by the wealthy, and they are the ultimate beneficiaries of the windfall corporate tax cuts. In other words, while working class people were confronting each other over culture war issues, the elites made off with a bundle of cash. The modest income tax cuts benefitting average people are set to expire in 2025, while the corporate tax cuts are intended to go on permanently.

THE QANON CONSPIRACY

QAnon is the umbrella term for a set of internet conspiracy theories that allege that the world is run by a cabal of Satan-worshiping pedophiles. QAnon was the offspring of a conspiracy theory known as "Pizzagate." In 2016, the website WikiLeaks released a trove of e-mails that Russian hackers had stolen from the account of John Podesta (b. 1949), Hillary Clinton's campaign chair for her 2016 presidential election bid. On the website 4chan—a notoriously toxic internet message board—anonymous users speculated that the use of the term "cheese pizza" in Podesta's e-mails was code for "child pornography" and that a Washington, DC pizzeria named Comet Ping Pong, from which Podesta had ordered, was engaged in the sexual exploitation of children. Ultimately, Pizzagate conspiracy theorists eventually invoked the existence of an elite conspiracy of satanic cannibals operating a child sex trafficking ring out of the basement of Comet Ping Pong, even though the restaurant does not, in fact, have a basement.

Subsequently, according to QAnon lore, former president Donald Trump was recruited by top military generals to run for president in 2016 to break up this criminal conspiracy and bring its members to justice. Many of those cabal members would be arrested, and some would be imprisoned at Guantánamo Bay, while others would face military tribunals and be executed. QAnon is a "big tent" conspiracy theory because it is constantly evolving and adding new features and claims. But the existence of a global pedophile conspiracy is the core tenet of QAnon, and the one that most, if not all, of its followers believe. According to QAnon, the satanic sex-trafficking pedophiles now include Hollywood celebrities, left-wing Democratic politicians, and a few billionaires.

In the first year of Trump's presidency in October 2017, a post appeared on 4chan from an anonymous account calling itself "Q Clearance

Patriot." This individual, who became known simply as "Q," claimed to be a high-ranking government insider—perhaps one of Donald Trump's inner circle—with access to classified information about Trump's war against the global cabal. In what has become known as a "QDrop," Q predicted that this war would soon culminate in "The Storm"—an appointed time when Trump would finally unmask the cabal, punish its members for their crimes, and restore America to greatness. It's a reference to a cryptic remark Trump made during an October 2017 photo op. Posing alongside military generals, Trump said, "You guys know what this represents? Maybe it's the calm before the storm."

QAnon believers pointed to this moment as proof that Trump was sending coded messages—breadcrumbs—about his plans to break up the global cabal. Donald Trump is the central and heroic figure in QAnon's core narrative—the brave patriot who was chosen to save America from the cabal. As a result, most QAnon believers expected that he would easily win re-election and spend his second term vanquishing the "deep state" and bringing the satanic pedophiles to justice.

Since the 2020 election, QAnon has become a stronghold of support for the false theory that the election was stolen from Donald Trump. Many QAnon believers maintain that he is still the lawful president. Despite a great mountain of evidence to the contrary, about 40 percent of Americans—and three quarters of Republicans—believe it is true. They are angry because they believe everything has been stolen from them. Not only the election, but white power, white culture, old-time manhood, Confederate statues, and the story of a heroic America.

JANUARY 6TH INSURRECTION

On January 6, 2021, following the defeat of Donald Trump in the 2020 election, a violent mob of his supporters attacked the United States Capitol Building in Washington, DC. The mob was seeking to keep Trump in power by preventing a joint session of Congress from the ceremonial counting of electoral college votes to formalize the victory of President-elect Joe Biden. More than 2,000 insurrectionists stormed the building and occupied, vandalized, and looted it. They assaulted Capitol Police officers and attempted to locate key lawmakers to capture and harm them. With building security breached, Capitol Police evacuated and locked down both chambers of Congress and several buildings in the Capitol Complex. Insurrectionists occupied the empty Senate chamber while federal law enforcement officers defended the evacuated House floor. The Capitol was clear of rioters by mid-evening, and the counting of the electoral votes resumed and was completed in the early morning hours of January 7. Seven people died as a result of that attempt. More than 140 police officers reported suffering injuries.

The many millions who watched the events unfold on their televisions instantly knew that it would rank among the most anguished and horrifying days in American history. But it was worse and more wretched than we imagined. Thanks to the exceptional work of the House Select Committee that investigated the January 6 attacks, we now know the details of a deliberate, coordinated, violent, multipart plan to overturn the 2020 presidential election. And the main actor was the nation's president. "The central cause of January 6 was one man, former President Donald Trump, whom many others followed," the report of the committee said. "None of the events of January 6 would have happened without him."

The attack on the Capitol was unmistakably an act of political violence, not merely an exercise in vandalism or trespassing amid a disorderly protest that had spiraled out of control. Writing in The Atlantic magazine, David A. Graham (b. 1983) described how pro-Trump factions are now trying to redefine January 6 as a mythic symbol, a "New Lost Cause."[8] The New Lost Cause, like the old one, seeks to convert a shameful catastrophe into a celebration of the valor and honor of the culprits and portray those who attacked the country as the true patriots. The original Lost Cause was a revisionist history that gained popularity in the 1890s. Law professor Michel Paradis (b. 1980), also writing in The Atlantic, said:

> *The Lost Cause recast the Confederacy's humiliating defeat in a treasonous war for slavery as the embodiment of the Framers' true vision for America. Supporters pushed the ideas that the Civil War was not actually about slavery; that Robert E. Lee was a brilliant general, gentleman, and patriot; and that the Ku Klux Klan had rescued the heritage of the old South, what came to be known as "the southern way of life."*[9]

The problem with these myths, the Lost Cause and the New Lost Cause, is that they emphasize the valor of the people involved while whitewashing what they were actually doing. The January 6 insurrectionists violently assaulted the seat of American government. They do not deserve revisionist celebration.

8. Graham, "New Lost Cause."
9. Paradis, "Lost Cause's Legacy."

THE CONSERVATIVE MIND

Fear and anxiety seem to be the hallmarks of contemporary life, but especially among conservatives. Our sense of anxiety is an interpretation of the primal fight-or-flight survival mechanism. Fear leads to a stance of self-preservation at the expense of others. Fear pits people against other people as competitors. It is the root of racism and heterosexism. It is the leading cause of gun ownership in the United States today. It diverts our treasury from the common good into the arsenals of never-ending war.

Psychologists have found that conservatives are fundamentally more anxious than liberals. Anxiety is an emotion that waxes and wanes in all of us, and as it swings up or down, our political views can shift in its wake. When most people feel safe and secure, they tend to become more liberal; when they feel threatened, they tend to become more conservative. Research conducted in the weeks after September 11, 2001, showed that people of all political persuasions became more conservative in the wake of the terrorist attacks.

Molly Ball (b. 1987), a national political correspondent for Time magazine, commented on the fear of Trump supporters in The Atlantic magazine on September 2, 2016:

> *Trump supporters, recent polling has shown, are disproportionately fearful. They fear crime and terror far more than other Americans; they are also disproportionately wary of foreign influence and social change.*[10]

An article in Psychology Today from December 2018 stated the science has shown that the conservative brain has an exaggerated fear response when faced with stimuli that may be perceived as threatening. A brain-imaging study published in Current Biology revealed that those who lean right politically tend to have a larger amygdala—an almond-shaped cluster of neurons inside each cerebral hemisphere. While the amygdala is deeply involved in the formation of emotions and emotional memories, it is primarily involved in the intense emotions of fear and anxiety rather than empathy. On the other hand, liberals had more grey matter in the anterior cingulate cortex (ACC), a region in both hemispheres of the brain that helps people cope with complexity. It has connections to both the emotional and rational functions of the brain. The activity of the ACC has been related to decision-making, socially driven interactions, and empathy-related responses. Individuals with a large amygdala are more sensitive to fear. On the other hand, those individuals with a larger ACC have a higher capacity

10. Ball, "Donald Trump and Politics."

to tolerate ambiguity and the psychological stress of cognitive dissonance, caused when a person is confronted with two or more contradictory beliefs, ideas, or values. On the whole, the research shows, conservatives desire security, predictability, and authority more than liberals do, and liberals are more comfortable with novelty, nuance, and complexity. While these findings are remarkably consistent, they are probabilities, not certainties— meaning there is plenty of individual variability.

NATURE VERSUS NURTURE

Such studies question whether these brain differences are determined at birth, or whether they arise from childhood experiences—the age-old nature versus nurture question in psychology. Does a larger amygdala arise from frightening family encounters such as authoritarian parenting and corporal punishment? In the same way, does the larger anterior cingulate cortex come from exposure to educational challenge, social diversity, or early childhood opportunities for creativity and curiosity?

In *Moral Politics: How Liberals and Conservatives Think*, cognitive linguist George Lakoff (b. 1941) argues that conservatives and liberals hold two very different conceptual models of morality. Conservative morals derive from a "strict father model," in which people are made good through self-discipline and hard work, and everyone is taken care of by taking care of themselves. The strict father insists on his moral authority, commands obedience, and when he doesn't get it, metes out retribution as fairly and justly as he knows how. For him, strictness is a form of nurturance and love—tough love. In the strict father model of the family, the mother is subordinated to running the day-to-day affairs of the home and raising the children according to the father's direction. It is the father that bears the major responsibility and makes the major decisions.

Liberal morals, on the other hand, derive from a "nurturant parent model" in which everyone is taken care of by helping each other. The family may consist of one or two parents. Two are preferable, but not always possible. The experience encountered in this model is one of being cared for and cared about, having one's desires for loving interactions met, living as happily as possible, and deriving meaning from one's community and from caring for others. Through empathizing and interacting positively with their children, parents develop close bonds with them and teach them empathy and responsibility towards others and toward society. The obedience of children comes out of love and respect for their parents, not out of fear of punishment. Children are taught self-discipline in the service of nurturance: to take care of themselves, to be responsible to others, and to realize their potential.

In *The Righteous Mind: Why Good People are Divided by Politics and Religion*, social psychologist Jonathan Haidt (b. 1963) describes why liberals and conservatives find it so hard to understand one another. He identifies six key areas of moral psychology: fairness, caring, liberty, loyalty, authority, and purity. Liberals, he says, tend to prioritize just two of them: caring for people who are vulnerable and fairness, which for liberals tends to mean equal access to resources. Conservatives care about those things, too, but for them fairness means proportionality—that people should get what they deserve based on the amount of effort they have put in. Conservatives also emphasize the values of loyalty, authority, and purity. Haidt contends that everybody values compassion and fairness, whether they are liberal or conservative. But then there are these three others: loyalty, authority, and purity. And what we find is that conservatives give relatively high marks to all five. Liberals tend to reject those last three, seeing them as possible foundations for exclusiveness.

Fairness and caring are *universal values* found in virtually every culture, as exemplified by the widespread formula of a "golden rule" in every major religion around the globe: "Do to others as you would have them do to you." In contrast, authority, loyalty, and purity are more *tribal values*, more concerned about "us" than "them." The *authority* value believes that certain authority figures have the right to tell people what to do. *Loyalty* believes that certain people are more deserving of our trust than others. And the *purity* value contends that certain behaviors, practices, or people are taboo, while others are often pure, holy, and sanctified. While these values can be helpful in some situations, they can also lead to authoritarianism and exclusivity.

Recent surveys have shown that former president Donald Trump has about a 40 percent approval rating among all adults. That works out to about 98 million people who approve of and share Trump's racist policies and beliefs. They anchor one end of the political spectrum. But what is more troubling is those enablers of evil who consider themselves not extremists, but political and religious moderates.

Chapter 9

the complicity of moderates

THE WELL-KNOWN QUOTE BY late eighteenth-century statesman and philosopher Edmund Burke perfectly describes the role played by moderates and political independents in any society—good people who do nothing to stop the triumph of evil. The persistence of evil in a nation is more due to the inaction and inattention of political and religious moderates than it is to the actions of dedicated white supremacists and authoritarian politicians. Throughout history, those who consider themselves political moderates, centrists, and independents have, by their relative silence, been complicit with the rule of autocrats and evil regimes. Whether they realize it or not, they are collaborators in evil. They have historically allowed racism, misogyny, heterosexism, antisemitism, ethnic cleansing, war, poverty, and oppression to flourish by their self-centered inattention and inaction.

In his "Letter from Birmingham Jail," Dr. King wrote:

> We will have to repent in this generation not merely for the hateful words and actions of the bad people but for the appalling silence of the good people. Human progress never rolls in on wheels of inevitability; it comes through the tireless efforts of men willing to be coworkers with God.[1]

Today, political moderates and centrists like to portray themselves as common-sense people who keep an open mind on issues, are willing to listen to different viewpoints, think for themselves, and are not extreme in their beliefs. These are the so-called independent voters who do not strongly affiliate with either major party or their ideologies. They often feel themselves to be above or turned off by the partisanship that afflicts the rest of us.

A critic might view moderates less charitably. They are what Richard Nixon called "the silent majority." They tend to take refuge in the safe middle, preferring to blend in so they do not stand out. Although they may lean one way or another, they fear that labels of liberal and conservative or Democrat and Republican may lump them with people with whom they do not completely agree. And for the most part, they are politically inactive. Independent voters are often portrayed as political free agents with the potential to alleviate the nation's rigid partisan divisions and capable of building a national consensus. They possess the numeric capacity to shift society toward good or evil ends. But they don't really care all that much about politics.

About 1 in 5 adult Americans are not registered to vote. Of those who are registered, according to Gallup in March 2019, 43 percent of voters said they were independent, 30 percent were Democratic, and 24 percent were Republican. Of the 43 percent who said they were independent, 17 percent tended to lean toward Democratic positions, 13 percent tended to lean toward the Republican Party, and about 10 percent did not lean toward either party. Studies show that the first two groups aren't all that different from the voters in the party they lean toward. But they do tend to be more averse to identifying themselves as a partisan when there is a negative stigma associated with partisanship. So, it's really the arguments, the hostility, the negativity that seems to be driving independents' behavior. But polling shows Americans of all political stripes really are tired of partisan bickering. Calling oneself an independent does not mean they lost their previous partisan

---

1. King, *We Can't Wait*, 99.

identity; they just became more inclined to hide it. Independents are still voting largely for one of the two major parties; they're just refusing to affiliate with them publicly. Those true independents (the other 10 percent) do not represent a clearly defined third way—an independent ideology. They tend to be the kind of people who glide through life unburdened by the need to take a stand on anything of substance.

LACK OF ENGAGEMENT AND ATTENTION

But recent studies have found that the inactivity is a larger problem than previously imagined. A 2021 study found of those who self-identified as independents, only under a third bother to vote. What we see is a curve like an inactive jump rope with high political engagement on both extremes and low engagement in the middle. They may lean toward one party or the other, but they do not care enough to take the time to vote. That is why turnout in elections is so important, and why both parties strive to make their case to drive up voter participation. But true independents often show a low level of interest in politics and a corresponding lack of knowledge about what is truly going on in our society. Political parties arose, in part, to establish a voting shorthand for citizens who don't pay a lot of attention to politics, which is most people. Surveys since the 1960s demonstrate that political knowledge directly correlates with ideological understanding and consistency.

A poll of Americans' attentiveness to the 2016 election revealed that 38 percent of respondents observed the election "somewhat closely," while 22 percent followed "not too closely," and 8 percent "not at all." A combination of the "not too closely" and "not at all" groups indicate 30 percent of the American electorate do not pay attention and do not care about the political issues of our time. These results are not at all surprising given the tedium of politics. People have better things to do. Plus, many often prefer entertainment over knowledge. Independents are more likely to know about the latest sports, reality TV, or Hollywood gossip than about the Trump impeachment hearings or the committee looking into the January 6th insurrection.

The term "low information voters" has been used to identify people who may vote yet are generally poorly informed about issues and candidates. When they do vote, they generally choose a candidate they find personally appealing, regardless of the candidate's stance on policy and issues, and regardless of the political ideology they represent. They know little about government or how the outcomes of elections might alter government policy. They also tend to lack what psychologists call a "need for cognition" or a desire to learn. High cognition people are more likely to devote the time and resources necessary to evaluating the complex issues of interest to well-informed voters. On the other hand, people with a low need for cognition find little reward in collection and evaluation of new information or consideration of competing positions. Martin Luther King Jr said, "Shallow understanding from people of good will is more frustrating than absolute misunderstanding from people of ill will."

In their desire to be neutral or nonpartisan, moderates and independents take a position whether they know it or not. When a person avoids taking sides or hides their true values, they lend support to current power structures and systems. By their silence, they enable and sustain the status quo. To speak or to remain silent become moral choices in times of injustice. As Desmond Tutu (1931–2021) said, "If you are neutral in situations of injustice, you have chosen the side of the oppressor." Elie Wiesel (1928–2016) made a similar point in his acceptance speech for the 1987 Nobel Peace Prize, "We must always take sides. Neutrality helps the oppressor, never the victim. Silence encourages the tormentor, never the tormented." And Martin Luther King Jr said, "The hottest place in Hell is reserved for those who remain neutral in times of great moral conflict . . . [an individual] who accepts evil without protesting against it is really cooperating with it."

MODERATE CHRISTIANS IN NAZI GERMANY

I will use an example from an earlier book.[2] It has to do with the Protestant Church in Nazi Germany, a nation of about 60 million people. In the early 1930s, two-thirds of the population was Protestant (about 40 million members) and the remaining third was Roman Catholic (about 20 million). Less than 1 percent (600,000) were Jewish.

Because the modern state of Germany was created from a number of small independent principalities and kingdoms in the late nineteenth century, the Lutheran and Reformed (Calvinist) Protestant churches of Germany remained separated as 28 independent regional bodies reflecting their origins as small state-sponsored churches (*Landeskirchen*) with the local secular ruler as head. In 1922, they formed a loose federation to participate jointly in mission activities, but they did not come together as one unified church until April 1933 when the German Evangelical Church (*Deutsche Evangelische Kirche*) was created under the direction of Adolf Hitler. (The term Evangelical was preferred over Lutheran or Reformed and was different from how the term is used in America today.)

2. Struckmeyer, *Conspiracy of Love*, 173–178.

Only months earlier, in January 1933, German President Paul von Hindenburg (1847–1934) had appointed Adolf Hitler as Chancellor of Germany. When Hindenburg died the following year, Hitler combined the offices of chancellor and president and became the nation's dictator. Many Christians in Germany openly welcomed Hitler's National Socialist (Nazi) party to power as a historic moment of Christ's work on earth for and through the Aryan *Volk* (German for *people*).

As it rose to power in the 1930s, the Nazi message was that despite their God-given destiny, the nation was threatened from within by the insidious presence of communists, Jews, and liberals in their midst. Hitler told the nation that their duty was to purify themselves of these influences to prepare for their divine vocation as God's anointed nation. His message was that he would make Germany great again. The truth is, Christian men and women widely supported Nazism because it benefited them, and it seemed to reinforce the cultural values that gave meaning and purpose to their lives. They believed God was in control and had blessed their culture and their leader for special greatness—and that outsiders and foreign influence needed to be subjugated or eradicated for Germans to protect themselves.

The newly formed German Evangelical Church was founded under the strong influence of an antisemitic faction called the German Christians (*Deutsche Christen*) who were proponents of the Nazi party and its belief that the nation could only fulfill its destiny by absolute obedience to a strong leader (*Führer*). This faction, representing about one out of six Protestant clergy, was not alone in its prejudice against Jews. Antisemitism had long been a characteristic of many Christians since the Middle Ages, especially in Northern Europe.

In September 1933, Ludwig Müller (1883–1945), a leader of the German Christian faction, was appointed by Adolf Hitler as Reich Bishop (*Reichsbischof*) of the newly unified church. Müller's task was to bring the church under the absolute control of the Third Reich and its Führer. Hitler believed that religion, along with other cultural elements, needed to be brought in line with the Nazi vision. He ordered members of the Nazi party to demonstrate a powerful religious presence by filling the pews of Christian churches in uniform every Sunday.

Reichsbischof Müller supported a revisionist view of the historical Jesus that proposed that Jesus had been a member of the Aryan race and was not Jewish at all. The German Christian faction envisioned a more "heroic" and "positive" interpretation of Jesus, who was seen as one who battled against corrupt Jewish influences in his society. Müller and others favored a plan to purify Christianity of "Jewish corruption," including eliminating large parts of the Old Testament from the Bible and focusing only on a revised New Testament. They rewrote the gospels, calling the region of Judea "Jewland" and suggesting that the people of Jesus' native Galilee were of Aryan descent.

Under Müller, the church implemented the "Aryan paragraph" of the Nazi-sponsored 1933 Civil Service Law that purged people of Jewish descent and those married to non-Aryan spouses from further participation in government-funded positions. This included clergy of the state-supported Protestant churches who were therefore employees and representatives of the state. Non-Aryan clergy were dismissed from their positions.

In May 1934, a minority of Protestant Christians who were opposed to the Nazi vision and infuriated by the Aryan Clause, met at the industrial city of Barmen in the Rhineland region of Germany. Known as the Confessing Church (*Bekennende Kirche*), the defiant pastors denounced Müller and his leadership and declared that they and their congregations constituted the true Evangelical Church of Germany. They opposed the theological ideas of the German Christian faction and affirmed that the church owed its ultimate allegiance to God and not to the leader of any state. They protested that the church was not an organ of the state and needed to be independent of political ideologies to be true to its calling. They declared that no person and no nation could be above the law of God. However, to their discredit, the Confessing Church only protested state manipulation of religious affairs. They did not take up defense of the Jews outside of the church.

During the first six years of Hitler's dictatorship, from 1933 until the outbreak of war in 1939, Jewish citizens felt the effects of more than 400 decrees and regulations that restricted all aspects of their public and private lives. In September 1935, Nazi leaders announced the Nuremberg Laws that excluded German Jews from Reich citizenship and prohibited them from marrying or having sexual relations with persons of German or German-related blood. They were deprived of most political rights, denied the right to vote, and not allowed to hold public office.

It is estimated that there were about 18,000 Protestant clergy in Germany at this time, ministering to 40 million church members. About 3,000 pastors were part of the German Christian faction and about 3,000 participated in the Confessing Church movement. That left the vast majority, about 12,000 pastors, who remained in the Nazi-controlled church and, not voicing strong opinions either way, simply went along to get along. To a great extent, they believed that their calling was a purely spiritual one and thus took an apolitical stance. And so, they remained silent in the face of increasing tyranny. For a time, this seemed like a very safe position, but ultimately it was destructive to the life of the church.

These 12,000 pastors considered themselves faithful moderates and centrists. They, in turn, represented most church-going Protestants, who likewise believed in the historic creeds and Lutheran confessions but remained silent about changes in the political climate. Only a small minority of Christians in Germany ever spoke out against the growing evil as Nazi ideology overtook their land, infiltrating their schools, churches, and institutions.

Historian, civil rights leader, and peace activist Howard Zinn (1922–2010) titled his autobiography *You Can't be Neutral on a Moving Train*. By that he meant that, at any given time, history is moving along a clear and observable path. The context of one's life is not a still point in time but a vector—a course or direction with velocity. Opting for the status quo is not a choice to avoid taking responsibility for historical consequences; it means one is moving along with the popular direction of one's time. To be neutral is not neutrality at all. It is to decide, to take a side, to support a direction, often a direction that can potentially lead to great evil and repression of people at the margins of society.

CHURCH-GOING CHRISTIANS TODAY

In 2014, a Washington Post/ABC News poll found that most Christians believed that CIA torture of suspected terrorist detainees was justified. In addition, Christian majorities often support an unquestioning acceptance of America's military engagement around the world and favor the use of capital punishment. The church-going majority express a very conservative stance on social issues—frequently declaring opposition to the legal reproductive rights of women, hostility toward same-sex marriage and transgender rights, and even resistance toward women in leadership roles, especially in the church. White Evangelicals voted overwhelmingly—81 percent—for Donald Trump in the 2016 election. But in addition, 58 percent of white Mainline Protestants and 52 percent of white Roman Catholics supported Trump.[3] Thus, most white American Christians voted for a radical right-wing social, political, and economic vision for their country and a leader with immoral, racist, and fascist views. This widespread political conservatism is hard to relate to a stance of unconditional love, acceptance, and care for those in dire need in our communities and our nation.

Some Christian clergy claim that being part of a church community makes people more loving, compassionate, and accepting. But based on significant bodies of research, that theory doesn't seem to be holding up.

3. Smith and Martinez, "How the Faithful Voted."

The majority of people who sit in pews on Sunday morning are simply not as loving and compassionate as claimed. They may demonstrate compassion on an interpersonal level, but corporately and politically, they act immorally.

In 1932, theologian Reinhold Neibuhr published *Moral Man and Immoral Society: A Study in Ethics and Politics*. His thesis was that a distinction must be drawn between the moral and social behavior of individuals and that of groups, including economic classes, political factions, and nations. As individuals, people are often able to transcend their interests to consider the needs of others. Aggregated into larger social groups, however, people seemingly lose the capacity for empathy. Neibuhr proposed that human beings lack the moral imagination to sympathize with others outside of their limited personal interactions. They cannot fully extend their compassion for others beyond a certain boundary.

Conservative politics is based on maximizing the self-interest of individuals; therefore, they want limited regulations and controls, laissez-faire economics, small government, low taxation, and little or no assistance to needy persons and families. Unfortunately, most Christians support those objectives, which are far from the teachings of Jesus. Whatever conservative Christians are hearing in church is something other than the gospel of compassion, peace, justice, and social inclusion that Jesus proclaimed. Most likely, most churches are feeding their members a message of spiritual comfort and a heavy dose of eternal security, while overtly or tacitly supporting the status quo of the worst aspects of American society.

PART 4

people of the Way

Chapter 10

a theology of liberation

It remains an experience of incomparable value that we have for once learnt to see the great events of world history from below, from the perspective of the outcasts, the suspects, the maltreated, the powerless, the oppressed, and reviled, in short from the perspective of the suffering.

—DIETRICH BONHOEFFER (1906–1945)

Where we stand is what we see.

—ROBERT MCAFEE BROWN (1920–2001)

MY LIFE EXPERIENCE HAS largely been as a college-educated, professional, white male Christian American of German ancestry. My forebearers came to America from Westfalen in Germany in 1872 (on my father's side) and from the German province of Posen (in today's Poland) in 1869 (on my mother's side) to seek opportunity. I grew up in the Midwest where they settled—in St. Louis, Missouri—raised by solidly middle-class parents. We weren't rich, but we weren't poor either. Yet I was born to a privilege that I did not see, and an ignorance about the reality of the world for people who didn't look like me.

For instance, I assumed that all veterans of the Second World War, like my father, were granted access to the GI Bill of Rights.[1] That law enabled veterans to obtain grants for school and college tuition, low-interest mortgage and small-business loans, job training, hiring privileges, and unemployment benefits. I later learned that over a million black Americans

---

1. Servicemen's Readjustment Act of 1944

served in uniform. Not only did they face continued brutal racism and discrimination when they returned home from the war, but the benefits of the GI Bill were denied to them by the government they fought for.

I didn't realize it at the time, but I profited from a white, male, and Christian power structure that paved the way for my modest success in life—in the educational opportunities I was given, the job opportunities I received, in the neighborhoods I was allowed to live in. But not all Americans were given the same opportunities.

In America, our cultural view of reality is one of climbing an economic ladder. As we climb, we tend to keep our eyes on the rung above us, towards those who have more than we do. Because a few are incredibly wealthy, we tend to think of ourselves as poorer than we really are. When we turn around, as Jesus calls us to do, we look back down the ladder. Then we can see most people who have far less than we do, and we begin to understand how incredibly wealthy we really are. It is a change of perspective, a shift of the mind, a whole new way of thinking. If embraced, one's life becomes transformed; one becomes fundamentally altered.

It's time to look at life from a different point of view—from the margins, the borders, and the periphery of society. It's time to listen to the people who dwell at the bottom of the economic ladder, people who live on the fringes, whose skin color may be different, whose gender and gender identity may be different, and whose sexuality may be different. It's time to try to understand their many perspectives.

I believe this is where liberation theology can help us. Broadly speaking, liberation theology is a social and political movement within the church that attempts to interpret the gospel through the lived experiences of oppressed people.

ORIGINS IN LATIN AMERICA

More than 60 years ago, a new way of understanding God began to be circulated among people at the grassroots in Latin America. They wanted to know God's response to people like themselves—people on the margins, in poverty, and in pain—with difficult questions about justice and hope. Their conversations and conclusions led to the emergence of a new system of theological reflection and action that has become known as "liberation theology."

The Second Vatican Council—or Vatican II—met in Rome for four annual sessions, each lasting between eight and twelve weeks, from 1962 to 1965. Pope John XXIII (1881–1963) called the council because he felt the church needed "updating." He saw that many church practices were outmoded and the church's teaching needed to be presented in a way that would be relevant and understandable in a secular world. One result was that the Latin mass was ended, and masses began to be said in the languages of ordinary people. In addition, salvation was no longer considered limited to the Roman Catholic Church, and the church itself was understood to be the entire people of God, a community rather than a hierarchy. Vatican II encouraged people to dialog with the world of rapid technological and social change. But from a Latin American perspective, the world was filled with structural poverty and oppression. Since colonization, the wealthy few have owned most of the land in Latin America, leaving most people poor and landless. It was unlikely that dialog would change those conditions. In the mid-1960s, revolution was in the air. An upheaval for change was going on in societies all over the globe.

The birth of the liberation theology movement is usually dated to a Latin American Bishops' Conference, which was held in Medellín, Columbia in August 1968. The bishops called for Christians to be involved in the transformation of society. They recognized that the social situation demands a church that goes beyond the preaching and the administration of sacraments, to one that is involved in social change. They maintained that poverty and hunger were preventable. The bishops declared that the church should take "a preferential option for the poor." This refers to a consistent call, heard throughout the Bible, of concern for the poor and powerless of society in the teachings and commands of God, as well as the voices of the prophets. The option for the poor does not mean pitting one group against another, but rather, it calls us to strengthen the whole community by assisting those who are most vulnerable. The bishops wrote that "a deafening cry pours from the throats of millions of persons, asking their pastors for a liberation that reaches them from nowhere else." The "inhuman wretchedness" of poverty, they argued, was the result of systematic injustice that structured the profound inequality of Latin American society. They called this "institutionalized violence." The goal of the bishops was to liberate the people from the violence of poverty. The attending bishops issued a document affirming the rights of the poor and asserting that industrialized nations enriched themselves at the expense of developing countries.

They strove "to encourage and favor the efforts of the people to create and develop their own grassroots organizations to restore and expand their rights and the search for true justice." They spoke of "Christian base communities," a term that had recently been coined to denote small lay-led groups of Christians, in which the illiterate poor might learn to read by reading the Bible. The first small communities began to appear in 1956 in

Brazil, six years before the opening of Vatican II. Few such communities existed then, but they would soon become widespread.

Liberation theology was a response to the poverty and the ill-treatment of ordinary people. It had its origins in the mid-1950s as economic development pushed the peasants in villages and barrios into desperate poverty. Peasants witnessed an increased concentration of land in the hands of wealthy owners and a subsequent decline in wages and standards of living. With the economic unrest came political unrest, and military dictators soon took over many governments in the name of national security.[2] A rise in the military state's political repression and violence, including mass detainment, torture, and the assassination of political opponents only served to oppress the poor further. Repressive governments began crushing labor unions, controlling the press, abolishing or neutralizing democratic congresses, and elevating the armed forces. Frequently, the church hierarchy was allied with the wealthy class and the military.

BASE CHRISTIAN COMMUNITIES

Liberation theologians believed that the church must be mobilized to fight poverty. But there was a problem. Because existing parishes were often miles away from a church building and a shortage of priests meant the sacraments were not always accessible, the church in many areas consisted of only lay people without ordained leadership. How could they mobilize? The answer was "base communities" (*communidades de base*), which were local groups, composed of 10 to 30 members each, that studied the Bible, reflected upon scripture, and applied its lessons to their situation. They attempted to meet material and practical needs for food, water, sewage disposal, and electricity. A great number of these base Christian communities, led by laypersons, sprang into being throughout Latin America. The word *base* refers to the foundations—the roots of society—where people can influence the structures and established order from below.

Phillip Berryman (b. 1938), a retired professor of Latin American studies, said that "the most important development within the church during this period was the quiet, steady growth of base Christian communities."

2. Military coups ushered in repressive governments in Brazil (1964), Bolivia (1971), Uruguay (1973), Chile (1973), and Argentina (1976). Existing military governments shifted rightward in Peru (1975) and Ecuador (1976). Repressive military rule continued in Paraguay and most of Central America. Only in Mexico, Columbia, Venezuela, and Costa Rica did formal democracies remain. Through the 1960s to the 1980s, many repressive governments in Latin America were supported either overtly or covertly by the United States.

They provided a space in which people could meet in an atmosphere of respect and reaffirm their own faith and hope. Where the media were censored and intimidated and where governments and armies impose their ideology of national security, the base communities provided a small space where the truth could be spoken, even if guardedly. In a situation that seemed to offer no human reason for believing things could be different, their message was that things had to change. They became a space where poor people could "speak their word" and where they heard that God was on their side, just as in the time of the Israelites and in the age of the apostles.[3]

Through the guidance of a priest or local lay leader, base Christian communities organized rural peasants and the urban poor into self-reliant transformational communities. Small groups of people in both cities and country would come together to study the Bible, analyze their social, political, and economic situation in light of the gospel, and then create a plan to work for social justice. They used Father Joseph Cardijn's "observe, judge, act" model that came to Latin America in the 1950s.

Joseph Leo Cardijn (1882–1967) was born in the booming Brussels suburb of Schaerbeek, Belgium. His working-class parents agreed to let Joseph continue his studies to become a priest instead of going to work in a factory that was the fate of many of his friends. He was a brilliant student, but during school vacations he observed old schoolmates working in the mines and mills, and believed the church had abandoned them. He realized that the church was focused solely on spiritual matters, whereas the struggles of his friends were found in the real world.

In 1912, Cardijn was given responsibility for social work projects for women in the factory town of Laeken, a suburb of Brussels. Within months, he launched his first study circles. Contacting young teenage female factory workers outside the parish structure, Cardijn began holding small group meetings that stressed not doctrine, but action around people's real problems, especially at work. Issues such as unjust treatment by a foreman, or union struggles, or a coworker's needs. The method was summed up in three words: observe, judge, and act. Participants would *observe* by discussing the relevant facts, *judge* by deciding whether the situation was in accord with the gospel, and agreed to *act* in some way, however small. At the next meeting, they would evaluate whether they had in fact fulfilled their commitment and what impact they might have had.

3. Berryman, *Liberation Theology*, 100.

Soon, Cardijn's work came to the attention of his superiors, and he was given responsibility for church social work for the whole Brussels region. In 1919, after the First World War in Europe ended, Cardijn started the Young Trade Unionists. By 1924, the name of the organization was changed to the Young Christian Workers (JOC or *Jeunesse Ouvrière Chrétienne* in French). The organization grew rapidly, and his small-group methodology spread throughout the world. By 1938, there were 500,000 JOC members throughout Europe. In 1967, this had increased to two million members in 69 countries.

OBSERVE, JUDGE, ACT

The small Latin American base communities adopted Cardijn's model. Their intimate structure encouraged discussion and solidarity within the community and created a power base that flows from the bottom of their society upward to influence change. Discussions within these communities were oriented toward understanding the kingdom of God as it relates to issues of social, economic, and political justice. Inevitably, organized and empowered peasants became a threat to the power and status quo of wealthy elites in Latin American societies.

Latin American liberation theology emerged as a biblical analysis of poverty out of these small groups. Practice came first, theology followed. Jesus was seen as the "liberator" who always stood firmly on the side of the poorest of the poor and defending the rights of the poor was seen as the central aspect of the gospel. Followers of Jesus were called to work toward a just society, bring about social and political change, and align themselves with the working class. It often called for reorganization of social, governmental, and economic structures so that the poor are not merely cared for but transformed into thriving people.

The original work on liberation theology was written by Peruvian priest Gustavo Gutiérrez (b. 1928). *A Theology of Liberation* (1971) gave the movement its name and emphasized the church's mission to those on the periphery of society. Gutiérrez said, "I come from a continent in which more than 60 percent of the population lives in a state of poverty, and 82 percent of those find themselves in extreme poverty." He felt the European theology he had studied did not reflect the oppressive material conditions in Latin America. To Gutiérrez, the source of the problems of Latin America was the sin manifested in an unjust social structure—the ancient domination system.

His theological focus aimed to connect salvation and liberation through the preferential option for the poor that emphasized improving the material conditions of the impoverished. Gutiérrez proposed that the church at large had focused on spiritual matters instead of bringing about the kingdom of God on earth. In this way, his methodology was often critical of the social and economic injustice he believed to be responsible for poverty in Latin America and the clergy within the Catholic church that he believed were complicit. The central pastoral question of his work was: "How do we convey to the poor that God loves them?"

Gutiérrez developed his theology in concert with education activist and philosopher Paulo Freire (1921–1997) who was born to a middle-class family in Recife, the capital of the northeastern Brazilian state of Pernambuco. He became familiar with poverty and hunger from an early age during of the Great Depression. During his childhood and adolescence, Freire ended up falling four grades behind. "I didn't understand anything because of my hunger. I wasn't dumb. It wasn't lack of interest. My social condition didn't allow me to have an education."

Paulo Freire eventually enrolled in law school at the University of Recife in 1943. Although admitted to the bar, he never practiced law and instead worked as a secondary school teacher of Portuguese. In 1946, Freire was appointed director of the Department of Education and Culture in Pernambuco. Working primarily among the illiterate poor, Freire began to develop an educational theory that would have an influence on the liberation theology movement of the 1970s.

In 1962, he had the first opportunity for large-scale application of his theories, when, in an experiment, three hundred sugarcane harvesters were taught to read and write in just 45 days. In response to this experiment, the Brazilian government approved the creation of thousands of study groups across the country. He published *Pedagogy of the Oppressed* (1969) based on his theories. He believed that traditional education used a "banking" concept of education, in which students are viewed as empty accounts to be filled by teachers. Instead, Freire believed that education should treat the learner as a participant. Such an education style would allow the oppressed person to regain a sense of human dignity. And this, in turn, would allow the oppressed person to play a role in their own liberation.

Liberation theologians believed that God speaks particularly through the poor and that the Bible can be understood only when seen from their perspective. Gutiérrez insisted that all theology must take its bearings from an "axis" of oppression and liberation. In the Bible, such an emphasis would focus on the exodus—God delivering his people from slavery—and on the laws and prophets that call Israel to have compassion for the poor. Those who had contempt for the poor would bear special judgment.

One of the most prominent clerics associated with liberation theology was the Archbishop of San Salvador, Óscar Romero (1917–1980). Initially considered a social conservative, he became increasingly an outspoken advocate for the poor and oppressed as the security situation in El Salvador deteriorated in the late 1970s. In the lead-up to El Salvador's 12-year civil war, Romero fought for agrarian reform for landless rural farmers. He mediated between labor unions, popular guerrilla organizations, and the military to try to prevent armed conflict. He established the country's foremost human rights and legal aid organization and urged President Jimmy Carter to cease the United States' financial support for El Salvador's military. In one of his last homilies, he pleaded with El Salvadoran soldiers to stop the killing. He was assassinated by government agents while saying mass in a cancer hospice in San Salvador on March 24, 1980.

RESISTANCE WITHIN THE CHURCH

Liberation theology was perceived as threatening to the power brokers, including the church hierarchy. Because of their insistence that ministry should include involvement in the political struggle of the poor against wealthy elites, liberation theologians were often criticized as naive purveyors of Marxism and advocates of leftist social activism.

Initially encouraged by the reforms of Vatican II, the subsequent conservative theological retractions under popes John Paul II (1920–2005) and Benedict XVI (1927–2023) have suppressed the movement and the positive influence of liberation theology on the lives of the poor. In 1984, Cardinal Joseph Ratzinger—later Pope Benedict XVI—stated that the theology of liberation was a thoroughly valid term, but he rejected certain forms of Latin American liberation theology for focusing on systemic sin and for identifying Catholic Church hierarchy in South America as members of the same privileged class that had long oppressed indigenous populations. The Vatican emphasized that the church's ministry was not social but was aimed toward the individual and personal nature of sin. By the mid-1980s, Pope John Paul II had begun to curb the movement's influence through the appointment of conservative cardinals and archbishops in Latin America. He closed institutions that taught Liberation Theology and he rebuked the movement's activists such as Gustavo Gutiérrez.

In 2013, a new pope was elected. Argentine-born Pope Francis—originally Jorge Mario Bergoglio (b. 1936)—has stood in marked contrast to his two predecessors. Born in Buenos Aires, Argentina, Bergoglio worked for a time as a bouncer and a janitor as a young man before training to be a chemist and working as a technician in a food science laboratory. After recovering from a severe illness, he was inspired to join the Society of Jesus (the Jesuits) in 1958. He was ordained a Catholic priest in 1969, and from 1973 to 1979 was the Jesuit provincial superior in Argentina. He became the archbishop of Buenos Aires in 1998 and was created a cardinal in 2001 by Pope John Paul II. The first pope from the Americas, he chose Francis as his papal name in honor of Saint Francis of Assisi who chose to live a life of poverty in solidarity with the poor.

In his first interview with journalists, Pope Francis declared "How much I wanted a poor church for the poor." He later reflected, "As long as the church places its hope on wealth, Jesus is not there. Poverty is at the center of the gospel." He has said that prioritizing the poor is "the key criterion of Christian authenticity."

> *Faith, hope and love necessarily push us towards this preference for those most in need, which goes beyond necessary assistance. Indeed, it implies walking together, letting ourselves be evangelized by them, who know the suffering Christ well, letting ourselves be "infected" by their experience of salvation, by their wisdom and by their creativity. Sharing with the poor means mutual enrichment. And, if there are unhealthy social structures that prevent them from dreaming of the future, we must work together to heal them, to change them. And we are led to this by the love of Christ, who loved us to the extreme, and reaches the boundaries, the margins, the existential frontiers.[4]*

Pope Francis is an outspoken critic of unbridled capitalism and free market economics, consumerism, and overdevelopment. He is also a champion of environmentalism. He views "Mother Earth" as one who has been raped and plundered. Francis has sought to revive base Christian community work in Latin America's slums and marginalized areas. In 2018, Pope Francis canonized Óscar Romero as the first native saint of Central America.

DECLINE OF BASE COMMUNITIES

In the twenty-first century, the rural poor are migrating to cities in search of employment. This migration has weakened base Christian communities, which were already decimated by years of military repression in the countryside. An ironic quip heard today in Latin American religious circles goes, "While liberation theologians made a preferential option for the poor, the

---

4. Francis, "Matthew, Chapter 25."

poor made a preferential option for Pentecostalism." The explosive growth of Pentecostal churches is contributing to a new religious reality in urban Latin America. Tens of millions of Latin Americans have left the Roman Catholic Church in recent decades and embraced Pentecostal Christianity. Indeed, nearly one-in-five Latin Americans now describe themselves as Protestant. Pentecostalism is now overwhelmingly anchored in Latin America, having originated in the United States. In Brazil, for example, the Assemblies of God, a Pentecostal denomination, has 10 to 12 million members, while the American Assemblies of God has only 2 to 3 million.

Some Latin Americans who grew up Catholic converted to Pentecostalism at a time of a health crisis, because Pentecostalism puts such a great emphasis on faith healing. This healing ministry is one of the drivers of the Pentecostal boom. In addition, the emphasis that some evangelical Protestant groups place on "prosperity" theology, make this new movement more compatible with capitalism. People are told that with sufficient faith and prayers to God, eventually the things that you want in life will be yours. That's a very powerful message to someone who has very little.

Pentecostal preachers tend to sound more like their congregants than educated priests. They are often uneducated, and they speak to their congregations in the same way that people in Latin American speak to each other. They also tend to look like their congregants. So, in Guatemala, many preachers are Mayan, and in Brazil they are Afro-Brazilian. By contrast, in the Catholic Church, most priests are white or mestizo, and many are actually from Europe.

There is a further point that impacts the embrace of the poor to the Pentecostal faith. When I was in El Salvador in 2005 for the 25th anniversary of the assassination of Óscar Romero, I was told by members of the base Christian community in the village of Nuevo Esperanza that some of the appeal to women was that the men could no longer drink. Many people are attracted to Pentecostalism because they are struggling with substance abuse or other problems. Pentecostalism promotes healthy lifestyles and serves as the largest detox center for Latin American men. Men who join these churches often stop hard drinking or gambling or womanizing. This new emphasis on piety and prosperity makes it likely that the base Christian communities will continue to decline in number and influence.

SMALL COMMUNITIES IN AFRICA

As they decline in Latin America, they are on the rise in Africa. In the thirty years since the First African Synod in Rome in 1994, Roman Catholic bishops in East Africa have insisted on the importance of "small Christian communities" or SCCs. Like the "base communities" in Latin America, small Christian communities are small neighborhood, parish-based groups in an urban or rural area in East Africa (Kenya, Tanzania, and Uganda; and the Horn of Africa, made up of Somalia, Djibouti, Eritrea, and Ethiopia). African bishops declared that they would be "a new way of being the church," rooted in the belief that small Christian communities are not optional but are the basic unit and most local expression of the Catholic church. The word "small" was specifically chosen to avoid certain negative undertones of the word "base."

Small Christian communities in Africa are groups where people can come together and share their lives, read the gospels, and ask themselves about the will of God for their lives. As the name implies, they are small so that people can really come to know one another and establish supportive relationships, in contrast to the rather impersonal links among people that are common in parish communities. Many SCCs try to address the reality of peoples' lives to find creative responses that will liberate them, allowing them to be more truly themselves and be of service to others.

They meet in one another's homes and usually rotate their place of gathering so that each has a turn in hosting the group. The meetings are held on a regular basis, usually once a week. They see that the lonely, sick, and impoverished of their neighborhood experience caring love and support. They are also actively involved in the affairs of their village or town. It is in these small communities that the average person will more readily speak about the inhuman conditions they experience, and it is these very neighborhood communities that can try to do something themselves about problems as they arise. Visits are made between the communities to meet to work or discuss together. In 2014, there were over 160,000 Small Christian Communities in the seven countries of East Africa.

OTHER VOICES FOR LIBERATION

Liberation Theology deals primarily with the relations of rich and poor. Other voices have been raised, particularly in the United States. Black Liberation Theology focuses more on race, and Feminist Liberation Theology more on gender. But for all these groups, it is a question of relations between one group who are considered oppressive, and another considered the oppressed. They argue that the Bible should be read from the perspective of those who are oppressed. The Bible looks different to poor and rich, black and white, female and male, gay and straight. There is no biblical interpretation that is socially, racially, economically, politically, or gender neutral.

BLACK LIBERATION THEOLOGY

James Hal Cone (1938–2018) was best known for his advocacy of black liberation theology. His book, *Black Theology and Black Power* (1969) provided a new way to comprehensively define the distinctiveness of theology in the black church. Cone wrote, "Exodus, the prophets, and Jesus—these three—defined the meaning of liberation in black theology."

Cone wrote of the inadequacy of white European theology: "What could Karl Barth possibly mean for black students who had come from the cotton fields of Arkansas, Louisiana, and Mississippi, seeking to change the structure of their lives in a society that had defined black as non-being?" Cone's theology came from a frustration with the black struggle for civil rights. Accordingly, his theology was heavily influenced by Malcolm X and the Black Power movement. But Martin Luther King Jr was also important. He describes King as a liberation theologian before the phrase existed.

Cone's message was that Black Power—defined as black people asserting the humanity that white supremacy denied—was the meaning of the gospel in America. He held that Jesus came to liberate the oppressed, advocating the same thing as the Black Power movement. Despite his associations with the movement, however, Cone was not entirely focused on ethnicity: "Being black in America has little to do with skin color. Being black means that your heart, your soul, your mind, and your body are where the dispossessed are."

By choosing Israelite slaves to be the people of God and by becoming the oppressed one in Jesus, God is known where human beings experience humiliation and suffering. Cone asked how we could have a rejected, beaten, crucified savior at the center of our faith and not recognize the similarity to the black condition in America? God has identified with the oppressed to the point that their experience becomes God's own experience. Cone asserted that this is the essence of the biblical revelation. Liberation is not an afterthought, but the very essence of divine activity.

FEMINIST LIBERATION THEOLOGY

Feminist theology claims to seek the equality, justice, and liberation of women from oppressive male systems of power and domination, especially in religion. Feminist theologians believe these systems of male power and privilege have shaped the history of the church, the history of traditional biblical interpretation—and sometimes even the content of the Bible (written *by* men *for* men)—and have justified and resulted in the oppression, silencing, and exclusion of women in all areas of life, especially in the church. Feminist theology seeks the equality and welfare of women by opposing and dismantling patriarchal systems of power, domination, and exclusion. Rosemary Radford Ruether (1936–2022) developed this thinking in her book, *Sexism and God Talk: Toward a Feminist Theology* (1983). The most important principle of feminist theology, according to Ruether, is the promotion of the full humanity of women in Christian theology and traditions.

There is not just one feminist theology but many, each arising from different historical, cultural, and global settings. In recent years, the concerns and methodologies of feminist theologians have broadened from a focus on women and gender relations to include the compounding effects of race, ethnicity, class, sexuality, and other dynamics of power and privilege. The interconnected, overlapping nature of these social categories is known as "intersectionality." In this analysis, the perspective and needs of the marginalized take priority over those of the privileged—among whom are white, well-educated, middle-class, Western, female feminists.

Feminist theology now employs a wide range of methods and perspectives reflecting the varied experiences of women around the globe; including African American women (womanist theology); Hispanic American women (*mujerista* theology); Korean women (*minjung* feminist theology); low-caste Indian women (*dalit* feminist theology); and those from the LGBTQ+ community—including transgender women (biological males at birth).

WOMANIST LIBERATION THEOLOGY

The term "womanist" was originally coined by author Alice Walker (b. 1944) to describe black feminists or feminists of color. Womanist theology joined black liberation theology in its call for the freedom of all human beings and joined white feminist theology in its assertion of women's dignity. Womanist theology critiqued white racist oppression, but it also identified and critiqued black male oppression of black females, and white feminist theology's participation in the perpetuation of white supremacy. In *Sisters in the Wilderness* (1993), womanist theologian Delores Williams (1937–2022) constructed her theology around the biblical character of Hagar, "a female slave of African descent who was forced to be a surrogate mother." Hagar was a concubine of Abraham, and slave to both Abraham and his wife Sarah. Williams notes parallels between Hagar's role as handmaiden, giving birth to Ishmael when Sarah and Abraham were unable to conceive, and the role of black women in caring for white children during and after slavery. The story of Hagar's ability to survive in the wilderness has resonated with many black women who have found the strength to survive and persevere through adversity by leaning on their God.

QUEER LIBERATION THEOLOGY

In the late 1960s, a new generation of young gay and lesbian Americans saw their struggle within a broader movement to dismantle racism, sexism, and traditional customs regarding human sexuality. Queer theology begins with an understanding that gender variances have always been present in human history, including faith traditions and their sacred texts. It was at one time separated into two separate theologies: gay theology and lesbian theology. Later, the two would merge and expand to become the more inclusive term of queer theology.

There are just eight verses in the Bible that are traditionally used to condemn perceived homosexuality, most of which are not descriptions of loving relationships. The minimal reference to homosexuality shows how minor a concern it is in comparison to more important things such as compassion and justice. Jesus himself never spoke about the subject. Queer theology seeks to return to the radical love of Jesus that has been misplaced by Christian theology.

Kelly Kraus, the author of *Queer Theology: Reclaiming Christianity for the LGBT Community* (2014), says:

> *Jesus was concerned with love above all else. He loved the outcasts of his day and he loved them fiercely. Jesus did not concern himself with what was considered a "proper" expression of love; rather, he loved freely . . . Jesus can be seen as a member of the gay and lesbian community, as he can be seen as a member of any loving community.*[5]

These many theologies all speak from the viewpoints of those on the margins, the borders, and the periphery of society. As Dietrich Bonhoeffer put it, "to see the great events of world history from below, from the perspective of the outcasts, the suspects, the maltreated, the powerless, the oppressed, and reviled, in short from the perspective of the suffering." And lawyer and activist Bryan Stevenson (b. 1959) has said, "We've got to find ways to get closer to the poor, the neglected, the abused, the excluded, the marginalized, because it's in proximity to these communities that we hear things that we will not otherwise hear; we will see things that we will not otherwise see."

5. Kraus, "Queer Theology."

It's time to listen to the people who dwell at the bottom of the economic ladder, people who live on the fringes of society, people whose skin color may be different, whose gender and gender identity may be different, and whose sexuality may be different. It's time to try to understand their many viewpoints and perspectives, and this in turn will enlighten our collaboration to liberate all people from oppression.

Chapter 11

a religionless Christianity

If religion is only a garment of Christianity—and even this garment has looked very different at different times—then what is a religionless Christianity?[1]

—DIETRICH BONHOEFFER (1906–1945)

Jesus does not call us to a new religion, but to life.[2]

—DIETRICH BONHOEFFER (1906–1945)

POSTMODERN PEOPLE SEEM TO be heading away from traditional "church Christianity" to some new mode of being a Christian in the world—Christianity developing outside of the walls of a church building. Nearly 80 years ago, Dietrich Bonhoeffer first conjectured on the possibility of this happening. Bonhoeffer began to see that the church could not continue to be concerned simply with the purity of its own life and practice. He believed the church was the church only when it lived for others. Bonhoeffer realized that the church needed to do more and become active in the resistance to systemic evil.

We are not to simply bandage the wounds of victims beneath the wheels of injustice, we are to drive a spoke into the wheel itself.[3]

---

1. Bonhoeffer, *Letters and Papers*, 280.
2. Bonhoeffer, *Letters and Papers*, 362.
3. Bonhoeffer, No *Rusty Swords.* 225.

Bonhoeffer became increasingly engaged in the work of a conspiracy committed to the overthrow of the Nazi government, especially within the *Abwehr* (the German Military Intelligence Office), that planned to assassinate Adolf Hitler and take over the government to broker a surrender to the Allies before Germany's destruction was complete. In March 1943, Bonhoeffer was arrested and imprisoned by the Gestapo because documents found in the Abwehr offices linked him to various subversive activities, specifically to his participation in "Operation 7," an undercover activity that spirited fourteen German Jews across the border to neutral Switzerland under the pretext that they were Abwehr agents.

In July 1944, an attempt was made to assassinate Hitler. It failed disastrously, and hundreds of political prisoners were executed afterwards. Bonhoeffer was eventually hanged at the Nazi concentration camp at Flossenbürg on April 9, 1945, only a month before the end of the war in Europe. He was 39 years old and had spent the last two years of his life as a prisoner.

CAN WE BE RELIGIOUS ANYMORE?

Nearly a year after his imprisonment, in a letter written on April 30, 1944, from cell 92 in Berlin's Tegel penitentiary, Dietrich Bonhoeffer described his thoughts about the state of Christianity to his good friend Eberhard Bethge (1909–2000), who later edited Bonhoeffer's writings.

> *You would be surprised, and perhaps even worried, by my theological thoughts and the conclusions that they lead to . . . What is bothering me incessantly is the question what Christianity really is, for us today.*[4]

Considering the depravity of the Nazi state and the horrific violence of the Second World War, perpetrated by religious people on all sides, Bonhoeffer questioned what Christianity represented any more. Why are Christians so unquestioningly captive to their culture? Why did German Christians not protest the persecution of the Jews? Why were they so unwilling to stand up to evil authorities and unjust laws? Bonhoeffer began struggling with what it means to claim to be religious in any real sense. And he saw a time coming in which religion would prove to be fundamentally irrelevant.

> *We are moving towards a completely religionless time; people as they are now simply cannot be religious anymore. Even those who honestly describe themselves as "religious" do not in the least act*

4. Bonhoeffer, *Letters and Papers*, 279.

up to it, and so they presumably mean something quite different by "religious" . . .

And if therefore man becomes radically religionless—and I think that is already more or less the case (else, how is it, for example, that this war, in contrast to all previous ones, is not calling forth any "religious" reaction?)—what does that mean for "Christianity?"[5]

Bonhoeffer was disappointed that religious people—lay and clergy alike—were not speaking out or taking a stand, and their social and political struggles were conducted without drawing on their faith—or more likely, that their faith had become so disjointed from social and political conditions that they saw no connection.

If religious institutions in every nation were willingly transforming themselves into servants of the state, and not raising a prophetic voice for peace and justice, was there another possibility for Christianity in the world? In his prison cell, Bonhoeffer questioned:

Are there religionless Christians? If religion is only a garment of Christianity—and even this garment has looked very different at different times—then what is a religionless Christianity?[6]

What would Christianity look like when it is stripped bare? Bonhoeffer began to struggle with what remains when the typical traits of a religion—clergy, religious institutions, sacred rites, orthodox beliefs, and an absolute morality—are eliminated. How would that redefine Christianity? What would be left?

What bothered Bonhoeffer was that a person could confess doctrinally correct beliefs, follow the accepted behaviors and practices of the church, and observe its moral codes, while simultaneously hating and oppressing other human beings. The question thus becomes: how is it possible that the practice of Christianity can become divorced from loving our neighbors in any real sense? How is it that religious practice—including word and sacrament—can leave a person ultimately unchanged at the core of his or her being?

CONTEMPLATION AND ACTION

Dietrich Bonhoeffer believed that, in the future, a new form of Christianity, stripped of its religious garments, would be limited to two things: prayer and doing justice in the world. He described his thoughts in a letter to the

5. Bonhoeffer, *Letters and Papers*, 279–280.
6. Bonhoeffer, *Letters and Papers*, 280.

infant son of his good friend Eberhard Bethge on the occasion of the child's baptism in May 1944. Bonhoeffer had been asked to be godfather for his namesake Dietrich Bethge (b. 1944), a duty he could perform only from a jail cell.

> *You are being baptized today as a Christian . . . Our church has been fighting during these years only for its self-preservation, as if that were an end in itself. It has become incapable of bringing the word of reconciliation and redemption to humankind and to the world . . . We can be Christians today in only two ways: through prayer and doing justice among human beings. All Christian thinking, talking, and organizing must be born anew, out of that prayer and action. By the time you grow up, the church will have changed considerably.*[7]

I often look at Bonhoeffer's letter as one that could have been addressed to me. I was born less than three years after Dietrich Bethge, who grew up to be a concert cellist. With others of my Baby Boomer generation, I have witnessed the increasing decline of "church Christianity" in Europe, Australia, and North America. Seventy years later, a new form of Christianity is struggling to be born in a secular world.

> *To be a Christian does not mean to be religious in a particular way, to cultivate some particular form of asceticism (as a sinner, a penitent, or a saint), but to be a human being. It is not some religious act which makes a Christian what he or she is, but participation in the suffering of God in the life of the world.*[8]
>
> *The religious act is always something partial; "faith" is something whole, involving the whole of one's life. Jesus calls us, not to a new religion, but to life.*[9]

In the life of Jesus, we can clearly see the two dimensions of religionless Christianity—contemplative prayer and righteous action or justice. The gospels describe Jesus continually moving between these two polarities. He often withdraws to the wilderness or to a quiet, lonely place to meditate and pray alone. And then he jumps back into the life of the world with healing actions and a bold prophetic voice. Prayer and righteous action were the key features of the life of Jesus. This is where Bonhoeffer believed that Christianity was heading in the future. Religionless Christianity is a life of caring for

7. Bonhoeffer, *Letters and Papers*, 299–300.

8. Bonhoeffer, *Letters and Papers*, 361. (This translation from Robinson, *Honest to God*, 83.)

9. Bonhoeffer, *Letters and Papers*, 362.

people and responding in concrete ways to heal wounds and alleviate the causes that lead to hurting people. That has been part of the church's mission over the centuries, but sometimes it seems to forget that it is central, not just a peripheral activity.

It will perhaps surprise many to say that the model for a religionless Christianity is Jesus himself. Jesus did not intend to establish a new religion. Christianity as we know it was not his objective. His life, teachings and actions were focused on creating a new kind of personal and community life amid the old. He set out to transform human life amid a great empire and to challenge those forces that oppress and divide people in every society.

CONTEMPLATIVE PRAYER

Bonhoeffer believed that regular contemplative prayer focused on the needs of others was important because it draws forth empathy and concern toward those whom we envision. Thinking deeply about other peoples' suffering—and not just our own problems—helps put everything into a larger perspective.

Today, contemplative prayer is often defined as "centering" prayer that involves rhythmic deep breathing while focusing on a single word or mantra. But that is not how Bonhoeffer used the term. For him, it was not about achieving a state of consciousness focused on inner peace and tranquility; it was about moving beyond ourselves into the lives of others. In contemplative prayer, Bonhoeffer said, "I move into the other person's place. I enter their life . . . their guilt and distress. I am afflicted by their sins and their infirmity."[10] Bonhoeffer believed that this sense of identity with the situations of others was the necessary motivating force that would lead us to act upon and affect the lives of men and women throughout the world.

Compassion is a feeling of empathy with the suffering of others, the capacity to feel how others feel. The Latin root of the word *compassion* is a compound of *com* (with) and *passio* (suffer), which gives us the meaning *to suffer with*. Compassion is entering into the pain of another and feeling their suffering—experiencing it, sharing it, tasting it. It is identifying with the sufferer, being in solidarity with the sufferer.

Contemplation is a matter of opening one's heart and letting oneself be moved with compassion. One scientific study showed that motor circuits in the brain lit up when people were feeling compassionate, as if they were getting ready to do something about the suffering they were sensing.

10. Bonhoeffer, *Sanctorum Communio*, 133. (I have taken the liberty to replace his male-oriented terms "man" and "his" with the words "person" and "their.")

The importance of contemplative prayer is that it can move us to act in real and tangible ways, rather than calling upon an omnipotent God to act supernaturally. Countless people typically pray for God to change conditions in the world. Their prayers may often sound as if they are reminding God what God's job is (to bring peace among warring nations, to bring healing to the sick, to be with those who suffer, etc.). They want to put everything in God's hands and let God deal with the mess we have created here below. That kind of prayer allows the petitioner to sit passively aside, waiting for God to act, ignoring the reality that the God of love can *only* work through us in the world.

Bonhoeffer likewise realized that the power we call God can *only* work through us in the world. It is not appropriate, nor is it realistic, to ask God to do things in the world independent of us. Contemplative prayer doesn't ask God to act; it is instead a motivating force for each of us to act in concrete ways. Bonhoeffer prayed so that he—acting as one of God's agents—would be motivated to change those things in the world that he could impact personally. He realized that instead of waiting for God to intervene, the God of love waits for us to act.

RIGHTEOUS ACTION

For many years, I used a 1971 edition of Bonhoeffer's *Letters and Papers From Prison* that used the words *righteous actions*. I recently purchased a 2015 translation from the original German that substitutes the word *justice*. The word *righteous* may need some clarification because the common understanding of righteousness is 1) being morally right, or 2) being right with God. These moralistic and relational understandings can sometimes lead the Christian to a sense of superior self-righteousness, which is certainly not what Bonhoeffer meant. When he used the term *righteous*, Bonhoeffer was not talking about the moral quality of the doer; he is talking about the nature of the deed. Bonhoeffer was referring to a more holistic biblical understanding of righteousness—standing up for what is right, doing what is right and just. Righteousness means seeking justice in human society.

The terms *righteousness* and *justice* are often linked in biblical texts. That is because they are synonymous, redundant terms. In the original languages of the Bible, the word for justice also means righteousness. The Greek word *dikaios* (*DIK-ah-yos*) in the New Testament and the word *tzedakah* (*tze-dah-KAH*) in the Hebrew Bible have this dual meaning. Righteousness implies a personal and individual dimension, while justice implies a social dimension, but they both have the same objectives—acting on behalf of those suffering from injustice.

CHARITY

Compassionate action usually takes three forms: charity, service, and justice. Although some would also include service under the category of charity, charity more specifically involves gifts of money, clothing, food, or other material goods, but does not necessarily involve an investment of our time and talents. Charity is very important but writing a check to a worthy cause does not necessarily transform our lives. We can remain distant from those we seek to help. Service, however, involves us face-to-face with those in need. It can be an immensely transformative experience that can change us from our natural state of self-centeredness into increasingly selfless people. Perhaps it is the only thing that can. Although generosity sometimes leads to self-satisfaction, service often becomes a very humbling and deeply moving experience.

Following Jesus can be costly, but we are not required to emulate Jesus by abandoning all our possessions and financial security. Instead, the idea that we should pool our resources to help one another is central to the communities that gathered around him. It became the most distinctive characteristic of early Christianity for nearly three hundred years. The kind of radical personal charity that Jesus recommended is rare. Regardless of our generosity, most of us are cautious in how we use our funds. We know we can do more, yet we hold back, not wanting to be taken advantage of by "undeserving" people. But no matter how generous we are, in the end, charity is only a Band-Aid. It fills the gaps left by an unjust society. Charity is important, but it is not enough.

SERVICE

Serving the needs of others is the path of transformation from egocentrism to humility and self-giving love. Our captivity to our ego causes us to value success, importance, and praise. But Jesus calls us to deny ourselves—our self-importance, our self-centeredness, our innate selfishness—and by humbling ourselves, serve others in need.

There are many ways to serve, but we should be aware of some pitfalls. Professor Rachel Remen (b. 1938) identifies our natural inclination to help others and to fix them as impediments to real service.

Service is not the same as helping. Helping is based on inequality; it's not a relationship between equals. When you help, you use your own strength to help someone with less strength. It's a one up, one down relationship, and people feel this inequality. When we help, we may inadvertently take away more than we give, diminishing the person's sense of self-worth and self-esteem . . . Helping incurs debt: when you help someone, they owe you. But service is mutual. When I help, I have a feeling of satisfaction, but when I serve, I have a feeling of gratitude.

Serving is also different to fixing. We fix broken pipes; we don't fix people. When I set about fixing another person, it's because I see them as broken. Fixing is a form of judgement that separates us from one another; it creates a distance.

We may help or fix many things in our lives, but when we serve, we are always in the service of wholeness.[11]

JUSTICE

Charity and service are both personal forms of compassionate action. Their objective is to alleviate the effects of suffering in the world. Justice, on the other hand, seeks to eliminate the root causes of suffering. William Sloane Coffin (1924–2006) has said: "The Bible is less concerned with alleviating the effects of injustice, than in eliminating the causes of it."[12] Martin Luther King Jr said:

We are called to play the Good Samaritan on life's roadside; but that will be only an initial act. One day the whole Jericho road must be transformed so that men and women will not be beaten and robbed as they make their journey through life. True compassion is more than flinging a coin to a beggar; it understands that an edifice that produces beggars needs restructuring.[13]

Loving one's neighbor calls us to much more than charity and service; it means working for a just and equitable society. Justice is ultimately the most important factor in loving our neighbors. Philosopher and activist Cornell West (b. 1953) once said, "Justice is what love looks like in public.

11. Remen, "Helping, Fixing, Serving."
12. Coffin, *Credo*, 50.
13. King, *Where Do We Go?* 198.

You can't talk about loving folk and not fight for justice."[14] So justice is not only the social form of compassion, but also the social form of love.

The word *justice* means different things to different people. For many people, it suggests *retributive* justice, which seeks to punish lawbreakers. To others, it calls to mind *procedural* justice, which makes sure that everyone gets fair treatment under the law. However, the biblical meaning of justice is *distributive* justice, which promises a fair share of the necessities of life. Biblical scholar John Dominic Crossan reacted to the suggestion by some conservatives that the equitable sharing of our resources is nothing more than liberalism, socialism, or communism by suggesting that if we need to give biblical justice an "ism," the best label would be "enoughism."

The question is why Christians nearly always favor the personal forms of charity and service over social justice. In an unjust world, only the first and more limited responses—charity and service—are acceptable to those in power. The work of faith-based charities is often lauded by government until they try to influence government policies to change the status quo. Television journalist Bill Moyers (b. 1934) has said:

> *Charity is commendable; everyone should be charitable. But justice aims to create a social order in which, if individuals choose not to be charitable, people still don't go hungry, unschooled, or sick without care. Charity depends on the vicissitudes of whim and personal wealth; justice depends on commitment instead of circumstance. Faith-based charity provides crumbs from the table; faith-based justice offers a place at the table.*[15]

Jesus himself taught his followers to do all three: charity, service, and justice.

> Charity: *Help and give without expecting a return.*[16]
> Service: *The greatest among you will be your servant.*[17]
> Justice: *Strive first for the kingdom of God and its justice.*[18]

All three of these compassionate practices—charity, service, and justice—are necessary components of what Bonhoeffer describes as justice or righteous action among humanity. The conspiracy of love is about doing for the entire human family what we do within our individual families. Loving the whole human family means ensuring that everyone gets a fair and

---

14. This comment by West is frequently quoted, but not cited.

15. Moyers' foreword to Wallis, *Faith Works*, xvii.

16. Luke 6:35. (*Message*).

17. Matt 23:11.

18. Matt 6:33.

equitable access to the necessary means of life: food, clean water, clothing, shelter, education, health care, meaningful employment, safety, and protection from violence. As followers of Jesus, it is up to us to figure out how to live together as a human community, how to love one another, and how to care for the earth and all its creatures.

The life of faith Jesus calls us to is lived in a global arena where two-thirds of the children are forced to survive on less than two dollars a day, where one-third live without shelter, and where thirty thousand children die every minute of every day of malnourishment and preventable disease. Some congregations talk about these issues frequently. Others don't. Some churches engage their members in social and political action to transform the world to reflect the conspiracy of love. But many do not. For Jesus, lip service to justice was not enough. The fruitfulness of one's life is what counts.

Acts of compassion—charity, service, and justice—not only help others, but they also transform us into better people. In becoming better people, we have a chance to create a better world. If we live our lives as followers of Jesus, if we engage in his mustard seed conspiracy of love and justice, his vision of the inbreaking reign of love will be fulfilled within us and around us one small sacred act at a time. Countless acts of kindness, generosity, and self-giving love are performed every day by people precisely because they are Christians. Their lives have been changed and transformed by their faith. And all we need is love.

Chapter 12

communities of conspiracy

The church is dead. Long live the church!

—ROBIN MEYERS (B. 1952)

*The greatness of a community is most accurately measured by the
compassionate actions of its members.*

—CORETTA SCOTT KING (1927–2006)

THIS BOOK WAS INTENDED to be about the future of the church. So now is
the time to call the question. As our churches grow smaller and grayer, they
will increasingly find it difficult to financially support a building that may be
aging and is typically used only a few times a week. They may also lack the
funds to pay clergy and other institutional staffing. Some will merge with
other congregations in the hope that they can put off the inevitable. As more
churches close their doors, there will be fewer jobs for clergy. Seminaries
are already consolidating and closing as fewer people seek to make their
livelihood in the church.

QUESTIONS ABOUT THE FUTURE

As the world changes and as postmodern generations grow increasingly distant from the church, is there still a viable future for it? What new shape(s)
will the church take in the postmodern world? Perhaps—learning from the
past—we can move to a different model, one of the church moving beyond

the church doors and into the streets to pursue ministry to the poor and marginalized and the pursuit of peace and justice.

Without the church, where will a religionless Christian find support and nurture? Who or what will call people to follow Jesus, if it is not the church in some new form? Will the church of the future be defined by the way we live and not by what we believe? The religious issue for postmoderns is not about rites, creeds, or worship—it is about a holistic way of life. How will such a life of faith be challenged to grow and mature?

Without the church, who will teach the faith? How will young people learn about Jesus, grasp his radical wisdom, and understand his call to righteous action—to a life of peace, justice, and compassion? How will we teach our children about the nonviolent transformation of the world and resistance to the forces of oppression, racism, sexism, militarism, and empire? Where will they learn about active service to others? Admittedly, the churches of today have failed in many of these roles. Future forms of the church must take these responsibilities seriously if they want to survive.

American youth are growing up in a diverse, pluralistic society and are exposed to many different belief systems. A variety of religious paths often appear to lead to the same God. For many of these young people who have friends from other faith traditions, Jesus is a path to God, but not the only path. Others have simply stopped looking for a God who is missing in action and instead are searching for real meaning in their lives.

I am convinced we are now moving toward a radically different form (or forms) of Christianity—smaller groups and smaller gatherings. We are setting off into the unknown without a map of the territory. But there are tentative models exploring the future, leading the way. New forms of being the church are springing up around the world. I am confident there is a future for the Christian faith; it just will not be the same, especially in the Global North. It will take some creativity to discern the path (or paths) to the future. Maybe a shift of the mind is required. As New York Times columnist David Brooks (b. 1961) wrote:

> *The core American idea is not the fortress, it's the frontier. First, we thrived by exploring a physical frontier during the migration west, and now we explore technological, scientific, social, and human frontiers. The core American attitude has been looking hopefully to the future, not looking resentfully toward some receding greatness. The hardship of the frontier calls forth energy, youthfulness, and labor, and these have always been the nation's defining traits. The frontier demands a certain sort of individual, a venturesome,*

hard-working, disciplined individual who goes off in search of personal transformation.[1]

A NEW REFORMATION

I believe that two things may be necessary if the church is to survive in a postmodern secular world. First, there needs to be a radical change in Christian theology that invites thinking people back into fellowship. This involves grounding our faith not in a supernatural dimension, but in the ordinary natural world. Second, there needs to be a radical change in the form of Christian community that will meet the needs of postmodern people. This calls for a Christian reformation every bit as significant as that of Luther's in the sixteenth century. It is about both the content of faith and the container. The exiles of the Christian church are looking for a more profound, yet basic theology based on the teachings of Jesus—a theology centered on radical love, lavish generosity, extravagant forgiveness, inclusive hospitality, compassionate action, selfless service, a passion for justice, creative nonviolence, and simple living. And they are looking for communities that embody those ideals. We need communities focused on the religion *of* Jesus—good news to the poor—and no longer a religion *about* Jesus. What are needed are countercultural groups committed to the way of Jesus.

We are called to a passionate faith, one that embraces resistance to those things in our culture that Jesus resisted in his. Following Jesus is a life of non-conformity to the dominant cultural values of our day. The Apostle Paul recognized this when he said, "Do not be conformed to this world, but be transformed by the renewing of your minds."[2] This act of turning around, of walking in a different direction, of opposing the norms of our society, is an act of revolution. Jesus was calling for a sudden, marked change in cultural values that would lead to a radical and pervasive change in society. Quaker pastor Philip Gulley (b. 1961) wondered what the church would be if it were truly Christian, following the way of Jesus.

> *If the church were Christian, Jesus would be a model for living, rather than an object of worship. Affirming our potential would be more important than condemning our brokenness. Reconciliation would be valued over judgment. Gracious behavior would be more important than right belief. Inviting questions would be valued more than supplying answers. Encouraging personal exploration*

1. Brooks, "Assault on Trumpism."
2. Rom 12:2.

would be more important than communal uniformity. Meeting needs would be more important than maintaining institutions. Peace would be more important than power. We would care more about love and less about sex. This life would be more important than the afterlife.[3]

COMMUNITIES OF RESISTANCE

The conspiracy of love is found in community. So, without the continued existence of the institutional church, we must replace it with some other form of community. One that is simpler, lighter, and more agile. Meeting in a home or in a public space, like a café or pub, may all be models for the future of the church. But if these groups focus on the needs of their members alone—personal or spiritual—and do not engage in service or the pursuit of justice, are they any better than the struggling churches of twenty-first century America? They must learn to see the world from the bottom and margins of society by embracing the cause of liberation. And they must begin to structure themselves around the demands of service, peace, and justice.

In his book *Spiritual Defiance: Building a Beloved Community of Resistance*, pastor Robin Meyers (b. 1952) explores the decline of the church as a community of believers and calls readers back to the church's roots as a community of resistance.

> *We mean well, of course. We sing our hearts out. We pray long prayers. But none of it can finally compensate for the fact as a change agent, we have all but disappeared. Instead of leaven, we are all like chameleons for Christ, absorbed into the very dominant culture we are called to critique and resist. In fact, this is precisely the word I cannot get out of my head, resistance. Who thinks of the church anymore as a defiant community?*[4]

The practice of spiritual resistance, Meyers proposes "must always be the self-conscious and intentional decision to obey, as a disciple, the radical demands of the kingdom of God." People are leaving the churches, Meyers concludes, not by their lack of spiritual hunger but "they are fleeing because so many churches now seem bereft of the very spirit that birthed them."

3. Gulley, "If Church Were Christian."
4. Meyers, *Spiritual Defiance*, xiii.

SMALL COMMUNITIES

The early Jesus communities were small and communal in nature. They were not hierarchical. Instead, they relied on egalitarian participation. The early church was based on a way of life that embodied compassion and servanthood. More profoundly, the Christian movement grew because at its core were small communities of compassion that integrated people from different social classes and provided comfort and care for the less privileged. This was the essence of the remarkable love that observers saw.

Jesus the storyteller frequently told parables of small things with the capability of affecting change in society: a mustard seed tossed in a tidy garden, a pinch of yeast in a large bowl of bread dough, a dash of salt in a pot of soup, or a small lamp in a darkened room, and a small group of committed people. The followers of Jesus were a "little flock," but they were the inheritors of the kingdom of God. Luke's gospel quotes him as saying, "Do not be afraid, little flock, for it is your Father's good pleasure to give you the kingdom."[5] In an article in America magazine, theology professor John W. Martens comments:

> By qualifying "flock" with "little," Jesus is saying something about the unassuming nature of his disciples, who might be little in number, little in power, little in social standing or some combination of all of them . . . The strength of the "little flock" becomes its willingness to live out its faith, not primarily as an intellectual assent to theological claims or grasping a list of dogmatic propositions but as a way of following Jesus wherever the Good Shepherd leads . . . Faith is following Jesus by attending to all the "little" things that seem unimportant or insignificant, as well as paying attention to all the "little" people we are tempted to forget or overlook.[6]

Postmodern people long for community. But for them it must be genuine, not just a loose gathering of people on Sunday for a weekly dose of comfort and contentment. The basis for true community must be friendship, intimacy, shared values, and a common vision of meaning and purpose. I doubt that a genuine community like that can exist in groups larger than a dozen people. A genuine community is a safe place, a place where grace happens, where people find acceptance, where differences are celebrated, where people communicate openly and honestly, where the truth is spoken, where people listen and understand, where people fight gracefully, where people

5. Luke 12:32.
6. Martens, "Little Flock."

experience growth and healing, where there is love and compassion, where people are cared for, and where people are challenged to care for others.

THE EMERGING CHURCH MOVEMENT

The emerging church movement takes its name from the idea that as culture changes in a secular world, a new church should emerge in response. It is a label that has been used to refer to Christians who are rethinking Christianity in the context of postmodernism. A postmodern church community will most likely have these elements:

- more focus on Jesus, less on the church
- more about personal transformation, less about personal salvation
- more about lifestyle, less about doctrine
- more about service, less about worship
- more about grace, less about fear
- more communal, less individualistic
- more loving, less legalistic
- more accepting, less judgmental
- more compassionate, less moralistic
- more inclusive, less exclusive
- more this-worldly, less other-worldly
- more organic, less institutional
- more intuitive, less rational
- more about listening, less about talking
- more about modeling, less about teaching
- more cross-cultural, less culturally bound

HOUSE, PUB, AND CAFÉ CHURCHES

Many emerging churches look to ancient models of the church to shape their life and worship. Some alternative communities try to overcome a church culture that is over-familiar and often irrelevant. Some groups meet in the evening, some meet every other week. In every century, Christians have met in homes in small groups to supplement their more formal church life. Others have left the established denominations altogether to form independent house churches.

A "house church" is a label used to describe a group of Christians who regularly gather in private homes. They see the house church as the primary form of Christian community. After the time of Jesus, the house church was the only viable option left to his followers after the destruction of the Jerusalem temple in 70 CE and later, their exclusion from Jewish synagogues. In fact, house-based ministry became so common in the New Testament that throughout the book of Acts, every mention of a local church or church meeting, whether for worship or fellowship, is a reference to a church meeting in a home. The churches that Paul established in the trading towns across the Aegean Sea were all house churches. Those in the house church movement are dissatisfied with a Christianity that emphasizes crowds, large and costly church buildings, and ecclesiastical hierarchies. They desire to go back to the values of simplicity and the priesthood of all believers, just like the early church. Simple church, organic church, essential church, relational church, and micro-church are all terms that identify these house churches.

In addition to houses, Christian communities may also meet in cafés, coffee shops, and pubs. People naturally gather around tables with food and drink, and they have in all cultures and at all times. The notion of table fellowship in the church goes back to the ministry of Jesus and has the potential to create significant encounters between people. It encourages them to explore the meaning of the gospel and mission of Jesus. What these new sorts of sacred spaces and communities have in common is they seem to be casual, creative, diverse, non-judgmental, informal, and inclusive. They draw people who would never attend a traditional church. Some say a bar or coffee house is a place that one would likely find Jesus if he were here today.

DINNER CHURCH

Another model of the church is the "dinner church." It is one of the fastest growing formats for Christian gathering in North America, according to Beth Ann Estock and Paul Nixon, co-authors of *Weird Church: Welcome to the Twenty-First Century*. It is a gathering of people weekly, bi-weekly, or monthly, where all the important things happen at the table. Think of a good dinner party with a spiritual variation, and then add music, singing, poetry, robust conversation, and prayer.

St. Lydia's dinner church in the Gowanus neighborhood of Brooklyn, New York, says that they are working to dispel isolation in New York City, reconnect neighbors, and subvert the status quo. A relatively new congregation of the Evangelical Lutheran Church in America (ELCA), it is named after a New Testament first-century businesswoman known for her hospitality. They place practice before belief, trusting that eating, praying, and singing together moves them deeper into faith. Instead of trying to narrow down what people believe, they are trying to live out their individual faiths. St. Lydia's is a church that gathers to share a meal, as the first followers of Jesus did. Simple unaccompanied music is sung, scripture explored, and prayers offered, all in the context of a home-cooked meal. Different communities gather each Sunday and Monday night to share a sacred meal.

Commenting on his experience in another dinner church, author Paul Nixon reports:

> *I attended a Dinner Church once where dinner started with the breaking of loaves of bread at each table, and the host said something like this: "As we begin our meal, we break bread, and we remember that though we are many, we are all connected—we are one body, one human family—all of us: friends of Jesus, who gave himself fully to human beings." At the end, we poured a little more wine, and we toasted, "To Jesus, who is alive, in us . . . luring us to take the way less travelled and to love our neighbors this week." With these simple rituals of bread and wine, book-ending the dinner and all that happened at the dinner, we had church that night. My, did we have church!*[7]

COFFEE SHOP MINISTRY

Community Covenant Church in Kirkwood, Missouri, were down to less than 40 members. They sold their church building to a local school, put the money in the bank, and began praying for the future. Olivia Tischler, a 20-something graduate of St. Louis University, had a degree in theology and entrepreneurship. She dreamed of starting a coffee shop, where she could pay people well, buy from local suppliers, and treat customers and her staff like family. But she had difficulty finding investors until she became connected with Community Covenant Church, who are now part owners in Teleo Coffee, home of the "Love Your Neighbor" Latte, which helps raise funds for charity. *Teleó* (*tel-EH-oh*) is the Greek for "finished." It is the root word of *tetelestai* (*teh-TEH-leh-sty*), meaning "It is finished," which were the last words of Jesus from the cross. But instead of a Christian-branded

7. Nixon, "What is Dinner Church?"

coffeehouse, Tischler said she wanted to run a business that lives out its faith in practice. For her, that has meant using local suppliers, like Bridge Bread, a bakery that helps people who had been homeless get off the streets, and the Switch Coffee Collective, a coffee roaster that helps employ people who had been incarcerated. The coffee house will also host a training program for students with special needs. As for Covenant, they are delighted with the arrangement. They have changed their name to Embrace Church, rented some new space, and began meeting for dinner church.

The danger of a dinner church, a house church, or church in a coffee house or a pub is that they may lack a mission element. Some may have as their mission evangelizing people, but they do not necessarily pursue the kingdom of God and its generosity, service, or justice. Many pub churches, coffee houses, and café churches are open to anyone, which is a good thing, but they may not go beyond simply attracting people or appealing to the unchurched, rather than calling them to follow the way of Jesus. We need more. Hymn sings and beer drinking, while enjoyable, do not necessarily mean engaging in service to others or the pursuit of justice in society.

INTENTIONAL COMMUNITIES

Intentional communities are another variation on the house church. They are residential communities designed from the start to have a high degree of unity and teamwork. The members typically hold a common social, political, religious, or spiritual vision; often follow an alternative lifestyle; and typically share responsibilities and even property. The multitude of intentional communities includes collective households, co-housing communities, co-living communities, ecovillages, and neo-monasteries.

The idea of "new monasticism" was developed by Jonathan Wilson in his 1998 book called *Living Faithfully in a Fragmented World*. Wilson called for a "new monasticism that would sustain the church's witness to the gospel of Jesus Christ through faithful living."[8] He built on the ideas of Dietrich Bonhoeffer, who said in 1935:

> *The restoration of the church will surely come only from a new type of monasticism that has nothing in common with the old but a complete lack of compromise in a life lived in accordance with the Sermon on the Mount in the discipleship of Christ.*[9]

8. Wilson, *Living Faithfully*, 69.

9. Bonhoeffer, *Testament to Freedom*, 424.

Most new monastic communities emphasize the following: thoughtful, prayerful, and contemplative lives; some form of communal life; a focus on hospitality; and practical engagement with the poor. The movement differs from other Christian monastic movements in several ways. Today's new monastics are not cloistered, they do not wear religious habits, nor do they take vows of obedience, chastity, and poverty. Communities do not always live in a single structure, but geographic proximity is emphasized. The new monastics are ordinary people—single and married—with jobs in the community. Their vision is simple: to incarnate the gospel message where they live.

They commit to follow a "rule of life" (which may include vows of prayer, hospitality, service, witness, and accountability) and they immerse themselves in community life and service, often working in inner city neighborhoods among the poor. Some communities provide housing for communal living for a small group of individuals, often young singles, but most simply live near one another in the same neighborhood to create an intentional community, gathering for weekly meals, worship, study, and service.

The Simple Way community in Philadelphia, formed by Shane Claiborne (b. 1975) in the mid-1990s, represents one form of the emerging monastic community. His ideas are contained in the book, *The Irresistible Revolution: Living as an Ordinary Radical.* According to Claiborne, *The Simple Way* represents a way of being faithful in the world. This focus on practice is designed to incarnate belief in a way of living. He views many churches today as strong in belief, but weak in the practice of that belief. Claiborne calls *The Simple Way* a movement of ordinary radicals—people who are not doing anything amazing, just living out the faith they claim to believe. He tells of hanging out with neighborhood children, sharing food with people in need, eating the food their neighbors share with them, running a community store, making gardens amid abandoned lots, and sharing life with their neighbors while trying to take care of each other. "We set out not to start programs, but simply to be good neighbors."[10]

In June 2004, representatives from several neo-monastic communities across the country met in Durham, North Carolina to discern a possible shape of a new monasticism. Participants in the conference identified twelve "marks" or common characteristics of these neo-monastic communities. Among those are:

- Relocation to the "abandoned places of empire" at the margins of society

- Sharing economic resources with fellow community members and the needy

10. Claiborne, *Irresistible Revolution*, 125.

- Hospitality to the stranger
- Nurturing common life among members of an intentional community
- Geographical proximity to community members who share a common rule of life
- Peacemaking amid a violent society
- Commitment to a disciplined contemplative life

THE CHURCH IN ACTION

Finally, one of the most remarkable models of a new form of community is that of the "Kirche in Aktion" (Church in Action) that operates 50 ministry locations in the Frankfurt Rhine-Main area, which is the second-largest metropolitan region in Germany with a total population exceeding 5.8 million.[11] Founded by brothers and co-pastors Philip and Cris Zimmermann, it holds worship services in fourteen locations, including coffee shops, movie theaters, retirement homes, and bars. The organization also operates a youth center, helps the elderly in nursing homes, and launched a ministry for victims of sex trafficking in a nation where prostitution is legal. Kirche in Aktion creates nonprofits, businesses, and other organizations that serve specific groups of people in sustainable ways. It also operates global missions, sending 150 people annually providing education, food, health care, and water projects around the world. The vision for the church at Kirche in Aktion is to align themelves as closely as possible to Jesus, his methods, his mindset, and his passion so that they can participate in bringing heaven into their world and their daily existence. They prioritize building the kingdom of God instead of building the church.

Their basic unit is called a *Community in Mission*, a small group of eight to ten people who meet in an every-other-week rhythm. One week, they meet to care for one another, build relationships, and share their lives. The other week, they serve together on a chosen project to make heaven visible in a specific area of their city and to build relationship to those that live there. According to Philip Zimmermann, "We don't define church around the worship gathering, but instead define the core of church around mission, which means sharing the love of God in word and deed."

The situation for the church in Germany is dire. For well over 1,000 years Germany had been at the center of Christianity in Europe. Today the influence of Christianity is still seen everywhere in modern Germany

11. Church in Action web site. https://churchinaction.com/

with church buildings in most villages and neighborhoods. Fifty-five percent of the population still identifies with the official Protestant or Catholic churches. Despite that, less than 10 percent of Catholics and only 3 percent of Protestants attend church. In 2019, over half a million Protestants and Catholics officially disassociated themselves from the church. The churches are empty, and an increasing number of Christians no longer believe the creeds and teachings of the faith.

In 2010, Cris Zimmermann, who is also an attorney and entrepreneur, and a small team of young people began meeting at the Berliner Pub in Frankfurt. They soon created social projects benefiting the homeless in the city as well as financing a well in Ethiopia where the pub owner was from. Their goal was to create one church in many locations. His brother Philip Zimmermann says, *"From the beginning, there was always one question that we asked: how can we as a church serve those who are marginalized?"* But *Kirche in Aktion* has never attempted to gather people in a church building. They take the gospel to the streets and put it into action. Their 10-year goal is to have 1,000 Communities in Mission in Germany and to have 10,000 world-wide by training pastors to spin off their model.

As we have seen, the possibilities for ministry in the secular world are seemingly endless: house churches, pub churches, coffee house churches, dinner churches, small Christian communities, intentional communities, new monastic communities, communities in mission. Those are all different containers for a life of faith. But what of the content? What will they exist for? I am attracted to the contemplation and action rhythm that some groups have established: one meeting to discuss the life to which we are called and to build community, and the next to serve human need or the cause of justice in some way. That is the cycle of a religionless Christianity—contemplation and action. And proof that there may be genuine life after the death of church Christianity.

THE RELIGIOUS LEFT

Since the mid-nineties, an increasingly influential religious movement has arisen on the left, mostly escaping the national presses' notice. The religious left has always had deep roots in American history, from the abolitionists to the civil rights movement. They are a somewhat loosely-connected movement of pastors and people and faith-based organizations that advocate for left-leaning policies and tend to support Democratic politicians. The movement expends its political energies not on the cultural concerns that primarily motivate conservative evangelicals, but instead on an array of labor, economic, and social justice issues affecting working families.

It draws its inspiration from the Christian social justice movement that formed in the late 1800s as a response to the emerging industrial economy, which many religious leaders viewed as brutal and unfair to workers. Largely rooted in Mainline Protestant churches, the Social Gospel movement emphasized how Jesus' ethical teachings could remedy the problems caused by "Gilded Age" capitalism, especially issues of social justice such as economic inequality, poverty, alcoholism, crime, racial tensions, slums, unclean environment, child labor, lack of unionization, poor schools, and the dangers of war. The Social Gospel was the religious wing of the Progressive movement (1890–1920) which had the aim of combating injustice, suffering, and poverty in society.

The Social Gospel movement is generally said to span the years from about 1870 to 1920. Liberals found an articulate voice in Walter Rauschenbusch (1861–1918), a Baptist minister and theologian who had worked with German immigrants and the poor in the area called Hell's Kitchen in New York City. Influenced by the New Testament vision of the kingdom of God, he articulated a progressive Christian vision of how to transform the unbridled capitalism in America into a cooperative Christian society. Rauschenbusch linked Christianity to emerging theories of democratic socialism which, he believed, would lead to equality and a just society. He asserted that religion's chief purpose was to create the highest quality of life for all citizens. Rauschenbusch believed that the best way to uplift the oppressed was to redistribute society's wealth and forge an egalitarian society. "It is not a matter of getting individuals to heaven, but of transforming the life on earth into the harmony of heaven," Rauschenbusch wrote in *Christianity and the Social Crisis* (1907). This Social Gospel pervaded the Protestant mainstream in the decades before the First World War. The Social Gospel movement faded into relative obscurity by the mid-twentieth century, although it had a brief renewal during the civil rights movement under the leadership of Martin Luther King Jr who wrote in *Stride Towards Freedom* in 1958:

> *It has been my conviction ever since reading Rauschenbusch that any religion which professes to be concerned about the souls of men and is not concerned about the social and economic conditions that scar the soul, is a spiritually moribund religion only waiting for the day to be buried.*[12]

---

12. King, *Stride towards Freedom*, 84.

Kate Rice, author of *Jesus Is Not Republican*, recounts what happened next. The Social Gospel, largely the domain of Mainline Protestants and Social Justice Catholics, gradually morphed into a progressive form of Christianity. But progressive Christians don't lay claim to any specific denominational brand; they cut across all denominations. They are spread out across the land like the kingdom of God. They stopped identifying as much with a religious brand, in favor of the larger social justice movements they supported. They are "Matthew 25 Christians."[13]

> *That tradition continued through the decades. It grew into a religious progressivism centered on openness and inclusiveness. But this also weakened the Christian progressive brand. Here's why. Christian progressives work (or worked) on many social justice fronts. If you were part of this group, you weren't flying the flag of your faith. You were flying the flag of the cause you advocated for. You're going to stand side by side with LGBTQ plus activists, advocates for refugees and immigrants, and protestors calling for equal rights for people of color and for reproductive freedom. Your religious identity is just one of many things that define you. And the world doesn't see you as progressive Protestants or social justice-minded Catholics; it may just see you as activists fighting for economic, racial or social justice.[14]*

With the rise of the vocally powerful religious right, progressive Christians became comparatively invisible. Rice quoted religion professor Bradley Onishi and co-host of the podcast *Straight White American Jesus.*

> *"One of the paradoxes of the story is that they were so successful they kind of became invisible." He calls this victorious invisibility. That means that the child of a Mainline Protestant preacher in 1965 can grow into an adult who says to herself, "Y'know, I can fight these battles without having to brand myself as a Methodist or a Baptist." Social justice movements and progressive Christians tend to have common beliefs about justice, inclusivity, equality and giving a helping hand. Social justice movements include many people of faith.[15]*

In America today, there is a resurgence of the Gilded Age as the pursuit of profits takes precedence over the pursuit of justice—and working families and the poor are suffering the consequences. But the problems facing us are far greater than economics alone, including the seeming success of a

13. Matt 25:35–40.
14. Rice, *Jesus Is Not Republican*, 25.
15. Rice, *Jesus Is Not Republican*, 25–26.

right-wing Christian agenda affecting all of us. These reactionary Christians are diligently working to achieve their goals: the suppression of women and LGBTQ+ people, racism toward blacks and Asians, Islamophobia and anti-semitism. They overwhelmingly supported Trump. Now we are threatened by the rise of white Christian nationalism, perhaps the most potent evil political movement in the country today.

We need a counternarrative from the religious left—a movement that includes people from different religions and spiritual people who may not have a specific tradition. This is the time for the remnants of a social justice faith—progressive Christians, humanists, liberal denominations, social justice churches, and activist religious communities—to speak up, to organize, to rally, to march, to educate, to train, and to morally wrestle with these threats to marginalized people.

In his book, *American Prophets: The Religious Roots of Progressive Politics and the Ongoing Fight for the Soul of the Country*, reporter Jack Jenkins (b. 1989), covers many religious activists on the left who are making a difference today. One of those is Rabbi Sharon Brous (b. 1973) who leads a Jewish community in Los Angeles called IKAR, which means "the essence" or "the heart of the matter."

> *My Jewish tradition is centered around obedience to God and observance of mitzvot—commandments—and yet the central charge of our tradition is to stand in defiance of unjust power structures. Our heroes are those who stood up for the vulnerable, who risked everything, challenging both God and man to fight for what is just and right . . . Faith is a rebellion against [the] world. The goal is not to be quieted, to feel good, to get comfortable and settled while the palace burns. It is to be awake and to fight—with love—for the courage we need, for the family we yearn for, for the beloved community we're called to be, for the world we want our children to inherit.*[16]

Rabbi Brous is just one of many women who lead progressive religious communities. Once women become religious leaders, they bring women's issues to the fore and that often leads to creating a society that is more just and compassionate. Similarly, as an ever more diverse band of faith leaders occupy positions of prominence—be they LGBTQ+, immigrants, or non-Christians—so too will the religious institutions they lead reflect a broader, more progressive slate of political concerns.

---

16. Jenkins. *American Prophets*, 268.

In his book, Jenkins reported on a conversation he had with a Union Theological Seminary professor about the possibility of the religious left attracting young people:

> *Religion scholar Simran Jeet Singh told me these kinds of bold, public-facing activist stances by houses of worship have the potential to attract a generation of younger, more justice-focused Americans. "Showing publicly the power of religion to produce and sustain justice makes religion more compelling," he said. "[Young people] have sincere empathy and sincere commitment to justice. They really feel like they want to be doing good in this world. A lot of people are having trouble finding a system of ideas—coherent ideas—that gives them a home, roots, and a place where they can look for guidance . . . And I think as we see more of a spotlight on the Religious Left, it will make religion more compelling for them."*[17]

That thought was amplified by an activist connected with Jim Wallis' "Sojourners" organization:

> *I think the focus on the person of Jesus is birthing a younger generation . . . Their political agenda is shaped by Jesus' call to feed the hungry, make sure the thirsty have clean water, make sure all have access to healthcare, transform America into a welcoming place for immigrants, fix our inequitable penal system, and end abject poverty abroad and in the forgotten corners of our urban and rural communities.*[18]

After much time spent investigating and listening to the leaders of the religious left, Jenkins concludes:

> *And that's precisely why the modern Religious Left, broadly defined, is likely to impact politics for years to come. It draws from a seemingly bottomless well of resilience that is paradoxically adaptable and immutable. It is undeterred by those who mock it, and even if the cameras vanish from the rallies, or the flood of activists slows to a trickle, or the politicians stop listening to them altogether, religious communities dedicated to progressive causes will endure. For they have the audacity to believe in a faith that gives them no other choice but to cry out.*[19]

<hr>

17. Jenkins. *American Prophets,* 272.

18. Merritt, "Rise of Christian Left."

19. Jenkins. *American Prophets,* 284–285.

CONCLUSION

Jesus invites us into communities of conspiracy to change the world—not to worship him, but to act on his behalf. He suggested this kind of conspiracy would create a manifestation of his ongoing presence among us—a sign of the resurrection, a sign of new life, a sign of dramatic change in the world. Our call is to become activists for a vision of a renewed human community and prophetic voices for compassion and justice on behalf of the poor, the marginalized, the excluded, and the oppressed.

We need to rethink and expand our boundaries. Communities of conspiracy may be Christian, but on the other hand, they may not. A religionless Christianity takes place completely in the secular world. Action and contemplation are the keys. Political and social action core groups may band together to both support their members and engage in righteous action. Welfare and social service activities, including homeless and domestic violence shelters, disaster relief programs, food pantries, clothing closets, and emergency aid centers may form the central focus of our ministries in the world.

We are called to follow Jesus in the real world—in a nation where guns are considered sacred, where violence is glorified, where market capitalism is deified, where consumerism is celebrated, and where selfishness is the dominant political value. The conspiracy of love is a movement of insurgency against unbridled militarism, a rebellion against institutional racism, an insurrection against unfettered capitalism, an uprising against unconstrained materialism, and a revolt against the destruction of the earth. It is an uprising against the powers that dominate our common life. As followers of Jesus, we don't have to ultimately solve all the issues facing us, but we cannot be silent in the face of injustice, oppression, and violence. Following Jesus calls us to passionately stand up to evil authorities and unjust laws. It is a resistance to the normalcy of civilization through acts of generosity, compassion, forgiveness, acceptance, nonviolence, and distributive justice.

Biblical scholar Walter Brueggemann (b. 1933) suggests that when facing a society in crisis, we often find ourselves caught between denial and despair. Perhaps small groups can attempt to find a third way to respond. The idea is to help people create tangible responses to current events without falling into a sense of helplessness, cynicism, and inaction. Rather than simply bemoaning the state of the world, they can seek to find a way to work through the social, political, and economic issues we face to create a more profound understanding of their root causes. We need to find ways to stir other faithful people from cynicism, indifference, and lethargy. Yet we need to follow Jesus in the company of others for insight, support, and encouragement. Most importantly, we will support one another in small actions to create a better world that our hearts know is possible.

The way of Jesus is a path toward a vision of the way the world ought to be, the way it is meant to be, the way we dream it to be. It is a freely chosen path but is not a way that is risk-free. There is never any assurance of success, only a promise of continuing challenge. It is a matter of trying and failing, and sometimes succeeding, but always continuing. Guided by the vision, the journey itself is the most important thing.

The way of Jesus led to the cross. That is where Jesus calls us to follow today. This is a passionate confrontation with the real world of power, violence, poverty, disease, suffering, and death. It is ugly and messy. It can be terrifying. But we are not alone. There are always others on the journey. The spirit of Jesus walks ahead. His vision leads the way. And his invitation bids us to join him in the conspiracy of love for a better world, a world our hearts know is possible.

So, go forth into the world and be of good courage. May you love freely, act compassionately, live justly, and seek peace.

Bibliography

2020 U.S. Religion Census. https://www.usreligioncensus.org/.

American Religious Identification Survey (ARIS). City University of New York, 2008. http://www.americanreligionsurvey-aris.org/reports/ARIS_Report_2008.pdf.

Anderson, Carol. *The Second: Race and Guns in a Fatally Unequal America*. New York: Bloomsbury, 2021. Kindle edition.

Arendt, Hannah. *Eichmann in Jerusalem: A Report on the Banality of Evil*. New York: Viking, 1963.

———. *The Origins of Totalitarianism*. New York: Harcourt Brace Jovanovich, 1951.

Ball, Molly. "Donald Trump and the Politics of Fear." *Atlantic*, September 2, 2016. https://www.theatlantic.com/politics/archive/2016/09/donald-trump-and-the-politics-of-fear/498116/.

Berryman, Phillip. *Liberation Theology: The Essential Facts about the Revolutionary Movement in Latin America and Beyond*. New York: Pantheon, 1987.

Berton, Pierre. *The Comfortable Pew: A Critical Look at Christianity and the Religious Establishment in the New Age*. Philadelphia: Lippencott, 1965.

Bonhoeffer, Dietrich. *The Cost of Discipleship*. New York: Macmillan, 1963.

———. *Discipleship*. Dietrich Bonhoeffer Works 4. Minneapolis: Fortress, 2003.

———. *Letters and Papers from Prison*. Dietrich Bonhoeffer Works 8. Minneapolis: Fortress, 2015.

———. *No Rusty Swords*. New York: Harper & Row, 1965. "The Church and the Jewish Question."

———. *Sanctorum Communio: A Theological Study of the Sociology of the Church*. Dietrich Bonhoeffer Works 1. Minneapolis: Fortress, 2009.

———. *Testament to Freedom*. San Francisco: HarperSanFrancisco, 1997.

Borg, Marcus. *The Heart of Christianity*. San Francisco: HarperSanFrancisco, 2003.

Borg, Marcus, and John Dominic Crossan. *The First Paul: Reclaiming the Radical Visionary behind the Church's Conservative Icon*. San Francisco: HarperOne, 2009.

Brooks, David. "The Philosophical Assault on Trumpism." *New York Times*, October 3, 2017. https://www.nytimes.com/2017/10/03/opinion/philosophical-assault-on-trumpism.html.

Claiborne, Shane. *The Irresistible Revolution: Living as an Ordinary Radical*. Grand Rapids: Zondervan, 2006.

Clement of Alexandria. *The Stromata*, bk. 7, ch. 12. https://www.newadvent.org/fathers/02107.htm.

Coffin, William Sloan. *Credo*. Louisville: Westminster, 2004.

Cohen, Elliot. "Are Evil People Crazy?" *Psychology Today*, August 29, 2011. https://www.psychologytoday.com/us/blog/what-would-aristotle-do/201108/are-evil-people-crazy.

Cone, James Hal. *Black Theology and Black Power*. New York: Seabury, 1969.

Cosper, Mike. "Aftermath: What Happens to Your Faith When Your Church Is Torn Apart?" *Christianity Today*, December 4, 2021. https://www.christianitytoday.com/ct/podcasts/rise-and-fall-of-mars-hill/mars-hill-podcast-driscoll-finale-aftermath.html.

Cramer, Katherine. *The Politics of Resentment: Rural Consciousness in Wisconsin and the Rise of Scott Walker*. Chicago: University of Chicago Press, 2016.

Day, Dorothy. *Loaves and Fishes*. Maryknoll, NY: Orbis, 1963.

Dean, Kenda Creasy. *Practicing Passion: Youth and the Quest for a Passionate Church*. Grand Rapids: Eerdmans, 2004.

———. *Starting Right: Thinking Theologically about Youth Ministry*. Grand Rapids: Zondervan, 2001.

Dowd, Maureen. "The Marjorie Taylor Greene-ing of America." *New York Times*, Nov. 5, 2022. https://www.nytimes.com/2022/11/05/opinion/election-republican-greene-vance.html.

Du Mez, Kristin Kobes. *Jesus and John Wayne: How White Evangelicals Corrupted a Faith and Fractured a Nation*. New York: Liveright, 2020.

Ellul, Jacques. *The Subversion of Christianity*. Grand Rapids: Eerdmans, 1986.

Estock, Beth Ann, and Paul Nixon. *Weird Church: Welcome to the Twenty-First Century*. Cleveland: Pilgrim, 2016. Kindle edition.

Florer-Bixler, Melissa. "Why Pastors Are Joining the Great Resignation." *Sojourners*, November 20, 2021. https://sojo.net/articles/why-pastors-are-joining-great-resignation.

Francis. Pope Francis General Audience Address. "Matthew, Chapter 25: A Key Criterion of Christian Authenticity." Catholic Culture, August 19, 2020. https://www.catholicculture.org/culture/library/view.cfm?recnum=12393

Freire, Paulo. *Pedagogy of the Oppressed*. London: Penguin, 2017.

Funk, Robert, and Roy Hoover. *The Five Gospels: The Search for the Authentic Words of Jesus*. New York: Macmillan, 1993.

Graham, David A. "The New Lost Cause." *Atlantic*, October 18, 2021. https://www.theatlantic.com/ideas/archive/2021/10/donald-trumps-new-lost-cause-centers-january-6/620407/.

Gloer, Hulitt. "Love Feast." Holman Bible Dictionary. https://www.studylight.org/dictionaries/eng/hbd/l/love-feast.html.

Gorski, Philip, and Samuel Perry. *The Flag and the Cross: White Christian Nationalism and the Threat to American Democracy*. New York: Oxford University Press, 2022.

Gulley, Philip. "If the Church Were Christian." *Huffpost*, May 25, 2011. https://www.huffpost.com/entry/if-the-church-were-christ_b_49538.

Gutiérrez, Gustavo. *A Theology of Liberation: History, Politics, and Salvation*. Maryknoll, NY: Orbis, 1973.

Haidt, Jonathan. *The Righteous Mind: Why Good People Are Divided by Politics and Religion*. New York: Vintage, 2013.

Hankey, Katherine. "The Old, Old Story." A fifty-stanza poem written in 1866.

Hart, David Bently. *The New Testament*. New Haven, CT: Yale University Press, 2017.

Herberg, Will. *Protestant-Catholic-Jew: An Essay in American Religious Sociology.* Garden City, NY: Anchor, 1960.

Hochschild, Arlie. *Strangers in Their Own Land: Anger and Mourning on the American Right.* New York: New Press, 2018.

Ireneaus of Lyon. *Against Heresies.* Bk. 4, ch. 8, para. 3. https://www.newadvent.org/fathers/0103413.htm.

Jenkins, Jack. *American Prophets: The Religious Roots of Progressive Politics and the Ongoing Fight for the Soul of the Country.* New York: HarperCollins, 2020. Kindle edition.

Jeremias, Joachim. *Jerusalem in the Time of Jesus.* Philadelphia: Fortress, 1969.

Jones, Jeffrey. "LGBT Identification in U.S. Ticks Up to 7.1%." *Gallup,* February 17, 2022. https://news.gallup.com/poll/389792/lgbt-identification-ticks-up.aspx.

Jordan, Clarence. *The Cotton Patch Version of Matthew and John.* Chicago: Follett, 1970.

———. *The Sermon on the Mount.* Valley Forge, PA: Judson, 1952.

King, Martin Luther, Jr. *Stride towards Freedom: The Montgomery Story.* New York: Harper & Brothers, 1958.

———. *Where Do We Go from Here: Chaos or Community?* Boston: Beacon, 1968.

———. *Why We Can't Wait.* New York: Signet Classics, 2000.

Kraus, Kelly. "Queer Theology: Reclaiming Christianity for the LGBT Community." *e-Research: A Journal of Undergraduate Work* 2. http://digitalcommons.chapman.edu/e-Research/vol2/iss3/4.

Lakoff, George. *Moral Politics: How Liberals and Conservatives Think.* Chicago: University of Chicago Press, 2016.

Loisy, Alfred. *The Gospel and the Church.* London: Isbister, 1902. Kindle edition.

Lumpkin, Joseph. *The Didache: The Teaching of the Twelve Apostles: A Different Faith—A Different Salvation.* Blountsville, AL: Fifth Estate, 2012. Kindle edition.

Mack, Burton. *The Lost Gospel: The Book of Q and Christian Origins.* San Francisco: HarperSanFrancisco, 1993.

———. *Who Wrote the New Testament?* San Francisco: HarperSanFrancisco, 1995.

Malkinson, Trevor. "N.T. Wright's Vision for a Post-Postmodern Christianity." February 3, 2012. https://www.beamsandstruts.com/bits-a-pieces/item/791-nt-wrights-vision-for-a-post-postmodern-christianity.html.

Martens, John W. "The Little Flock." *America: The Jesuit Review,* July 2016. https://www.americamagazine.org/content/the-word/little-flock.

Martyr, Justin. *The First Apology.* Chapter 14. https://www.newadvent.org/fathers/0126.htm.

McLaren, Brian. *Everything Must Change.* Nashville: Thomas Nelson, 2007.

Merritt, Jonathon. "The Rise of the Christian Left in America." *The Atlantic,* July 25, 2013. https://www.theatlantic.com/politics/archive/2013/07/the-rise-of-the-christian-left-in-america/278086/.

Meyers, Robin. *Spiritual Defiance: Building a Beloved Community of Resistance.* New Haven, CT: Yale University Press, 2015.

Myers, Ched. *Binding the Strong Man: A Political Reading of Mark's Story of Jesus.* Maryknoll, NY: Orbis, 1988.

Neibuhr, Reinhold. *Moral Man and Immoral Society: A Study in Ethics and Politics.* Louisville: Westminster John Knox, 2021.

Newport, Frank. "More U.S. Protestants Have No Specific Denominational Identity." Gallup, July 18, 2017. https://news.gallup.com/poll/214208/protestants-no-specific-denominational-identity.aspx.

Nixon, Paul. "What Is Dinner Church?" https://www.gnjumc.org.

Nolan, Albert. *Jesus before Christianity*. Maryknoll, NY: Orbis, 1976.

Paradis, Michel. "The Lost Cause's Long Legacy." *The Atlantic*, June 26, 2020. https://www.theatlantic.com/ideas/archive/2020/06/the-lost-causes-long-legacy/613288/.

Peterson, Eugene H. *The Message: The New Testament, Proverbs, and Psalms*. Colorado Springs, CO: NavPress, 1993.

Plumer, Brad. "What a Liberal Sociologist Learned from Spending Five Years in Trump's America." Vox, October 25, 2016. https://www.vox.com/2016/9/6/12803636/arlie-hochschild-strangers-land-louisiana-trump.

Powelson, Mark, and Ray Riegert. *The Lost Gospel Q: The Original Sayings of Jesus*. Berkeley, CA: Ulysses, 1999.

Rauschenbusch, Walter. *Christianity and the Social Crisis in the 21st Century*. San Francisco: HarperOne, 2007.

Remen, Rachel. "Helping, Fixing, Serving." *Awakin*. https://www.awakin.org/v2/read/view.php?tid=127.

Rice, Kate. *Jesus Is Not Republican: A Secular Liberal's Adventures with Religion, Politics and Sex*. Cleveland: Seat of My Pants, 2021. Kindle edition.

Robbins, Michael, and David Bentley Hart. "Only God Could Join Us to God." Commonweal, August 30, 2022. https://www.commonwealmagazine.org/only-god-could-join-us-god.

Robinson, John A. T. *Honest to God*. London: SCM, 1963.

Root, Andrew. "Ministry inside the Immanent Frame: Public Lecture at Ridley Hall, Cambridge." November 2, 2022. YouTube.

Roozen, David A. "Twenty Years of Congregational Change: The 2020 Faith Communities Today Overview." Hartford Institute for Religion Research. https://faithcommunitiestoday.org/.

Ruether, Rosemary Radford. *Sexism and God Talk: Toward a Feminist Theology*. Boston: Beacon, 1983.

Smith, Gregory A., and Jessica Martinez. "How the Faithful Voted: A Preliminary 2016 Analysis." *Pew Research Center*, November 9, 2016. http://www.pewresearch.org/fact-tank/2016/11/09/how-the-faithful-voted-a-preliminary-2016-analysis/.

Solnit, Rebecca. "The American Civil War Didn't End." *Guardian*, November 2018. http://rebeccasolnit.net/essay/the-american-civil-war-didnt-end/.

Solzhenitsyn, Alexander. *The Gulag Archipelago: An Experiment in Literary Investigation*. 3 vols. New York: Harper Perennial Modern Classics, 2007.

Struckmeyer, Kurt. *A Conspiracy of Love: Following Jesus in a Postmodern World*. Eugene, OR: Wipf and Stock, 2016.

Strauss, William, and Neil Howe. *The Fourth Turning: An American Prophecy—What the Cycles of History Tell Us about America's Next Rendezvous with Destiny*. New York: Crown, 1997.

Taylor, Charles. *A Secular Age*. Cambridge, MA: Belknap, 2018. Kindle edition.

Tertullian. *Apology*. Ch. 39. http://www.logoslibrary.org/tertullian/apology/39.html.

Van Denburgh, Tom. "Why Do Christian Nationalists Sound So Much Like the KKK?" *Newsweek*, November 7, 2022. https://www.newsweek.com/why-do-christian-nationalists-sound-so-much-like-kkk-opinion-1757242.

Wallis, Claudia. "Trump's Victory and the Politics of Resentment." *Scientific American*, November 12, 2016. https://www.scientificamerican.com/article/trump-s-victory-and-the-politics-of-resentment/.

Wallis, Jim. *Faith Works: Lessons from the Life of an Activist Preacher*. Foreword by Bill Moyers. New York: Random House, 2000.

Wehner, Peter. "Evangelical Christianity Is Breaking Apart." *Atlantic*, October 2021. https://www.theatlantic.com/ideas/archive/2021/10/evangelical-trump-christians-politics/620469/.

Williams, Delores. *Sisters in the Wilderness: The Challenge of Womanist God-talk*. Maryknoll, NY: Orbis, 1993.

Wilson, Jonathan. *Living Faithfully in a Fragmented World: Lessons for the Church from MacIntyre's "After Virtue."* Harrisburg, PA: Trinity International, 1998.

Winfield, Mark. "Most Comprehensive Study Yet of COVID's Impact on Churches Finds Uneven Results." *Baptist News Global* website, November 12, 2021. https://baptistnews.com/article/most-comprehensive-study-yet-of-covids-impact-on-churches-finds-uneven-results/.

Wink, Walter. *The Human Being: Jesus and the Enigma of the Son of the Man*. Minneapolis: Fortress Press, 2002.

———. *The Powers That Be*. New York: Doubleday, 1998.

Zinn, Howard. *You Can't Be Neutral on a Moving Train: A Personal History of Our Times*. Boston: Beacon, 2002.

Zito, Selena, and Brad Todd. *The Great Revolt: Inside the Populist Coalition Reshaping American Politics*. New York: Crown Forum, 2018.